APOCALYPSE AND ARMAGEDDON.

THE SECRET ORIGINS OF CHRISTIANITY

*The First Shall be Last
and the Last Shall be First*

HEKATAIOS AMERIKOS

Copyright © 2015 Hekataios Amerikos.

All rights reserved. No part of this book may be reproduced, stored, or transmitted by any means—whether auditory, graphic, mechanical, or electronic—without written permission of both publisher and author, except in the case of brief excerpts used in critical articles and reviews. Unauthorized reproduction of any part of this work is illegal and is punishable by law.

Scripture taken from the NEW AMERICAN STANDARD BIBLE®, Copyright © 1960, 1962, 1963, 1968, 1971, 1972, 1973, 1975, 1977, 1995 by the Lockman Foundation. Used by permission.

Selections from the *Gospel of Thomas* taken from Pagels, Elaine. The Other Gospels: Non-Canonical Gospel Texts. Ron Cameron, ed. Philadelphia: The Westminster P., 1982. Other sources indicated within text.

Italics, both within and outside of quotes, are generally mine.

ISBN: 978-1-4834-3332-5 (sc)
ISBN: 978-1-4834-3331-8 (e)

Because of the dynamic nature of the Internet, any web addresses or links contained in this book may have changed since publication and may no longer be valid. The views expressed in this work are solely those of the author and do not necessarily reflect the views of the publisher, and the publisher hereby disclaims any responsibility for them.

Any people depicted in stock imagery provided by Thinkstock are models, and such images are being used for illustrative purposes only. Certain stock imagery © Thinkstock.

Lulu Publishing Services rev. date: 6/23/2015

To the real Jesus, whoever he was:

Jesus said, "The Pharisees and the scribes have taken the keys of Knowledge and hidden them. They themselves have not entered, nor have they allowed to enter those who wish to . . ." (Pagels, Elaine 30; *The Gospel of Thomas*, 39).

CONTENTS

Would You Be Surprised to Learn That: xi
Prologue: Proprietary Religion xiii

Chapter 1. The First Monotheists 1
    The First Prophet 1
    Development and Spread of Initial Monotheism 2
    Mithraism 4
    Akhenaten and the Aten 5
    Moses the Egyptian 8
    Moses and the Aten 11
    Akhenaten the Tyrant 13
    Moses' "New" Religion 14
    The Real Exodus 16
    The Great Compromise 21
    The Triumph of Yahu and the Remains From History 23
    Conclusions 25

Chapter 2. Hellenization, Christianity and the
               Deterioration of Religion and Philosophy 44
    Hellenization: the Forgotten Ingredient... 44
    Hellenization Surrounds Judea... 47
    Hellenization Dominates 49
    "Persecution" by Antiokhos (Antiochus) 51
    The Jewish Temples... 53
    The Gnostics and the Birth of the Son of Man.................................. 57
    Then Cometh the Romans 59
    Conclusions 61

Chapter 3. The Real John and the Real Jesus - The Apocalyptic Baptizer and the Revolutionary Son of Man 65
The Reality of the Egyptian Connection 65
John, The True Messiah 68
And They Were Gnostic Essenes Influenced by Zoroastrianism 70
The Qumran Connection 74
Jesus and the Temple 77
The Coming Apocalyptic Kingdom 81
The Essenes Were Apocalyptic Gnostics 85
Conclusions 89

Chapter 4. The Real Christianity and What Actually Happened to the Disciples 109
A Confused Christianity 109
Revolution and Hysteria 119
It Started in Roma 122
The Demise of Paul 126
The Roman Response to The Way and Its Results 132
The Effect of the Temple's Destruction Upon Judaism 135
The Egyptian Connection Revealed 137
The Egyptian Files 140
The Divided Church 143
The True New Covenant 145
The Failure of the Qumranites 147
The Roman Connection 149
The Christian Connection 154
The Roman Messiah Who Happened to be Pagan 156
The True Gentile Church 159
Paul the Egyptian? 161
Treading Upon Roman Victory, Before and After 163
Jesus, the Failed Warrior Messiah 167
Surviving Original Christianity 171
Conclusions 174

Chapter 5. The New Testament, the Dead Sea Scrolls and the Nag Hammadi Manuscripts 185
    The Problem of the Canonical Gospels 185
    John Was FIRST! 188
    The Esoteric Christ 195
    John and Peter 197
    When Were the Books Actually Written? 199
    The Torch Passes Back to Egypt 202
    The Dead Sea Scrolls 205
    The Nag Hammadi Library 209
    The Apocalypses 211
    Conclusions 214

Select Historical Timeline: 223
Timeline of Apostolic (separate, secret, hidden) vs.
    Pauline (revealed) Efforts: 225
Epilogue: A Call for a Brave New (non-apocalyptic) World 229
Acknowledgments 239
Select Bibliography 241
About the Author 249

WOULD YOU BE SURPRISED TO LEARN THAT:

1. Everything traces back to Egypt?
2. Moses was likely an Egyptian who followed the religion of the Aten?
3. Hellenization, put into effect by Alexander the Great, started the process that created Christianity well before the first century CE?
4. There was a major pre-Christian Jewish Gnostic movement in Alexandria, Egypt during the last two centuries BCE which, combined with Neoplatonism, greatly contributed to the development of Christianity; that Christianity didn't just pop up out of nowhere with the advent of John and Jesus?
5. Jewish Egyptian Atenists had survived the death of the Egyptian Pharaoh Akhenaten and eventually coalesced into the Essenes who moved to Qumran and that John and Jesus had been among these Essenes?
6. John the Baptizer did not invent the rite of baptism and that Christians were not the only ones to make use of it?
7. The Jesus portrayed in the gospels has little to do with the real Jesus; that Jesus clearly instigated an insurrection against the Romans, expecting his Essene allies from Qumran to help him, but when they failed to arrive Jesus was captured, arrested, and executed?
8. There were major divisions within the earliest Christian church; factions led by different apostles (mainly James the Just, Peter,

John and Paul) with different territories and that Paul meddled in just about all of them?
9. Christianity was meant to be led by a hereditary priesthood through the family of Jesus with the center of operation in Jerusalem, but that these priests were not to marry or have children because the apocalypse was to happen within the lifetime of the first believers?
10. The first known book-burning in all of history, at Ephesos (found in the book of *Acts*), brought Paul to the attention of the Roman imperator Nero and that the riot at Ephesos only a couple of years later *really* got his attention?
11. James the Just, brother of Jesus, was the main rival of Paul and that James caused Paul to be arrested by the Roman authorities, with Paul eventually having to stand before Nero for judgment?
12. There is a direct connection between the Great Fire in Roma and the beginning of the first major Jewish revolt against the Romans of 66-74 CE and that some of the apostles were probably killed when the Romans took Jerusalem, the rest escaping into Egypt?
13. The books contained within the New Testament were written in an entirely different order than we find them within the canon today with the *Apocalypse of John* being among the first, but they have deliberately been arranged as they are presently as an effort to deceive and that we actually have two "New Testaments" from two major factions combined into one today, the gospels having been written last of all, mainly in Egypt?
14. It all *does* matter to our modern world?

The information and analysis contained within the pages of this book are the result of many years of research and are based upon solid fact derived from extant evidence, not faith or supposition. This is a work of history, not fiction. It is meant to inform the reader. It is meant for those who wish to finally break out of the bounds set for them by those with religious and political agendas - for those who want to know about the true origins of the religion we today call Christianity. This work is meant to be controversial, but is not meant to offend. It is meant to set the record straight with insights that can truly be found nowhere else.

PROLOGUE: PROPRIETARY RELIGION

People often claim that they want to know the truth. But, when pressed in any way, especially about religion, one finds that they often prefer to adhere to the beliefs they already have rather than accepting a new fact or two that might lead them to something more in line with truth. And, after all, in order to get to truth one must first have some facts. Right? But often people believe that they have facts when they only really have supposition.

As an undergraduate in college I was struck by the fact that I was being taught things about religion that I had never heard of before even though I had attended church and studied my *Bible* from the time I was able to read. And I gradually began to realize that the material that I was being taught was, in a way, seen as proprietary to the ministerial profession and that ministerial students would graduate from college with absolutely no desire to share much, if any, of it with the folk. I came to realize that religious authorities generally preferred to keep the folk as ignorant of true religious history as possible so that they could continue to have a monopoly on such knowledge. Thus, nothing had really changed in that regard since the days of Jesus himself. My studies since that time have only tended to reinforce my original observation.

This investigation did not take place overnight and it has not been rushed by some university system that requires professors to pump out books in order to maintain their status. There is no way that it could have been completed and presented to the folk in, say, sixty to ninety days or even a year. And even if some may suggest that I did not, perhaps, look at all of the evidence available, I think that they would have to admit that I have evaluated and considered things in such a way as to obtain information that has been overlooked by others.

There are all kinds of books out there, even at this very moment in time, purporting to tell the truth of Jesus and/or Christianity. And all of these books come from differing viewpoints and serve up different supposed facts. And these books are, in the main, quite popular, judging from sales figures. But people somehow seem to realize that something is missing from the earliest history of Christianity, yet they don't know what it is and their efforts to discover it are like trying to grasp air. So they latch onto these histories and pseudo-histories in an effort to obtain the knowledge that they can't seem to obtain from just reading the *Bible* or attending Sunday School classes. After many years of research, I have concluded that even the best histories of earliest Christianity leave out some important points. Usually this is simply a sin of omission rather than being deliberate. After all, no one can know everything about that period in time, take it from me. And neither do I purport to know all about it or even to have every fact that can be obtained about that time. This would simply be impossible. So people, generally, are still left wanting.

Still, the overall picture, in my view, is even more daunting than most can even realize. They have no idea what the true origins of Christianity were. They depend upon what they have always been taught or what their preacher says or what they read in the gospels and the book of *Acts* and don't even bother to look further. But I couldn't do that, so I searched and researched even well beyond the attainment of my multiple college degrees in religions/historical studies. I continued because I knew that there was more to know. I found that people in general have no idea that the beginnings of Christianity go back further than the first century CE and actually go back to at least the first and second centuries BCE. They don't realize that John the Baptizer and Jesus didn't just suddenly pop up out of nowhere, somehow fulfilling biblical prophecy, and start leading their movements. And they don't realize that what they have studied and believed is actually history in a vacuum with little or no real reference to the wider world of the time. So all of these sensationalisms and pseudo-histories about Jesus and Christianity are a symptom of the emptiness that we are witnessing here.

For even if Christianity had really begun with the first century CE, we would still be left wanting because the gospels and other writings of the time don't really seem to fill in several gaps.

My purpose here is very simple - to give the folk that which they are looking for, but are unable to find because the powers that be have long decided that they don't need to know more than that which they are taught. Much of that which will be found within the pages of this book emanates from sources that had long been buried, literally, and believed to have been destroyed almost two thousand years ago. But modern archaeology and science has ensured that those documents, which the religious authorities of the past did not want us to *ever* read, are available to us after all. And they actually tell us things that we could have never believed possible.

This work will take the reader from a brief history of the first known monotheistic religion, Zoroastrianism, and its accompanying Persian religion, Mithraism, on to the Egyptian religion of the Aten and its influence upon the Hebrews/Israelites, and from there on to the very genesis of Christianity within Hellenization, Neoplatonism, Jewish Gnosticism and the Essenes, on to who John the Baptizer and Jesus really were. Then it will proceed to the disciples/apostles and reveal what likely really happened to them, especially Paul, as well as the infighting that existed within earliest Christianity between those who wished to follow Torah and those who wished to reject it. Then it will proceed to the process of creating the New Testament, the true order in which events took place as well as the true order that the New Testament books were written in. And, finally, it will proceed to the Dead Sea Scrolls and the Nag Hammadi manuscripts and show their relationship to the entire scenario. In the end, the reader will see that the history that has been provided via the book of *Acts*, the gospels, and other traditional sources is very different from that which actually took place. This work follows the evidence and the facts as they exist without the blinders of faith. I choose to believe only that which I can observe scientifically, discern through extant historical and archaeological evidence, deduce through the use of reason and logic, and/or accept by way of personal experience.

Now, this work is not meant to be comprehensive on the subject at hand, but it is meant to be substantive. Again, it is based upon actual FACTS, unlike certain pseudo-histories of late. Some will find it disturbing to their faith while others will find it freeing and enlightening. I am not writing this history in an effort to please anyone. And, again, I am not writing it as an academic exercise since I have had so many more years to produce this than your average academic, who often has to pump out books in quick succession in order to meet the standard of the university where he or she teaches. And a good part of it actually comes from papers I wrote years ago while I was in college, which I have expanded upon. So the detractor may well state that most of this is just old scholarship with some new insights. In fact, that is *exactly* what it is - old scholarship given new and crucial updates. The simple point is that I want the folk to know what I know. So here it is.

I
THE FIRST MONOTHEISTS

The First Prophet

Any treatment of monotheism (belief in and worship of only one god) should rightly begin, contrary to popular opinion, with Zoroastrianism because, based on extant historical evidence, it is the oldest extant form of this belief system. Thus, in the present work, Zoroastrianism is briefly introduced prior to the introduction of other forms of monotheism. The brevity here is due, in part, to the lack of knowledge of this religion and its origins for the most part and also to the fact that a long, detailed analysis of this religion is unnecessary to the point of this work. The important thing is to detail it succinctly and to emphasize the fact that it has influenced both Judaism and Christianity not only with reference to its monotheism or dualism, but also in its apocalyptic overtones. And Mithraism, although it cannot be classed as monotheism, is very briefly detailed mainly because it was a competing religion among the ancient Persians which had, frankly, an influence upon the western world more directly than Zoroastrianism did until the advent of Christianity.

The religion we today call Zoroastrianism (or, sometimes, Zarathushtranism) was promulgated by an ancient prophet from an area around southern Russia, Afghanistan or eastern Iran. His name was Zarathushtra Spitama. During the fourth century BCE it was calculated by the Greeks that Zarathushtra had lived 258 years before the conquest of the Persian Achaemenid Empire by Alexander the Great. That would place his life in the seventh century BCE. Exactly how they arrived at this calculation is uncertain. However, the linguistics of his surviving writings are such that he must instead have lived *much* earlier, sometime between the eleventh and sixteenth centuries BCE.

The prophet, Zarathushtra, or (in Greek) Zoroaster, founded this religion, having had a vision which led him to begin preaching his new faith. When Zarathushtra lived is, again, in debate. But, like all other prophets, he was at first rejected by his own people. He then journeyed westward into unknown areas, finally returning and encountering a king who was willing to convert to his new religion, who is believed to have been an ancestor of the Achaemenid king, Kūruš (Cyrus) the Great.

Again, although dates vary, the most likely time period for his writings and teachings was about 1500 BCE, making his the *oldest known form* of monotheistic, or at least dualistic, religious teaching. It does not really seem to be known what *name* this religion itself first went by - this piece of information seemingly lost to history. The adherents of this religion refer to themselves as "Mazdayasna", referring to their devotion or worship of Mazda. An older means by which they were referred was as "Behdin", meaning a follower of "Daena" or "Good Religion".

Development and Spread of Initial Monotheism

In any case, it is known that the basic thrust of this religion was that there was a good force, Ahura-Mazda, and an evil force. These forces were at odds with each other, but the good force would eventually win out at some future time. The name Ahura-Mazda is derived from ancient Persia in that, following their conquest of Bactria and the neighboring North-Indian land of the Asurs, the Persians began to adopt the most important deity of the Asurs, Asura Mazda "the Lord of High Knowledge", by way of the Indo-Aryans. The corresponding name in Persian was Ahura, thus Ahura Mazda (Oesterley 85-86). This religion was very anti-polytheistic although it still retained some elements of polytheism. It was almost from the beginning opposed to the use of sacrifice to propitiate deities while at the same time prescribing proper sacrifices for all the deities (a conflict which was never quite resolved, it seems). So, like other forms of monotheism, there was somewhat of a mix at first gradually being overcome by more or less total monotheism over time. Since the Indo-Aryan peoples of this area had been polytheistic Pagans prior to the advent of Zarathushtra, the changes he called for were not well-accepted for some time. But, eventually, under royal patronage, Zarathushtra's religion became accepted and slowly came to dominate Persian lands. So it had virtually no success until, as already mentioned, one Persian ruler adopted and promulgated it. This is a pattern that should be taken note of here as it is a recurrent pattern with monotheism.

Now, the Zoroastrians believed that humankind existed for a purpose and that purpose was a divine mission. Human beings held a critical place in the universe. They were created by the force of good but they possessed the capacity to choose between good or evil. One had the freedom of choice. By choice humankind ultimately determined the outcome of the kosmos. Their role was to ultimately serve as the determining factor in the victory of good or evil. And each person had only one life in which to make his or her own determination - no reincarnation. The good people adhered to ethics and joined the forces of good. Those who ignored ethics joined the forces of evil. Divine destiny itself, then, depended upon humankind learning to be good. And adherence required nothing more than a simple declaration. There was no initiation ritual. However, this had to be a voluntary act. Those who did not adhere to this way of living were to be left in peace.

One observed the faith, then, by simply living in an ethical manner. There was, therefore, no necessary conflict with any other established religion. Sadly, however, this religion eventually used military force to attempt to reach its goal of conversion of others. The Zoroastrian religion was male-dominated or patriarchal. It combined both predestination *and* personal choice - one was predestined to make the choice one made. And it emphasized a resurrection of the dead (and even a rapture) and a final judgment for all. This gave it apocalyptic overtones.

The priests/prophets of the Zoroastrian religion were the *Magoi* (singular, *Magos*), the Latin form of the term, *Magi* (singular, *Magus*), characteristically being used in literature (from which the terms *magic* and *magician* come). These are the "wise men" who, according to the Christian gospels, went to see the baby Jesus. And, later on in the book of *Acts* we encounter one "Simon Magus", who was rejected by the early church. Another connection with Christianity was the belief that a son named Saoshyant, who was to become the messianic savior of the world, would be born by way of a *virgin* named Hvov; in so many words, the first real concept of the virgin birth. And, following the salvific work of Saoshyant the apocalyptic end of the world and final judgment would come (Oesterley 88). All of this being laid out in writing well prior to the advent of Christianity.

Again, Zarathushtra stood against all forms of polytheism, including Mithraism. He found animal sacrifice, especially the Mithraic sacrifice of the bulls, to be hideous. Zoroastrianism endured, weakly, after the conquest of the Achaemenid Persian Empire by Alexander the Great, but Mithraism seems to have been stamped out there following his conquest. Still, three-hundred years later Mithraism is again found in the areas between the Parthian Empire and the Mediterranean, specifically in Armenia. Neither religion reached into the Greco-Roman world, especially not into Greece itself, because the Greeks refused to adopt the religions of their Persian enemies, for some time. Still, Mithraism, or at least the Sacred Mysteries thereof, did eventually make its way to Roma, although it is unknown how this took place. It was found mainly among the Roman armies in the legions on the Roman frontiers, the Romans, unlike the Greeks, having no qualms about adopting an enemy religion in this instance.

Mithraism

In any case, Roma had a tendency to accept practically any religion to be imported into the city, so it should not be surprising that the Romans accepted this one also since it was also polytheistic and included animal sacrifice. The actual origins of Mithraism, as with Zoroastrianism, are almost completely obscure. But the more mysterious thing is that this religion survived the advent of Zoroastrianism at all and then the conquest of Alexander, to spread elsewhere later. Most likely it was first introduced to the Romans by some Persian who joined the Roman army and had some notable successes so that his religion came to be of interest to the other soldiers who served along with him.

The sacrifice of a bull in Mithraism was prominent as Mithras was commanded to sacrifice a bull by the sun god, which Mithras reluctantly did. The slaying of the bull brought about a celestial miracle which created the world. So the killing of the bull was a reenactment of the creation of the world. From the bull's tail and from his blood came ears of corn and the vine. Afterward came the four elements, all of the trees and plants, the winds and the seasons. The seed of the bull produced the good animals and all living things.

The cult of Mithras became very popular among Romans over time, especially among soldiers. However, upon the ascendancy of Flavius Valerius Aurelius Constantinus (Constantine I "The Great", c272-337 CE) it lost imperial favor. Constantine's support of Christianity is one main cause for the demise of Mithraism, and genuine Mithraic Mysteries ceased. Still, this religion endured so that there are several dated Mithraic monuments as late as 321 CE. But, after this date, only one is found and it was located on the empire's frontier. Mithras is also mentioned in a collection of inscriptions from Roma, dated from 357 to 387 CE. These originated from a group of Pagan senators who were then in rebellion against the new Christian régime in Konstantinopolis (Constantinople). And these senators were also associated with Flavius Claudius Iulianus (Julian "the Apostate"). But Constantine's and his successor's support for Christianity ensured that the Christians would erect basilicas on top of the underground Mithraic caverns located at Roma and elsewhere, thus replacing them.

Akhenaten and the Aten

Amenhotep IV, who changed his name to Akhenaten (sometimes transliterated as Iknaten) after creating his new religion of the *Aten* (actually a combination of the great Egyptian gods *Ra*, *Horus* and *Aten*; an all-male trinity), was a pharaoh of Egypt during the Eighteenth Dynasty. He ruled for seventeen years and his rule was controversial. He was very much hated, so much so that, following his death, the

Egyptians moved to *totally* erase his memory from history. He reigned in either 1353-1336 BCE or 1351-1334 BCE, dying in about 1336 or 1334 BCE, depending upon how one calculates the dates.

Again, his main claim to fame was his effort to reform Egyptian religion, abandoning the traditional Egyptian polytheism for the strictly monotheistic worship of the Aten. It is not known what prompted Amenhotep IV to proceed as he did. There appears to have been no influence whatsoever from Zoroastrianism, the only other monotheistic religion known to have existed at such an early date. But a possible influence cannot be completely discounted.

Aten was represented by the sun disk, often with rays penetrating downward. This was modified within Egypt and the Near East at a later date into a sun disk with wings. But ultimately his new religion would not generally be accepted by the Egyptian people and it was gradually abandoned following his death, although it is known to have survived among a very few in Egypt for quite some time; at least two generations after Akhenaten's death. Tutankhhamun or "King Tut" is now known to have been the certain son of Akhenaten. He reversed his father's religious policies, returning Egypt to its traditional polytheistic form of worship.

Akhenaten was all but forgotten to history until the 19th century discovery of Amarna or Akhetaten, the new capital city of Akhenaten. But why was Akhenaten so hated by his subjects? Mainly, but not solely, due to his religious reforms. It is known that during his reign Akhenaten began to exclude any reference to other gods in any inscriptions or other writings, even going so far as to erase their names from previous monuments and inscriptions. This was especially so of Amun, the greatest of the Egyptian gods. But even so, he was fairly tolerant of the other religions at first and much was never erased. Still, for some unknown reason, toward the end of his reign, he became much more tyrannical and less interested in religious toleration. So it seems that, at first, he had intended for the changes to take place in a gradual manner, probably expecting the people to happily accept his changes without much resistance. But, when that did not happen, he sought to use force in his effort to effect this change. Because of his tyrannical measures, within a decade following his death an Egyptian reformation took place, bringing the people back, for the most part, to the traditional religions. And much from Akhenaten's reign was destroyed and/or defaced as the Egyptians sought to erase his legacy forever. In this they almost succeeded.

But, in addition to his hated religious reforms, there were other factors which contributed to the desire of the Egyptians to erase Akhenaten's very memory. Under his reign, due to neglect, the Egyptian Empire virtually crumbled, leaving territories in the Near East open to invasion. Indeed, Akhenaten ignored repeated pleas for help from vassal territories, preferring to concentrate on his internal religious reforms.

Now, it was in year five of his reign that Amenhotep IV moved decisively to establish the Aten as the exclusive, monotheistic, god of Egypt. He disbanded the priesthoods of all other cults and diverted their funds to the support of the Aten cult. And it is at this time that he changed his name to Akhenaten. And, in that same year, he began construction of his new capital. There he centralized Egyptian religious authority. By year nine of his reign Akhenaten declared that the Aten was not the supreme god, but the *only* god, and that he himself was the *only* intermediary between Aten and humankind. He also ordered the defacing of the temples of Amun and, where possible, any reference to multiple deities. Religious persecution, then, came into full existence in Egypt! And by this time the people were to worship Akhenaten himself. Only he and his wife, Nefertiti, could worship Aten directly and mediate between the Aten and the people. In the Great Hymn to Aten, written by Akhenaten himself, the Aten is referred to in this way - "O Sole God besides whom there is none". This is clearly monotheism and is a step beyond using the epithet "The Most High God", which was rather common in Egypt and the Near East during that time period.

By year nine of his reign Akhenaten instituted a ban on depictions of other gods, with the Aten as a sun disk the only legal representation of deity. By this time the Aten was not only thought of as a sun god, but also as a universal deity. Aten's representations were always accompanied with the disclaimer that they were exactly that, representations of something transcendent which could not really be represented. He also forbade the worship of other gods and forbade the veneration of "idols", even in private homes!

So, during the Eighteenth Dynasty of Egypt, when she had her glorious empire which stretched from Nubia in the south to Libya in the west to the borders of the Hittite Empire in the north, including Canaan, which had Jerusalem as one of its principle cities at that time, Akhenaten came to the throne, quickly and publicly changing his religion, and beginning to neglect the outer reaches of the Egyptian Empire. Akhenaten increasingly, as the years passed, became more and more assertive and tyrannical about his religion and quickly began to force his religion upon everyone else, persecuting those who preferred not to adopt his new faith.

In addition to all of this, it is known that at Akhenaten's new capital city, Akhetaten, the deceased were not allowed to be embalmed, but were instead buried in a cemetery nearby. They were buried directly into the ground without having gone through any type of embalming, on the orders of Akhenaten. Eventually, because of this, the decaying bodies of the deceased and their handling caused the spread of disease and a plague raged throughout his beautiful new city! This is probably one of the causes for his downfall since the people would naturally begin to suspect that the ancient deities were angry with them *and* with him. Once Akhenaten was dead, his new city was soon abandoned forever and the structures were demolished and used as fill in buildings in other parts of Egypt. At least some of those who remained loyal to the cult of the Aten would have fled - thus, the *Exodus*. Egypt was in turmoil following the death of Akhenaten and these people, who continued to worship Aten, no longer felt welcome within Egypt.

Moses the Egyptian

Now, perhaps the first to propose the theory that Judaism was a result of Akhenaten's monotheism was the Jewish psychoanalyst Sigmund Freud, although his theory is hotly debated and is actually dismissed out of hand by most. Ahmed Osman, for example, posited that Akhenaten's maternal grandfather, Yuya, was actually the Joseph of the book of *Genesis*. Yuya, he said, held the title of Overseer of the Cattle of Min at Akhmin. But Yuya is known to have had strong ties with the city of

Akhmim in Upper Egypt, so he is unlikely to have been a foreigner since most of them settled in Lower Egypt in and around the Nile Delta. Of course, none of that is proven. In his book, Moses and Monotheism, Freud stated his belief that Moses had likely been a priest of Aten who had left Egypt, along with his followers, following the death of Akhenaten.

Frankly, it is moderately surprising to me that no scholar that I have read has even entertained this as a possibility because, once one dispenses with the barrier of religious faith, it becomes quite obvious, in my view. Moses almost *had* to have been an Egyptian. However, I do think that Freud's analysis still has its faults, mainly the fact that he remained too wedded to the idea of the biblical Exodus rather than entertaining some other scenario. Still, as Freud himself put it:

> To deny a people the man whom it praises as the greatest of its sons is not a deed to be undertaken lightheartedly— especially by one belonging to that people. No consideration, however, will move me to set aside truth in favour of supposed national interests (Freud 3).

This, to me, is a very commendable statement. Freud, seeing something that others had either not seen before or could not bear admitting to having seen before, demonstrates his own personal determination to tell what he believes to be the *truth*. And I follow him in this.

First, Freud, citing James Henry Breasted's The Dawn of Conscience (p. 350), posited that, if Moses actually lived - if he was a real person - then it was during the thirteenth or fourteenth century BCE, the time of Akhenaten. He explained what should be obvious to most, but which is not - that the very name "Moses", the Hebrew being *Mosche*, is actually an *Egyptian name* itself. The explanation for Moses' name given in the Book of *Exodus* - that it means "he that was drawn out of the water", is actually incorrect and is, instead, actually later folk etymology. The name, Freud stated, can at best only mean "the drawer out" in Hebrew. In addition, he added that it made no sense at all to give credit to an Egyptian princess for knowing anything about Hebrew etymology and naming a baby accordingly (Freud 3-4), thereby showing her recognition that he was a Hebrew baby. But, of course, we would not know even this much if not for modern archaeology because we were, for almost 1500 years, unable to read ancient Egyptian. Until the Rosetta Stone was found, the closest thing we had to ancient Egyptian was the Coptic language, which really wasn't very helpful.

In any case, while mentioning that others before him had come to this very same understanding, Freud asserts that the name "Moses" derived from the Egyptian vocabulary directly, not the Hebrew. He again quotes James Henry Breasted and his The Dawn of Conscience (p. 350) in which Breasted openly states that the name "Moses" was actually the Egyptian word "*mose*" which simply meant "child". This word is found among Egyptian names in combination with the fuller form of a person's given name, examples being "Amen-mose", meaning "Amon-a-child" and "Ptah-mose", meaning "Ptah-a-child". Also, these examples are abbreviations of the more complete forms "Amon- (has given) -a child", etc. And it was early on that the abbreviation "child" itself became the convenient form of the full name. Thus, the name "Mose" became relatively common on Egyptian monuments (Freud 5). So, Moses himself would have had a prefix of some kind as part of his name and this prefix *would* necessarily have been of an Egyptian deity as in other instances. But which deity?

It is currently well-known to scholars that the story of Moses has striking similarities to other such hero stories of ancient times, especially that of Sargon of Agade who founded Babylon about 2800 BCE, which story I will not reproduce here. But this was not something that was commonly known until modern times because the records have only recently been unearthed by archaeologists. Like Moses, Sargon was born, placed into a basket, and set upon the water of a river where he was later found and saved. Many details are different, but the similarities cannot be ignored. And others who had similar stories written about them include Cyrus the Persian and Romulus, founder of Roma, along with other heroes, such as Oedipus, Karna, Paris, Telephos, Perseus, Herakles (Hercules), Gilgamesh, Amphion, Zethos, etc. So exposure in a basket clearly symbolized birth since the basket represented the womb and the stream symbolized the water of birth (Freud 8-9).

However, the story of the birth of Moses differs from all the others mainly in one important point - that the real family of Moses was among the lower classes, in fact, slaves, whereas the families of the others were of the royal classes. So, in the story of Moses, he was saved by royalty whereas with the others, except for that of Oedipus, they were saved by either deities or lower-class families. It is believed by some, as Freud points out, that there must have been an original story in which these roles were reversed so that the story of Moses was more like these other stories (Freud 10-11), but there is no need to detail that here either. In any case, Freud disputes that latter hypothesis.

Freud concludes that the truth is that one family in the story of Moses is real while the other is fictitious, as in all the other such hero stories, and that the fictitious family was invented by the use of myth to make Moses fit into this type of hero mythology. In so many words, Moses being found and brought up by an Egyptian princess is a *false* story and was made up in order to provide Moses with the types of heroic qualities that those in these other myths already possessed. But that does not automatically mean that the family of Moses was the Hebrew one, for who would it have been that made up the myth if not the Hebrews? No, Moses' real family was, in fact, the Egyptian one, but the myth-maker made him into a Hebrew rather than an Egyptian and wove his story in such a way as to make this plausible. Thus the *reversal* of families as compared to other myths of the same type. Moses the Egyptian is thus transformed into a Hebrew through a mythological hero story. And, whereas in all of the other similar stories the hero rises from humble origins, Moses descends from eminence to the very level of the Hebrew slaves (Freud 13). The atypical myth itself was, thus, *reversed.*

Moses and the Aten

In any case, it is well-understood that Moses was the law-giver and presenter of a new religion to the Hebrews. Yes, supposedly it was the same as that of the patriarchs but, somehow, the Hebrews had forgotten it and had to be re-taught. Freud stated that the Hebrew people who resided in Egypt undoubtedly had their own religion and if the presumed Egyptian, Moses, gave them a new one, then that other new religion almost had to have been that of the Aten (Freud 18). So, did Moses simply make up a religion out of thin air for the Hebrew people? Certainly not. What, then, might this "new" religion have been - the ancient Egyptian religion with its many deities? Obviously not. After all, practically anyone with even a minimal knowledge of ancient Egyptian religion would recognize the golden calf that Moses was so angry with the Hebrews for making while out in the desert was the Egyptian goddess Hathor. In addition, the Egyptian religion greatly emphasized magic through amulets and formulas in the service of their deities as well as in the daily lives of the Egyptians (Freud 19). The Hebrews clearly rejected this Egyptian polytheism along with its use of magic.

The fact of the matter is that, if Moses was an Egyptian, which he appears to have been, then the religion that he instituted among the Hebrews was clearly not the ancient Egyptian polytheistic religion with its emphasis upon magic and the afterlife. And, again, if Moses did not simply make up a religion, then what religion might he have presented to these Hebrews which they could have accepted? There is really only one answer and it has to do with Akhenaten.

To show this Freud goes on to cite what could possibly be the most important difference between the Egyptian religion and that of the ancient Hebrews. That difference was that the Egyptian religion emphasized death whereas the Hebrew religion essentially ignored death. In other words, the Egyptians made provision very carefully for the afterlife and worshipped Osiris in this regard. He was, in fact, their most popular god. But the ancient Hebrews "entirely relinquished immortality; the possibility of an existence after death was never mentioned in any place" (Freud 20). For them, death was the end and there was no reason to emphasize it in any way. So the Hebrews followed suit with the Atenists thus:

> Neither hymns nor inscriptions on graves know anything of what was perhaps nearest to the Egyptian's heart. The contrast with the popular religion cannot be expressed more vividly (Freud 26).

Akhenaten the Tyrant

Now, one of the more striking assertions that Freud makes is that not only was this the first instance known in history in which a monarch attempted to force his own monotheistic religion upon his subjects (although he leaves out Zoroastrianism here, probably not really knowing its history), but it was also the first instance in history (according to Freud), therefore, of religious intolerance, which he further asserted had been foreign to antiquity before this time and also for a long time afterward (Freud 21). And such intolerance was born with the belief in *one god*. And I submit that Freud was, in fact, correct. Monotheism, by its very nature, has historically tended to breed intolerance.

And Akhenaten went even further than to force his subjects to worship only his god, through him and his family, but added, along with his doctrine of monotheism, that of the concept of the "universal god" by inserting the quality of exclusiveness. An example provided from one of Akhenaten's hymns reads "O Thou only God, there is no other God than Thou" (Freud 24; Breasted: <u>History of Egypt</u>, p. 374). Thus, Aten was a god meant to be worshipped not only in Egypt, but everywhere.

To further his aims, Akhenaten initiated an overall persecution of the ancient Egyptian religions in an effort to force his subjects to turn to the religion of the Aten. This persecution was mainly directed against the religion of Amon, which had been the most important religion in Egypt up to that time. But the persecution was, of course, not limited to those who worshipped Amon, but extended to all others as well.

> Everywhere in the Empire the temples were closed, the services forbidden, and the ecclesiastical property seized. Indeed, the king's zeal went so far as to cause an inquiry to be made into the inscriptions on old monuments in order to efface the word "God" whenever it was used in the plural (Freud 25; Breasted: <u>History of Egypt</u>, p. 368).

Yes, for either the first or the second time in *all of known history*, depending on whether such occurred within the Persian realm during the initial spread of Zoroastrianism or not, the monotheists openly and aggressively attacked the polytheists by denying them the right to worship, by closing their temples, and even by defacing their monuments. It is clear even at this point that monotheism possessed a natural hatred for polytheism which rather automatically resulted in the destruction of anything seen as polytheistic. And, indeed, it seems to me, the very elimination of prefixes to Egyptian names such as "Mose" must have, in part, been a result of these persecutions since the deity's names had to be eliminated or, at least, left out on monuments and tomb records.

Moses' "New" Religion

Again, a comparison of the ancient Hebrew religion with that of the Aten reveals the first striking resemblance between the two for Freud, which is the fact that in its earliest form, the Hebrew religion spoke nothing whatsoever about any afterlife - about anything beyond the grave. So it appears that the ancient Hebrews took this lack of acknowledgment of the afterlife from the religion of the Aten, which was a necessary feature of this religion for Akhenaten since his main effort was in opposing religions that did emphasize death and the afterlife, such as that of the Egyptian trinity Isis, Osiris and Horus.

Also, as part of the "new" religion that Moses gave to the Hebrews, it is said that he instituted the rite of circumcision. All male infants had to be circumcised. But from whence did he get this idea? The book of *Genesis* states that the patriarchs did it. However, if they did, it is yet another part of their religion that the Hebrews had somehow forgotten while in Egypt. So it is uncertain whether the ancient Hebrews had ever practiced such a thing before Moses instituted it. Still, there is one thing that is certain. The ancient *Egyptians* practiced circumcision. So, contrary to modern popular opinion, the Hebrews appear to have adopted the rite of circumcision *from* the Egyptians!

But how do we know that the ancient Egyptians practiced circumcision? First, the ancient Greek historian, Herodotos (Ἡρόδοτος) stated as much and added that they had practiced this rite from very ancient times. Second, the examination of ancient Egyptian mummies confirms that this rite was practiced among them. Third, drawings on the walls of tombs also confirm it. And it appears that no other people of the eastern Mediterranean practiced this rite, it being certain that the ancient Semites, Babylonians, Sumerians and Canaanites did *not* practice it. So it becomes obvious that the Hebrews somehow adopted this rite directly from the Egyptians and did not invent it (Freud 30). Thus, if any Hebrews had ever resided in Egypt, one has to conclude that, if the Egyptians practiced circumcision then the Hebrews must have gotten the rite from them rather than vice versa. If this rite had been instituted by the ancient Hebrews, why would the Egyptians have adopted it from them? After all, the Egyptians despised them. So, as Freud insisted, Moses appears to have given the Hebrews/Israelites not only a new religion, but also the law of circumcision and, if this be the case, then Moses was not Hebrew, but Egyptian (Freud 31).

Still, Freud counters that what Moses did - leading the Israelites to the promised land from Egypt - is unintelligible if he were an Egyptian rather than a Hebrew, for why would he take up their cause if he were an Egyptian? But he then points out that the placement of Moses during the time of or shortly after the reign of Akhenaten solves the problem. Moses was obviously a man of some importance and close to the pharaoh. He probably expected to have and retain a high place in the Egyptian government for some time. But, once Akhenaten died and a negative reaction toward his new monotheistic religion ensued, Moses saw all of his hopes dissipate. If he could not or would not recant, then Egypt no longer held any promise for him. So Moses, rejected by his own people, decided that, as the Egyptian Empire crumbled, he would give this new religion to a new people and create a new empire with them. Freud goes on to speculate that Moses may have been a governor of some internal Egyptian province, such as Goshen, where some Hebrews had possibly settled, whom he chose for his new mission (Freud 31-32).

Unfortunately, although this is an amazing insight, this is where, I think, Freud made his most critical error. As stated earlier, I feel that Freud was a bit too wedded to the idea of the Exodus and, in fact, he utilizes the Exodus to help explain the later Israelites and their attitudes, with excellent effect. But, as I will show, most, if not all, of his points can be made in any case even if we dispense with the biblical Exodus story and consider another, more reasonable, possibility. That possibility, I submit, is that Moses who, as Freud points out, according to Josephus, had at some point in his career been an Egyptian field-marshal in a campaign against the Ethiopians in which he was victorious, is that, rather than being a governor of some Egyptian province *within* Egypt, might have been a governor or some other high official in an Egyptian province somewhere just a bit further away.

I submit that the area over which he had authority was none other than that which later became Judea, along with its most important city, Jerusalem. There Moses found himself essentially stranded when the Egyptian Empire began to crumble. There he was already in authority over whatever tribes inhabited the region, including, probably, some Hebrews and, certainly, the Jebusites and Canaanites. He was already in a position of power and already a strict adherent to the religion of the Aten which, I submit, he was already indoctrinating his subjects into from his base in Jerusalem. After all, there is no reason to suppose that the religion of Aten did not incorporate within itself the one element shared between *all* other monotheistic faiths - that of proselytization and expansion. So where, then, might this religion have logically spread? To places like Nubia, Ethiopia and Canaan; the latter under the direction of Moses. In addition, Moses must have allowed those Atenists who were fleeing from Egypt, probably led by Aaron, to enter Jerusalem and remain there. After all, to what other fortified, protected city could they have fled?

The Real Exodus

Freud goes on to emphasize that, according to his reconstruction of events, the Exodus would have had to have taken place between 1358 and 1350 BCE. Even the Jewish Rabbis calculated that Moses likely lived from about 1391 BCE to 1271 BCE (from the *Seder Olam Rabbah*). And this time-period fits quite well. So, for the moment forgetting that there was likely only a small Exodus from Egypt while accepting these dates as important when considering when the Hebrews probably entered Canaan en masse, let us continue with Freud's analysis since it still possess some important points. Freud arrives at the above dates because he states that these events must have taken place after the death of Akhenaten and prior to the reestablishment of authority of the Egyptian state by Haremhab. The dating he provides makes perfect sense. Whatever occurred did so during a time of turmoil, which did historically occur after the death of Akhenaten, and before the reinstatement of Egyptian authority, where possible. That hypothesis is more than reasonable.

Freud further points out, accurately, that following the collapse of Egyptian authority in Canaan, hordes of various peoples flooded into that area from the east. And what is it that Egyptian letters from Amarna, Akhenaten's capitol city, found in 1887 CE called these peoples? "*Habiru*" (Freud 33). But, I must point out here, there was no forty-year gap between the collapse of the Egyptian frontier and the invasions that took place as noted in the Amarna letters. These invasions were rather immediate. So, what must have really happened is that when that frontier area of the Egyptian Empire collapsed, Moses and his subjects, still within the walls of Jerusalem, found themselves essentially trapped with no one from Egypt to help them while hordes of vicious, savage, brutal, terroristic invaders (just read the book of *Joshua*) took over the surrounding territories and Atenist refugees from Egypt itself also had to be accommodated.

After all, the Egyptians had likely not pulled their forces completely out of such frontier areas so, regardless of whether it was Moses or someone else, there would have been Egyptians who found themselves in such a frightening situation. There can be little doubt of this, at least. Jerusalem was well-fortified and practically impregnable to attack from barbarian invaders lacking sophisticated weaponry, after all, we know from the Hebrew Bible that the Israelites had still not taken Jerusalem even up to the time of King David. But it would still have taken a very strong leader to have been able to prevent chaos from ensuing within the city walls during this time. And that man, more likely than not, would still have been an Egyptian, whatever his real name may have been.

Now Moses, as Freud continues, must have been circumcised himself since he was an Egyptian and this was their custom. He further points out that the attitude of those who have been circumcised, today, as in ancient times, is often one of superiority - that they are, somehow, special because of it. This while others who do not practice the rite often find it rather abhorrent. This Egyptian attitude of superiority is well-attested by the Greek historian, Herodotos, who, while visiting Egypt around 450 BCE, encountered it first-hand. He cited the extreme piety of the Egyptians as well as their tendency to remain separate from other peoples in all that they did.

And why shouldn't the Egyptians have felt exactly this way? After all, their religion and institutions had stood the test of time for thousands of years already. Compared with other religions and other cultures, the Egyptians were indeed far superior as evidenced by the very fact that their civilization had endured for so long. This was the attitude that they held. To them, *everyone* else was simply inferior. Period. But as Freud further points out, the Israelites who had accepted circumcision from Moses had to find a way to show that it was *not* connected to the Egyptians in any way (Freud 35). Moses, then, would have shared this attitude of superiority with those who shared the custom with him. They were special, separate, people (Freud 33). And, in fact, if Moses and his followers were surrounded by hordes of uncircumcised, barbarian invaders, then they were separate indeed. And his people must by no means be seen as inferior to the Egyptians! So circumcision had to be adopted by the converted populace in order to demonstrate their superiority over all others.

Now, at some level there still had to be communication and interaction between those who resided in Jerusalem and those who did not. And, again, there is no reason to believe that the one trait of all monotheistic religions was not also present within that of the Aten. That trait was a desire to spread out and proselytize whoever could be reached. That is the very first reason why it is reasonable to assume that it would have been found within the walls of Jerusalem in the first place while Jerusalem was still under Egyptian control. And that is the reason why it would also have remained there even after the collapse of the Egyptian Empire in that area. The Hebrews, then, could not and did not conquer Jerusalem. But those who still resided in Jerusalem were gradually able to impress their religious views onto many of the Hebrews, some of whom, apparently, who called themselves *Israelites*.

In addition, as Freud points out, it is said that Moses spoke with a stutter or had some other form of speech impediment (Freud 38). Could it have been, then, that Moses, who spoke Egyptian, had trouble speaking Hebrew and, therefore, required the services of someone else in order to communicate with them? This is entirely possible and plausible.

Freud further points out that, although practically all concur in that the Israelites did accept a new religion from Moses at some point in time, this event did not take place in the location that we are given. Freud is adamant that it did *not* take place at Mt. Sinai, but instead took place at Meribat-Qadeš (Freud 39). He suggests that the main reason why it took place there rather than at Sinai is because it possessed an abundance of springs and wells which could have supported the people, whereas Sinai did not. And it was here, he states that these people adopted the worship of a god he refers repeatedly throughout the rest of his work as "Jahve" (Freud 39). This is one and the same god as "Yahu" or "Yahweh".

Thus, Freud infers that the Israelites, during the Exodus, went to this place rather than to Mt. Sinai and there received their new religion, delivered by Moses. This Moses, as the Hebrew Bible indicates, was the son-in-law of the Midianite priest, Jethro, and Jethro, Freud states, visited Moses at that location in order to offer him directions as to how to proceed (Freud 39). However, because Freud accepts this scenario, he has to create two separate men who, he indicates, with time came to be seen as one and the same person and both given the name "Moses". This, in my view, is an astonishing and unnecessary reach. Much more plausible is the possibility that the Israelites, one of the Hebrew tribes, came from this area carrying with them their religion of Yahu, and entered the land of Canaan along with all the other Hebrew tribes at about the same time. They were separate and distinct from the other Hebrew tribes, not by race, but by religion. They already possessed monotheistic tendencies, but were not really monotheistic, since Yahu had a consort and there were also other deities whom they paid tribute to.

In any event, Freud continues by drawing yet another new picture of Moses - not of the man who died rather peacefully on Mt. Nebo while viewing the promised land, which he was never to set foot in himself, but of a leader who had been murdered by his own people in some sort of rebellion. Freud further states that at that time the religion that Moses had practically forced upon the people was abandoned. He gets this idea, first, from a passage in the book by the prophet *Hosea* (but he does not cite which passage), and adds that it is a concept repeated by most of the later prophets. The idea that Moses would return to lead his people became the basis for the concept of the messiah (Freud 42-43). Freud believed that this messiah concept became one of the surviving elements of the Aten religion - that, perhaps, Akhenaten himself was to possibly return at some later date. In effect, both Akhenaten and Moses came to be seen as personalities who would return someday to finish the job they had started, but had not been able to complete during their lifetimes.

That the man, Moses, might have met with some kind of violent end upon a mountain which was actually relatively near to Jerusalem, as Freud suggests, is quite plausible. Even as an Egyptian official who had remained in Jerusalem following the collapse of the Egyptian Empire, this would make perfect sense because he may well have had some cause to leave the defenses of Jerusalem at some point to fight some enemy - perhaps the very Hebrews themselves. If he were a military commander of any note at all, this could have been even more imperative for him in that he may have been forced to tip his hand, to prove himself, in order to retain control of the situation in Jerusalem. And, even though he was killed in this effort, his religion would have, after all, survived among those who remained in Jerusalem under Aaron's leadership and, thus began the myth that even Moses would return someday in some form. Jerusalem, after all, remained unconquered, so why would they have had any cause to change or modify their religion? This is part of what, I think, Freud refused to see. But he did see that Moses would have had a tendency to force his subjects to adhere to his religion because that is the very nature of monotheism. And he deduced that Moses must have met some sort of a violent end. I submit that his last military effort was one against those who would not accept his authority nor adhere to his religion and, thus, in the end, Moses led a failed effort against them, thus espousing violence in the end. After all, his violent tendencies are alluded to in the book of *Exodus*.

It is also entirely plausible that only some of those who later became the Jewish people had undergone possible slavery in Egypt, the tribe returning from Egypt having combined later with other related tribes

(Freud 43-44). Put even better, since there is absolutely no evidence that the Hebrew people were ever enslaved in Egypt, only a part of the people who later became the Jewish people had endured some sort of trauma which somehow made them into who they became and which they were able, at some later date, to share with all of the other Hebrew tribes with whom they combined. That this trauma became known as the Exodus from Egypt was the work of priests and scribes, perhaps descended from the Israelite faction.

But, how does Freud arrive at his astonishing conclusion? He first points out that in later times Egyptian names were only found among the Levites. The Levites were the survivors of the followers of Moses. They fused with the rest of the tribes, but remained loyal to Moses and his memory, including his religion. They were culturally superior to the other tribes with whom they eventually formed an alliance (Freud 46). And I concur with Freud here. So those who had actually been former Egyptians were likely fewer in number than other peoples, but they were culturally on a higher level and, therefore, exercised a greater influence on the ultimate development of the people, bringing to those other people a tradition that they had lacked. And, he further states, they may also have provided something more tangible than tradition.

> It is not credible that a great gentleman like the Egyptian Moses approached a people strange to him without an escort. He must have brought his retinue with him, his nearest adherents, his scribes, his servants. These [Freud posits] were the original Levites. Tradition maintains that Moses was a Levite. This seems a transparent distortion of the actual state of affairs: the Levites were Moses' people (Freud 45).

The Great Compromise

In the mean time, these peoples adopted the Israelite god Yahu, rather than Aten, whose religion was to be accepted by all tribes, along with the rite of circumcision. These tribes were expected at the same time to dispense with any other deities, including Yahu's consort. In this way it became a monotheistic religion and it began its pogrom of force in an effort to solidify the Hebrew people under one religion. But by itself it lacked something, some essential element that would have held it together among all of these tribes, so it broke in two resulting in the opposing kingdoms of Israel and Judah (Freud 44).

Still, some sort of compromise had been reached between the various tribes. Freud states that it occurred at Qadeš before they entered the land of Canaan (Freud 46). It seems more reasonable to assume, however, that it was a state of compromise reached, not all at once in one place, but over time, gradually, among tribes which had already entered Canaan. This seems much more probable and, although probability does not necessarily equal truth, the only reason to adhere to the notion that it occurred all at once in a single place is a determination to accept the biblical Exodus as historical fact, which it cannot be.

Freud states that since the people of Moses viewed their Exodus experience with such great importance, Yahu had to be given the credit for having freed them, thus also establishing his greatness with stories of the pillar of fire and the parting of the waters (Freud 48). Freud also brings out another important point in that, since the institution of circumcision was adopted by all, then this must have been a concession of the other tribes to those who followed the teachings of Moses. There had to be some connection to Moses, and this was to be it (along with the idea that he would someday return). The followers of Moses, the Levites, would not forsake this badge of superiority. They agreed to recognize the "new" deity, Yahu, as their part of the compromise for the sake of unity (Freud 47), but insisted upon retaining the rite of circumcision. And they came up with the idea that the name of their god must not be uttered as a way of eliminating the conflict that would have resulted over one faction calling him "Aten" and another faction calling him "Yahu". But this, as Freud points out, is also a primeval taboo in and of itself and, as I will point out, it is also a feature of chthonic deities in any case. Be that as it may, this primeval taboo imposed upon the people would have made the situation much easier to control.

So, in effect, the name Aten (and any connection to Egypt other than the biblical Exodus story) was completely eliminated with time and replaced with Yahu. In addition, the attributes of Yahu became the attributes of Aten, replacing his. Over time, Aten was essentially forgotten. But a few remembered, mainly Levites, some of whom became prophets and wrote books. These writings tended to focus upon the attributes originally given to Aten and wound up attributing these Atenist attributes to Yahu or YHWH. And some of these Levites migrated to a place in Egypt called Elephantiné and established a temple there. This will become important to our story. At Elephantiné in Egypt, where the second most ancient Hebrew/Jewish temple was located, papyri from there shows that they worshipped Anat-Yahu, Anat being the wife or consort of Yahu. And, at Elephantiné the Tetragrammaton was not written as YHWH, but as YHW. So, in effect, it is more like Yahu than Yahweh.

The Triumph of Yahu and the Remains From History

In any case, eventually, the people became true monotheists since that part of the Aten's character was adopted in total. Also, through the prophets and latent tradition, the people came to adhere to the belief that their god rejected ceremony and animal sacrifice, both of which had been the hallmarks of the Atenist religion. Belief in him as well as a life of truth and justice replaced sacrifice and the ceremonial (Freud 80).

Now, obviously, these latter were not replaced in their entirety, but they did become much more prominent and important. In so many words, the refugees from Akhetaten who arrived in Jerusalem kept their history of exodus, embellishing it, and that story eventually became transmuted into a journey of the soul into the afterlife for the Hebrews, thus replacing any obscure reference left to either Aten or Osiris for the Hebrews since it became attached to Yahu. Thus, a ceremonial meal developed as a means by which the Hebrews commemorated it, something which all Hebrews would have been more or less glad to participate in. And the sharing of a meal among the Hebrews had a flip-side - the exclusion of foreigners from the table so that no Hebrew was allowed to eat with a foreigner (Gentile). They could not share the Passover meal, or any meal. For to do so was to profane oneself.

Now, it is known that Yahu was originally part of the Canaanite pantheon. He was a war god. The earliest known occurrence of the name "Yahu" appears as an incorporation in reference to "the land of Shasu-Y/iw" found in a list of Egyptian place-names which are located in the temple of Amon at Soleb from the time of Amenhotep III, father of Akhenaten. This reference appears to be associated with Asiatic nomads. Another mention from the reign of Ramesses II (c1303-1213) associates Yahu with Mt. Seir, which is in the area of Moab and Edom.

Yahu appears to have first been worshipped in the areas of Moab, Edom and Midian, beginning as far back as the fourteenth century BCE. Scholars generally agree that his worship was carried northward into Canaan by the Kenites, who had formerly dwelt in Midian. In fact, the "Kenite Hypothesis" basically states that the Hebrews adopted the cult of Yahu from the Midianites via the Kenites. This hypothesis was first proposed by F. W. Ghillany. Hints found in the Hebrew Bible include the assertion that Moses spent time in Midian and also that his wife and father-in-law were Kenites. And, of course, Moses' father-in-law, Jethro, was a priest. But never is it stated - priest of whom?

In any case, the first known extant mention of the name "Israel" occurs with reference to the Egyptian pharaoh Merneptah, whom it is said defeated the Libyans and the Sea Peoples and also attacked Israel. He ruled from July/August of 1213 BCE to May 2, 1203 BCE - only ten years. It is known that he fought the Libyans and the Sea Peoples in year five of his reign. It is also known that his invasion of Israel occurred just prior to year five of his reign and it is stated that he "wiped out" Israel so that his seed was no more. And Ramesses III once again battled the Sea Peoples in 1178 BCE.

The last archaeological evidence of Egypt in Canaan was during the reign of Ramesses VI (1141-1133 BCE), which occurs on a statue base located at *Megiddo* in Northern Canaan. The first settlement at what would become the city of Jerusalem occurred between 4500 to 3500 BCE. So it was there long before the Egyptians ruled that area. The first mention of the city is found in Egyptian texts from about 2000 BCE, in which it is referred to as Rusalimum. It became a vassal city to the Egyptian Empire between about 1550 to 1400 BCE, between one-thousand and five-hundred years or so before the destruction of Minoan civilization on Krete.

The Jebusites, who controlled Jerusalem until Davidic times, observed an astral cult involving Shalem, a deity identified with the Evening Star in Ugraitic mythology. The god Tzedek/Sydyk personified "righteousness". And the Jebusites also worshipped El Elyon, the "Most High God".

Conclusions

The destruction of the Persian Achaemenid Empire under Alexander the Great actually helped to cause the spread of the Mithraic Mysteries to other areas, including Roma, just as the conquest of Egypt by the Roman imperator, Gaius Octavius "Augustus", ensured that the Sacred Mysteries of Isis would likewise spread. In the same way, the destruction of Jerusalem ensured the spread of Judaism and Christianity. As the religions of Dionysos, Kybele and Rhea, among others, were first accepted into the Greco-Roman world as mystery cults, so too those of Mithras, Isis and of Judaism were accepted. This is a process that took place over and over again from almost as far back as history records. This knowledge is useful to illustrate the fact that Christianity was simply another mystery religion, but in a monotheistic form. At least, that is the way that the Romans first saw it and they misunderstood it because of this due to the fact that they did not factor in the apocalyptic, which made all the difference. The apocalyptic made it something entirely different from just another mystery religion. And from where did Christianity obtain this apocalyptic outlook, not directly from Zoroastrianism, but from Zoroastrianism by way of earlier Jewish Gnosticism which had incorporated the apocalyptic into itself. For it was Zoroastrianism that first promulgated the concept of the end of time, the end of the world, a final judgment and a general resurrection of the dead with accompanying rewards and punishments. This, in an of itself, is the very definition of "apocalyptic".

Frankly, the national religions of vanquished nations "evolved" into mystery cults and spread throughout the Roman Empire due to the erasure of political boundaries. It is interesting to note that from Persia, it was Mithraism rather than Zoroastrianism that did so. It would seem that the key here must be that the polytheism of Mithraism allowed it to more readily evolve into a mystery religion, something that might have been rather difficult for Zoroastrianism to do. The addition of the apocalyptic within Zoroastrianism, along with the corruption of the religion overall making it akin to the Medieval Roman Catholic Church, made this a virtual impossibility. And one must remember that Zoroastrianism was the state religion of the Persians, whom the Greeks and Romans hated. However, as difficult as it may have been, Judaism still did what Zoroastrianism found impossible to do in the forms of Jewish Gnosticism and Christianity because of the added admixture of the process of Hellenization, which produced Neoplatonism. So, with the additional inclusion of Zoroastrian and Essene apocalyptic elements within Christianity, which will be discussed in more detail later, it became possible for Judaism to do what Zoroastrianism on its own was unable to do.

> From *Genesis* 14: 18-22:
> And Melchizedek king of Salem brought forth
> bread and wine; now he was a priest of *El Elyon*.
> He blessed him and said,
> Blessed be Abram of *El Elyon*,
> Possessor of heaven and earth;
> And blessed be *El Elyon*,
> Who hath delivered your enemies into your hand. . . .
> And Abram said to the king of Sodom, I have
> sworn unto YHWH, *El Elyon*, possessor of heaven
> and earth. . . ." (my translation for proper effect,
> based on the *New American Standard Bible*).

Here we can clearly see that *two* names are actually being used in the very same passage for the Hebrew god. But there is no confusion among those present. Whatever name their god is being called, they see him as one and the same regardless. This term *El Elyon* is often translated in some Bibles as the *Most High God*. It should be noted that the phrase is not "The Only God". The question arises as to just who, during that period in time in this Egyptian-controlled area of the world, based upon what we know of real history, was called the *Most High God*? The answer to that question is the *Aten*! In so many words, although there are traces of it here, the term *Aten* has been skillfully left out of the Hebrew Bible so that no reference is directly made to that particular deity by name.

A hint to the possibility that Moses had first worshipped Aten is the fact that, when Amenhotep IV began his reign and instituted the almost exclusive worship of the Aten, he changed his name to Akhenaten. As far as I can determine, this is the very first instance in a historical record of someone who changed his name for religious reasons - because he switched gods. The name of Moses was changed simply by dropping the prefix "Aten" as previously described. And, in the Hebrew Bible, Abram is said to have changed his name to Abraham after an encounter with his god and Jacob did the same, to Israel, after an encounter with his god through an angel. So the name change is significant as it shows a linear progression from the Egyptians and Atenism to the Hebrews. That both Abram and Jacob are supposed to have lived well before Amenhotep IV is not significant since no part of the Hebrew Bible was written as early as Amenhotep IV as the oldest extant copies of the Hebrew Bible date to about the second century BCE (unless one counts some of the Dead Sea Scrolls, which may be older), although they were, in fact, originally penned and revised earlier than this.

Frankly, it was the inevitable result of Akhenaten's religious revolution that the previous priesthoods, along with their temples, would be damaged or destroyed and that economic turmoil would ensue. Thus, the breakup of an empire built on polytheism. This must also have been the result within the Persian realm as Zoroastrianism spread, although we do not seem to have records to actually show this, since they were destroyed. This has been the result of the forced spread of monotheism wherever it has been taken - destruction of the economic stability of a given society as well as social dissolution, eventually resulting in the fall of that particular civilization. And this all because the rulers who adhered to or adopted these monotheistic faiths seemed rather automatically to become tyrants with apocalyptic expectations of some sort. So it seems that tyranny is somehow a natural result of monotheism combined with the apocalyptic. It seems to, more often than not, bring out the worst in rulers, rather than the best.

Akhenaten, whom some today revere as a person with great foresight but who, in reality, was little more than some weird creep who happened to be pharaoh, tried to replace the original Egyptian trinity of Osiris, Isis and Horus with his own all-male trinity, but failed. He tried to totally *reverse* Egyptian religion and this was carried forward by the Hebrews/Israelites who invented the story of Moses, reversing earlier hero stories of this same type. In his attempt, Akhenaten destroyed the Egyptian Empire and created the Israelites. So the Israelites were the children of the Egyptians, not the patriarchs. Thus, Akhenaten set the stage for those who would come later. And the Atenist revolution did not fail among the Egyptians so much because, after the death of Akhenaten, the religion of Amun took back over as because the Egyptian people simply *hated* it!

Following his death, the memory of the tyrannical Akhenaten was ruthlessly erased from the record and his new city of Amarna destroyed, the building blocks from it used as fill for building projects elsewhere. He and his religion were so hated that the Egyptians felt that this had to be done. There is even some evidence that both Akhenaten and his wife may have been murdered. But, he became no martyr thereby (although it was thought that he might return). So, some 1,330 years before the birth of Jesus, Akhenaten died and was essentially forgotten to history, only to be uncovered again by archaeologists centuries later.

Amenhotep IV, again, is the first person in history known to have changed his name (to Akhenaten) for religious reasons, i.e., after having an encounter with his deity. And Moses, it seems, followed suit as he was only known as Moses, rather than "Atenmoses", once he had an encounter with his god. Indeed, again, even in the Hebrew Bible this scenario plays out for us at least twice in a major way; Abram changing his name to Abraham and Jacob changing his name to Israel, both following encounters with their god. Is it any wonder, then, that the later Christians followed suit with the New Testament providing the perfect example when Saul had an encounter with his god and thereafter

Apocalypse and Armageddon, The Secret Origins of Christianity:

was referred to as Paul? And, at first, Christians did often change their names at baptism, which is essentially an encounter with their god.

Freud recognized that there had been two distinct factions within the religion of the early Hebrews that, over time, found a way to come together basically into one, with some compromise on both sides. And, although Freud never alludes to having ever been aware of this, Jesus himself said as much when, in *Matthew* 5:17, he stated: "Do not think that I came to abolish the Law or the Prophets; I did not come to abolish but to fulfill." Here Jesus clearly identified both factions openly. The *Law* and the *Prophets* are ways to identify these two factions, which still in some respects existed, though in basic cooperation. This is exactly why the question had to be answered in the first place, because both factions still existed in one form or another. But what one does not see here is that, later, the followers of Jesus did seek to abolish the Law (*Torah*) in favor of the Prophets. The Prophets were repeatedly used to bolster the Christian position within Judaism until the logically expected break-up occurred. And, if we take Freud's views here, which faction within early Judaism could be identified with the Prophets? It was the Atenists. So the earliest Christians were de facto followers of *Aten*. But how could this be thousands of years after the death of Akhenaten? The answer, which we will get to, resides in just who John the Baptizer and Jesus really were.

It can also clearly be seen here, and from further investigation if the reader has a desire to do so, that trinities were by no means new or novel to the ancient world by the time of Jesus. Trinities were actually quite common. Why exactly this is the case is still an open question. But they were by no means foreign to Paganism. So, they were actually perfectly acceptable among Pagans. All-male trinities, however, were considered anathema mainly due to their sheer lack of logic. And, in the instance of Akhenaten and his Aten trinity, all-male trinities were obviously a trend toward monotheism which, I submit, the people and the priests of the other religions realized would be the inevitable result. And this is exactly what Akhenaten had in mind, after all. The Egyptian people came to recognize, because of this episode, that all-male, all-powerful trinities or singular deities were to be studiously avoided at all costs.

The religion that we today call Judaism has at its core the Torah (Law of Moses), the Prophets and an amalgam of stories, some reasonably historical and some quite fanciful, which everyone among the "three great religions" (Judaism, Christianity and Islam) are supposed to believe. But let us just take two of these stories and ask some relevant, though not all-inclusive, questions.

The first story out of many possibilities to be questioned here is that of Noah's flood. Aside from the obvious discrepancies as to how supposedly every animal on earth could have entered the ark, two-by-two, except for those that the humans were allowed to consume, which somehow came on board in groups of seven so they would have something to eat (I guess they ate raw meat so as not to burn the ship down), how is it that every animal aboard could have had enough food for itself during such a long journey and how did the waste from all of these animals become disposed of? All of this, not to mention, how they all got along, the one question that I have never heard anyone so much as propose is just exactly how much might such a ship have weighed with all of those humans, animals, food and water aboard? Once this question is asked it seems quite absurd that a ship made of gopher wood could have withstood the undoubtedly rough waters, winds, etc. with such a load and survived. But we are expected to disengage our minds and accept that god could have made this happen! But the real truth is that if god could have made humans and animals get along and survive for such a period of time under such circumstances, he could have found some way of doing the same for humanity and nature for the rest of time without resorting to creating a flood that would destroy the whole world! After all, he was powerful enough, wasn't he? And the ancient Christian fathers laughed at Pagans for the stories told in the Greek myths while believing things such as this literally!

The second such story is that of the Exodus, the very core of Hebrew history as written in the *Bible*. We are supposed to believe that Moses led the Hebrews out of Egypt under the direction of god, who somehow became visible a number of times and in a number of ways in this story, so that he could actually be seen - as fire burning a bush, as a pillar of fire and as a pillar of smoke, not to mention whatever Moses is supposed to have seen upon Mt. Sinai. We are supposed to believe that the Hebrews followed Moses out of Egypt under these circumstances, probably taking with them little in the way of food or water, but while taking lots of treasure that the Egyptians gave them so they would go away. And some even try to prove the parting of the "Red Sea" as having been accomplished by a strong wind, discounting the fact that such a wind would have to have been so strong that it would have blown everybody away and, if it didn't, well, just walk around in the desert and see what happens when the wind kicks up just a little and you get sand in your eyes. It isn't pleasant.

We are also expected to believe, according to biblical tabulations, that there were some 600,000 men able to bear arms that went out into the desert along with all of the members of their families. By the best estimates, then, the population would have had to have totaled about 1 to 2.5 million which, if they walked ten abreast, the length of their movement would have been 150 miles! Not only is this patently absurd, but this population would have totaled more than the total estimated population of all of Egypt during that time period, which is estimated to have been between 2 and 5 million. One would have to totally suspend one's intellectual faculties to believe such. And some estimates of this population go up as high as 6 million - even more ludicrous. In any case, by just the original calculation, the population would require about 1,500 tons of food, 4,000 tons of wood, and 11 million gallons of water each and every day! Not possible.

Now, to be fair, there are those who work out differing methods for determining how big this population could have been which are more reasonable. But I will not get into the details of these alternative estimates. Suffice it to say that the best of these estimates shows that the maximum number could better be estimated as a total of 7,500 people altogether (Gebhart, *How many came out of the exodus of Egypt?*). But how can one even believe in a supposed Exodus even of these dimension after observing for some three weeks the plight of the Yazidi refugees on Mt. Sinjar in 2014? The best estimate for the number of refugees that were trapped there were about 40,000 people. That being almost five times as much as the best estimate of the Exodus population, they didn't have to remain on that mountain for 40 years! But we are expected to believe that the Israelites wandered around in the inhospitable Sinai desert, eating only manna and quail and occasionally getting water, for 40 years. Preposterous! The best that we can accept here is that the story is an exaggeration just like those in some Greek and other histories. So a much smaller group must have left Egypt. It is not belief that gets us here, but scientific analysis.

According to the best chronologies of Egyptian history, if some Hebrews were indeed enslaved in Egypt, it would have occurred during the reign of Hatshepsut's step-son, Thutmose III. Akhenaten and Ramesses came afterward. And it seems obvious that it was several-hundred years from the time that they might have been enslaved to the time of their invasion of Canaan. This seems pretty far-fetched, that an entire people could have been enslaved in a foreign land for so long a time. So it is actually unlikely that they were. But *a few* may have been. Those who were in Egypt obviously did not influence the Egyptians toward monotheism while there if they stayed that long, or even if they were there for a shorter time. So it seems only logical, then, that the Hebrews were, instead, first influenced by the Egyptians themselves and later influenced toward more strict monotheism by others. They must have been influenced by Akhenaten and his followers and the fact that this monotheistic religion was suppressed, but not destroyed, in Egypt caused some Atenists to leave Egypt. Thus the continued worship of the Aten, the sun, in the form of the Ark, was the impetus for their monotheism.

For those who want to dismiss the fact that the god of Israel was the Yahu from Moab, one can find this fact within the Hebrew language itself. The very name Matityahu (the real surname of the Jewish historian, Flavius Josephus showing his direct relationship with the Maccabean dynasty), meaning "god has given/gift from god", incorporates it. Here, god = *Yahu*. It is actually the same as the English and French name Nathaniel - the *el* meaning god. But, even more than that, one can easily see that Yahu is, within this name, referred to as a *Titan*, essentially a chthonic deity. That emanates from the part of the name here "tit". I say it is easily seen, but, frankly, it is actually easily missed. Nevertheless, it is true.

Now, I don't claim to be a linguist, but I do a pretty good job when I work at it. And I have noticed something else that, apparently, everyone else has overlooked (and if they haven't, I have not seen their work). After much pondering over the name "Moses" and knowing that it had to have been derived, as already discussed, from Egyptian names, a simple correlation almost automatically began to present itself. See, if the Hebrew form is Moshe and the Egyptian form is Mose, where did the form "Moses" come from? Well, the answer is actually obvious for those who have studied Greek and Latin and have also studied the Septuagint (the translation of the Hebrew Scriptures into Greek begun about 280 BCE and completed by the beginning of the Common Era), which is otherwise known as the Greek Bible or, better put, the Hebrew Bible written in Greek during ancient times. In so many words, the Hebrew Scriptures were translated into Greek so that those who spoke Greek could read them. And this was done in Alexandria, Egypt, by the way.

So, getting back to the name itself, it was translated from the Hebrew "Moshe" or "Mosheh" to the Greek "Moses" (Μωσῆς) or "Mouses" and from there to the Latin "Moses" or "Moyses". Now, also knowing that certain "Greek" families were actually originally Egyptian families something began to stand out for me. The ending of many names being "os", as in Hekataios, for example suddenly lent itself to comparison with the ending of "Moses", which is "es". That some Greeks and almost all of the later Romans ended their names with "us", as in Praetextatus, for example, is also significant here. And even "barbarians", the supposedly mythical Hyperboreans, had similar name endings as in Abaris, for example, with his name ending in "is".

Now, since the Egyptian "mose" really means "a son" rather than "a child" and these endings are exclusively used for masculine names, the correlation becomes apparent. The earliest "Greeks" who predated the Mycenaean invasions - mainly those who resided on the island of Krete and at Athenai (Athens) on the mainland - had come to utilize the ending "os" as an equivalent to the Egyptian "mose". So, a Greek name like Hekataios could at first have been written as "Hekate-mose". But it was shortened to the form known to have been used. And one of the things inherent within ancient Greek was always the desire to "beautify", just as in everything else. Thus, the shortened form, which simply sounds nicer. And if the Greeks had really known the likely true name of Moses, it would likely have been rendered as "Atenos" which is incredibly close to the Latin name "Antinoüs".

Now, as the reader has already seen, I have a tendency *not* to anglicize the ancient names by, as they so often do, cutting off these endings. In my view, the effort to persist in this is yet another way of hiding the truth from the folk. In this case, it is a way of skewing the names so that what I have proposed above will not be recognized by the common person. To me, this is very sinister indeed.

In any case, it is interesting that one can accept without much thought that the ancient Hebrews used Egyptian measurements, but one would reject with horror the idea that they embraced any form of Egyptian religion. The faithful simply cannot conceive of anything approaching this! The Hebrews took from the Egyptians and denied that fact just as, many centuries later, the Christians would take from the Greeks and the Romans and deny that. It appears to be a trait of monotheism to take from previous belief systems and then to deny having done it - in a word, theft.

Atenism appears to have rejected blood animal sacrifice along with magic and the concept of the afterlife. It had only one symbol for god just as the Hebrews also had only one symbol for god - the Ark. But the Hebrews, for whatever reason, could not reject blood animal sacrifice in total, even once influenced by Zoroastrianism. This is one of the things that made them at least moderately acceptable to Pagans because sacrifice was of utmost importance to Pagans. Augustus Caesar did not ask the Jews to pray for him, he asked that they make sacrifice on his behalf. To the Roman mind, that was at least as good as bringing the Jewish deity to Roma.

Later, when the early Christians would not even make sacrifice to the imperator that showed the Romans that they were not even willing to do as much for the welfare of the Roman state as the Jews were. *That*, for the Romans, was a clear difference. That the Jews were unable to make sacrifice anymore once their temple was destroyed in 70 CE was irrelevant. The Jews were already exempt from this obligation. But if the Christians wanted the same exemption they needed to establish reasonable grounds for it. This they were unable to do because their religion was *not* old. There was no precedent for it. And such a stance made them seem to the Romans that much more like the hated Zoroastrians who did not perform animal sacrifice (at least not officially). And when the Romans accused the Christians of practicing magic they were indirectly accusing them of being Zoroastrians. Perhaps this is really why the story of Simon Magus appears in the book of *Acts* - to show that Christians rejected Zoroastrianism and magic.

But I digress here. The point is that Christianity has always tried to have it both ways from the very beginning. Jesus and the apostles are said to have performed miracles, i.e., magic, but they rejected a magician who wanted their power. Christianity also rejected blood animal sacrifice even though, as will be shown, Jesus' parents performed such sacrifice themselves. They rejected said sacrifice in favor of the sacrificial death of their savior. Christianity rejected circumcision, even though Jesus had been circumcised as an infant, in favor of castration. They rejected marriage in favor of celibacy. They eventually rejected Torah in favor of freedom. They rejected family in favor of dissension. They even rejected Judaism but usurped the Hebrew Bible as their own. They rejected the Paganism of most of the known world while usurping its ethics and philosophy. And they rejected the world order in favor of apocalyptic chaos!

In any case, there is just as much actual evidence for the existence of Herakles (Hercules) as there is for Abraham - practically none for both. Yet millions claim descent from Abraham in one form or another, physically and/or spiritually. The concept of Melchizedek was a way of hearkening back to the religion of Aten. It is a way to remember Atenism, of whom he was a priest, without directly mentioning it. But during the Babylonian captivity Judaism had become heavily influenced by Zoroastrianism (the pseudo-Greek form of the word which, admittedly, does indeed sound nicer than Zarathushtranism, I think we can all agree). Those who were allowed to return to Jerusalem went so far as to request to take part of the Zoroastrian eternal flame as their guide back, a replacement for the column of flame and smoke that had, according to *Exodus*, guided the Hebrews to the Promised Land in the first place long before. So those influenced by Zoroastrianism had the Zoroastrian flame as their guide (which went out either just before or just after their entry into Jerusalem) while the earlier Hebrews, the Atenists, had a pillar of flame and smoke to guide them. Once in Jerusalem the returning exiles instilled their new Zoroastrian beliefs into the framework of Judaism to create a new religion there. Freud touched on this himself, in a way.

Though they have long forgotten this, the reason that the Jewish Sabbath begins at sundown, and because even in the book of *Genesis* days actually begin with the darkness of nighttime, is because Yahu was a chthonic deity. Aten, by contrast, was not. That is another reason why an intermediary was eventually needed to stand between the Hebrew god (Yahu) and humankind. It is a reversal, of sorts. Also, the biblical book of *Genesis* begins with the creation story that we are all familiar with in which Adam and Eve, supposedly the first created human beings, dwelt within a beautiful garden along with the animals (all animals, one would suspect) until the serpent beguiled Eve into presenting Adam with fruit of the tree of knowledge of good and evil (commonly depicted as an apple) and they were cast out forever to a future of toil and pain. And, naturally, an added curse was placed upon Eve and every woman from that point on in history that she and they would have to endure pain in the very act of childbirth. But, still, the very first commandment given by god remained in place, to have descendants that would continue to care for the earth. So it became an integral part of the Hebrew psyche that to have descendants was among the most important of things to be done.

But then jump ahead a few thousand years. Certainly, the apostle Paul, a follower of "The Way", an obscure Jewish sect, advocated celibacy as, it would seem, most of the other apostles also did. According to the earliest Jewish/Christian Gnostics - those who wrote some of the Nag Hammadi manuscripts, including that of the *Gospel of Eve* and the *Apocalypse of Moses*, the feminine was actually the good principle. It was Eve who tacitly gave Adam knowledge and, thus, gave knowledge to the whole of humankind. So, in effect, she did a good thing rather than a bad thing. And, when they both had knowledge, they were both awakened or *enlightened*. And this may also have been a subtle hint that matriarchy preceded patriarchy.

Similarly, the ancient goddess in practically every other Euro-Mediterranean culture gave knowledge to humankind through the agency of the ancient Sacred Mysteries. And that which scholars have missed for centuries is that, for Eve, the giving of the apple was actually equivalent to the giving of the symbol at the end of the Sacred Mystery enactment, the Tree of the Knowledge of Good and Evil symbolizing the actual Sacred Mystery. In so many words, the story of Adam and Eve *is* a Sacred Mystery play *full of reversals*. Knowledge was not imparted directly, but through the agency of the tree (symbolizing the Sacred Mystery) whose symbol was the fruit, presumably the apple. The assurance of salvation was symbolized *by* this fruit. So it was, effectively, that one piece of knowledge that one had to possess in order to know that one had salvation. It was that one symbol that led to understanding/Wisdom; that led to enlightenment. Again, the *Genesis* story also reveals several things in reverse when compared to other Sacred Mysteries of ancient times - the trials that one must go through occur *after* the receiving of knowledge once one is thrown out of the garden and, thus, has to then be concerned about salvation. But it is still essentially the same type of Sacred Mystery. It *is* a Mystery play.

The concept of forbidden knowledge (not necessarily to be equated with hidden knowledge) is a core concept among monotheists. After all, if one knows or learns certain things then one may wish to usurp even god and, thereby, make him angry. But, for the Pagan, there was no forbidden knowledge. There was *hidden* knowledge in the form of the Sacred Mysteries. But everyone historically could become an initiate and, thus, proceed along any one or more of multiple paths toward the knowledge that provided assurance of salvation, or enlightenment. And, frankly, some people understand better when presented with a mystery or a parable, as demonstrated in the gospels.

In addition, the Hebrews tried to make monotheism older than it really was by writing the book of *Genesis*, etc., providing a skewed history. But monotheism actually appears to have begun with Zarathushtra in Persia and then independently with Akhenaten in Egypt. The Hebrews, then, were first influenced by the form from Egypt and later it was reinforced by the form from Persia. *Genesis* was written for this reason just as the New Testament book of *Acts* was written to, in part, make it seem that Christianity spread more rapidly and easily than it did.

And, in fact, a case can be made that the early Hebrew patriarchs were really little more than ancient Canaanite deities made into human form - another *reversal* of sorts. This is shown in the following table. This table is important not in that it *proves* anything, for proof may never be obtained. This table is important because it shows that such a scenario is *possible* at all and, if it is possible, then it *could* have happened.

Biblical (& Egyptian)	Canaanite/ Ugrit/Hebrew (& Greek)	Mesopotamian (& Syrian)	Arabian (& Persian/ Parthian)
Adam	El/Il/Adonai	Apsu "water"	Ilāh
Eve	Elat/Anat/ Asherah/Astarte	Tiamat/Ba'alat	al-Lat/al-'Ilāhat
Cain	Mot (Hades)	Enlil	Sin
Abel	Ba'al Hadad (Zeus)	Adad/Anu	Abgal
Seth	Yam/Yatha (Poseidon)	Enki	Yatha
Enosh	El Shaddai	Enkimdu	Atarsamain (Asura)
Enoch	El Elyon	Enbilulu	Al-Qaum
Methuselah	Moloch/ Tzedek/Sydyk	Marduk	Malakbel
Noah (Nu)	Shahar/El Elyon	Ea	Nuha
NaamahEmzara (Naunet)	Ishtar/Astarte	Inanna	Atarsamain
Ham (Kuk)	Sin	Adad	Shams/Samas/ Shamash
Ne'elatama'uk (Kauket)	Kathirat	Lahamu	al-'Uzzá
Japeth (Amun)	Yarikh	Enki	Ya'uq
'Adataneses (Amaunet)	Asherah/Elat	Tiamat	al-Lat/al-'Ilāhat

Apocalypse and Armageddon, The Secret Origins of Christianity:

Shem (Huh)	Shalem/El Olam	Enlil	Suwá
Sedeqetelebab (Hauhet)	Ba'alat/Ba'alit	Ninlit	Manuāt
Abram/Abraham	Elohim	Dumuzid	Bēl-Samin/ Beelshamen
Isaac	Yahu/Yahweh YHW/YHWH	Tammuz (Adonis)	Yaghūth YGUH (Ahura)
Jacob	Israel	Asaruludu	Yarhibol
Laban	Latpan	lahar	Hubal
Melchizedek (Aten)	Moloch/ Tzedek/Sydyk	Marduk	Malakbel

Within the above table one can clearly see two almost distinct sections, which detail two almost distinct creation accounts, containing nine names within each. Again, it should be stated that it is not really important to absolutely *prove* here that the synchronization shown above is absolutely true and accurate, for after so long a passage of time and after so much destruction of ancient records, that is simply impossible. What is important, however, is the need to understand, since it was actually rather easy for me to work this up, that it was possible for such a synchronization to, in fact, *be* worked up (and more could have been done). The very fact that it could be done at all speaks volumes. It shows that, even after all these millennia, it is possible to see that which potentially underlies the whole account of *Genesis-Exodus*. And that there actually is something that underlies this account should concern any serious religious scholar and student. It would seem, then, that the truth really is that the ancient patriarchs of the *Bible*, especially those shown above, with few exceptions, must have originally been a part of some mostly forgotten ancient pantheon.

This, it would seem, then, is the whole reason that the characters in *Genesis* are not spared from exposure for the horrible things that they are sometimes shown as having done. Just as the ancient Greeks wrote of their gods and goddesses sometimes committing unsavory acts, the writer(s) of *Genesis* did the same with the patriarchs. After this, in *Exodus* and the following books, it was simply convention to continue this theme of human imperfection. But the point is that, in whatever original mythology or mythologies this might have all been taken from, the Hebrew deities did the same kinds of things as the Greek deities. They were not portrayed as perfect just because they were deities. And they became cleverly transformed into humans by the biblical writer(s). It's too simple and too obvious once one notices it. The writer(s) created a new myth with humans rather than gods (except for one) which actually utilized one creation story (that of Adam and Eve) and then another creation story (that of Noah and his family) and added genealogies in order to get to actual humankind.

In the Greek myths the deities sometimes did rather perverse things. In the Hebrew epic, their own ancestors sometimes did perverse things. In a way this is fitting as the Greeks would have proverbially said that they were descendants of their deities. Problem was, the Hebrews came to believe their writings as literal history that *had* to be accepted *as* literal. And the Christians were even more determined in this. Thus they (the Christians) also perverted the Greek myths by trying to also read and understand them literally. So, in all probability, the patriarchs really are members of a long lost pantheon. And as others accused the Greeks of worshipping deified humans, perhaps the Hebrews actually made their gods into humans so that they could continue to venerate them and still claim to worship only one god.

The whole reason that the biblical patriarchs are given incredible (and humanly impossible) life-spans is actually not because they, as humans, lived so long (for they were never even real people), but because they were now practically forgotten primordial deities - a pantheon that was made human so that these deities could continue to be venerated within a monotheistic system. The most important of these primordial deities are those detailed in the foregoing table. And only after these now human deities are detailed do we begin to see real human beings, such as Moses. The most important clue to this in the book of *Genesis* being the fact that it is stated that it was during the time of Enosh, son of Seth, that people began to call upon the name of the Lord (*Genesis* 4:26). Obviously, then, prior to this no one called upon the name of Yahu/El Shaddai. Only by this point did humankind begin the move toward monotheism. That is the reason that the above chart is divided in the way that it is. So all prior to Enosh/Abram are clearly ancient deities and after that a transition from deity and humankind takes place (deities to demi-humans).

Also, as shown on the above chart, the second set (that of Noah and his family) most strongly resembles the Egyptian chthonic deities known as the Ogdoad. Thus, Noah would be Nu, his wife, Naamah (whose name comes from Genesis Rabba midrash; the alternate name Emzara found in the book of *Jubilees*) would be Naunet (this couple representing the primordial waters), Japeth would be Amun, his wife, 'Adataneses (from the book of *Jubilees*) would be Amaunet (this couple representing air), Shem would be Huh, his wife, Sedeqetelebab (according to the book of *Jubilees*) would be Hauhet (this couple representing eternity), Ham would be Kuk and his wife, Ne'elatama'uk/Na'eltama'uk (from the book of *Jubilees*) would be Kauket (this couple representing darkness). That only leaves "god" who, in the Egyptian myth of the Ogdoad, was basically represented by Ra (representing light). The two stories are almost perfectly identical in many ways. So the biblical flood story was another creation story with basically the same primordial deities in different guise. Or it was an incorporation of a different and competing creation story with slightly different deities. Either way, we have two basic primordial creation stories embedded within the pages of *Genesis*. And, thus, like the Greeks, the twelve tribes of Israel could subtly claim that they were descendants of their ancient gods.

Embedded within all of this are smaller, but not less significant, allusions to whatever ancient mythology that existed along with the rites associated with it. One of these primordial rites was that of circumcision. That the Hebrews may have originally obtained this rite from the Egyptians is still debatable, although the preponderance of the actual evidence suggests that they did. Be that as it may, circumcision, in its most primordial reason for existing, would seem to have a direct correlation with the female menstrual cycle. That women bled on a monthly basis is something that abhorred ancient man. Even the ancient Greeks, lovers of all that was beautiful, including the female body, were horrified by this monthly cycle - by the blood. And ancient man had little appreciation for the potential causal connection between this blood, which was actually life-giving, and the conception of children.

They did not possess the scientific knowledge about this subject that we do today.

Still, that man himself did not bleed in such a manner and that woman, since she did, possessed something somehow that man did not, became the very impetus for circumcision because, within the quasi-logic of primordial man, he wanted to be able to bleed from his genitals too. And the very reason that the ancient Hebrews proposed that an eight day old male child should be circumcised is exactly because there were eight souls upon the ark (or, in reality, eight primordial chthonic creation deities which were probably very similar to the Egyptian Ogdoad). Thus the male child not only bled, but he bled long before the female did, in this way surpassing her in this patriarchal system with yet another *reversal*. Thus the patriarchal deities were made dominant.

Before this, and even after this, it was understood that the woman bled and experienced pain and man saw this as a curse upon her - the fact that she had to endure this monthly. But the woman understood that it was actually no curse, but was instead a blessing because only the woman could actually give life. So, although the man mimicked womanhood through the act of circumcision, he was still unable to produce life.

So some ancient Canaanite gods and goddesses were made into humans by the ancient Hebrews/Israelites. Thus, they became "demi-humans". Therefore, when the concept of the "Son of Man" was first postulated, that was exactly the same conceptual process, although this time it was making the only "Omni" creator god into a human by having him take on human flesh. It is *exactly* the same process carried a bit further. That the demiurge was transformed into a being of evil flesh (in the form of Jesus) would have been logical if one can accept that he was evil and the creation was, therefore, also evil. That Jesus himself was supposed to have been good and able to overcome this is exactly because he possessed special or *secret* knowledge. Be that as it may, the very concept that god or gods can become human stems from the ancient Israelite's ability to actually reduce their gods to humans. If they had drawn out this concept to its logical conclusion, rather than making it into some mystical proposition, then they might have actually developed a viable means by which salvation could be expounded to the folk in that the gods were obviously spirit/soul and upon becoming a part of the human-being, they would tend toward that being's salvation by instilling it with Knowledge which would allow it to transcend itself. But instead, their god-humans came into existence in a world with no hope other than procreation and rest in she'ol. In other words, there was no real concept of soul. So humans were actually left with no hope other than that their physical seed would survive. The sheer emptiness of this is mesmerizing! But the gospel-created Jesus added a Platonic soul to this mix and, thus, the hope of salvation.

Finally, a further comparison of ancient Hebraic religion, as exemplified by the books of *Genesis* and *Exodus*, with the Sacred Mysteries of the Egyptian and Greco-Roman world shows many contrasts beyond the reversals described here. In the Sacred Mysteries only the virtuous could enter. The initiate went through various "tests" and, in the end, beheld or received *hidden* (but not forbidden) Knowledge, which was a *symbol* of salvation. By this means, they were enlightened or assured of salvation. But, in the *Genesis/Exodus* scenario the sinful were made to exit paradise (thus, the development of the concept of sin). Adam and Eve lived in the garden/paradise naming the animals and Eve was tempted by the serpent. Eve was induced to take the fruit of the tree of the knowledge of good and evil, which was *forbidden* knowledge. She gave the fruit, which symbolized this knowledge, to Adam. The receipt of this knowledge effectively damned both to lives of toil and heartache. They had to exit paradise because they had been *made* sinful through knowledge. So the *Genesis/Exodus* scenario was actually a reversal and/or a perversion of the ancient Sacred Mysteries. But we will not dwell further on these Sacred Mysteries themselves in this work other than to show that Christianity was actually a form of a Sacred Mystery itself.

2

HELLENIZATION, CHRISTIANITY AND THE DETERIORATION OF RELIGION AND PHILOSOPHY

Hellenization: the Forgotten Ingredient

Hellenization was one of the results of the conquests of Alexander the Great (Ἀλέξανδρος ὁ Μέγας) of Makedonia. Alexander's father, Philip, had conquered Greece (Hellas) and also had his son, Alexander, educated at the feet of the great Greek philosopher, Aristoteles (Ἀριστοτέλης), better known as Aristotle, successor to Platon (Πλάτων), better known today as Plato (428-348 BCE). So Alexander was brought up to be both a philosopher and a warrior - more or less, the *philosopher-king* of Platon's writings. This was what many Greeks had sought for ever since Platon formulated the idea, just as the Jews were looking for a messiah, although the Jews had not completely formulated their concept yet.

Alexander, who strove to pattern himself after his hero, Achilles/Achileus (Ἀχιλλεύς), did not disappoint his father's legacy, for he went on to defeat and completely subjugate the mighty Achaemenid Empire of Persia, the arch enemy of Greece. But even this was not enough for the great Alexander, for he wished to conquer the entire world! And he might have almost succeeded, at least as far as the known ancient world was concerned, had it not been for the fact that his men *finally* refused to go further after they conquered southern India, which was beyond even the area of the former Achaemenid Empire.

Now, prior to Alexander's conquests, both Greece and Judea existed in separate spheres and had little or no influence upon one another. And the kingdom of Israel was already a distant memory. They didn't even trade with one another. Thus, they developed in completely different ways. Judea existed mainly as a strongly religious agricultural society while Greece existed very much as a philosophical/intellectual society with warlike tendencies. In other words, Judea was mainly populated by illiterate farmers while Greece was mainly populated by literate intellectuals and warriors. In fact, Greece was among the most literate societies of ancient times. Books were everywhere for purchase by anyone who could read and could afford to buy them. Not so in Judea, where not so much as a library, private or otherwise, existed except, perhaps, within the temple in Jerusalem.

But when Alexander conquered the Achaemenid Empire, all of this began to change. The previous nationalism and exclusiveness between nations was changed into a period of communication and amalgamation between the nations creating a somewhat cosmopolitan culture over time. A form of national syncretism was thus produced. In fact, the unity of East and West culturally and intellectually was, following the defeat of the Achaemenid Empire, Alexander's most cherished desire. Alexander's intention here was to create a cosmopolitan empire by way of a great fusion of ideas between East and West and, in this way, to "advance the work of humanity and give expression to the Hellenic spirit" (Bentwich 28-29), which envisioned humanity as good rather than evil. He therefore attempted to initiate an evolution toward human goodness. To this end Alexander established new cities throughout his new empire, many named after himself, which were meant to function as examples of progress and cooperation. And the populations of these new cities were diverse in every way, a mixture of all of the peoples of his vast empire and, in some cases, even from beyond.

As part of this effort, Alexander established many cities and colonies other than his multiple Alexandria's, which also included subjects from his vast empire and beyond, including the Jews, placed at his empire's most vital points (Bentwich 28-29). In fact, the Jews were considered valuable to this overall effort and the effect of settling Jews in various parts of his empire marked a new and advanced stage in the Jewish

Diaspora, begun under the Assyrians (Bentwich 31). This was the true beginning of the Jewish Diaspora over a wide geographical area.

But they were not the only ones who were spread throughout Alexander's empire, as previously noted. The Greeks and Makedonians also colonized many places throughout the empire and often resided side-by-side with the Jews, although usually within separate communities within the same city. Still, all of these people interacted to some degree. This interaction, over time, produced both positive and negative results. But the overall intent and effect was that *knowledge* was shared between all of these diverse peoples, and that was a success.

One cannot fault Alexander for believing, because of his philosophical training, that the creation of an amalgamation of philosophies and religions, mainly based upon the Greek Hellenic model, would work. Indeed, it *should* have worked, in theory. But, in practice, although it started out well, it did not work and it turned out to be anything but that which Alexander might have hoped for in the long run. However, that is not to say that there was nothing positive about the Hellenistic system. The system which survived the death of Alexander, again, worked quite well for the most part, judging from its survival even though Alexander's empire was fragmented following his death. But the philosophers of this age began to speculate upon subjects like the nature of reality rather than attempting to determine what was truly real, as in the past. Philosophy, then, began to lose its grounding in truth and seriousness and was, thus, weakened as a moral influence. Hellenization attempted to combine the search for the truth of things with the harmonization of life, but these two were naturally in conflict (Bentwich 58).

> The saying that Hellenism paid regard to beauty and Judaism to conduct has this amount of truth: in Hellas it was the feeling for beauty, in Judea the law of righteousness which impregnated the mass and determined the character of the people. And when Judaism and Hellenism expanded outside their national boundaries, these were the contrasted ideas which they carried with them into the diaspora (Bentwich 60).

So, although some positive effort was indeed made on both sides, the mixing of Jewish populations and Greek populations was not entirely successful anywhere because, as already noted, both communities originated from entirely different world concepts. Even the efforts of the eminent Jewish philosopher, Philo Judaeus of Alexandria, simply created a system that tended toward the very destruction of the civilization which it was designed to perpetuate, i.e., Judaism. As Marvin Meyer so aptly states:

> The Hellenistic world was not simply another classical world with Greek values and classical deities. Rather, it was more 'cosmopolitan': the *kosmos*, or 'world,' was the polis, and the citizens and gods of the world were not only Greek, but also Anatolian, Asian, African, and Indian (Meyer 2).

Another factor was that of astrology. As astrology spread from Babylonia westward it became, more or less, an obsession among the Jews, Greeks and others. It was opposed by Jewish leaders, who denounced it continuously, but many people continued to devoutly believe in it anyway (Bentwich 62).

Hellenization Surrounds Judea

Still, elements continued to exist that favored Hellenization. Also, in other parts of what had once been Alexander's empire, Hellenization was still the dominant theme, even among the Jewish populations dispersed there. Indeed, the Greek way was so prevalent that Jewish populations in the Diaspora had generally ceased to speak either Hebrew or Aramaic, speaking Greek instead. The result was the necessity that the Hebrew Scriptures be translated into Greek. And this translation served the second purpose of also bringing the Jewish religion to the Gentiles who could now read it.

Eventually the process of Hellenization, along with the strong efforts toward conversion of Gentiles, produced a system of biblical interpretation known as *allegory* as opposed to literalism. This was a way of explaining the basics of Judaism to a world which could otherwise by no means understand it. The frank fact of the matter was that the Greeks were not stupid enough to attempt to read and interpret the Hebrew scriptures literally as they even read their own myths allegorically.

Another result of Hellenization was that "[h]ellenistic Jewry became a medley of struggling heresies and sects. Animated by the desire to convert the gentiles, it had sacrificed its particularism and weakened its defenses. . . ." (Bentwich 341). Thus, this allegorical method of interpretation eventually produced two major systems of religious belief, Neoplatonism and Jewish Gnosticism, which were not in all cases mutually exclusive.

Now, Alexander and his successors went even further than that which has already been described. They also established colonies of Greeks and Makedonians, as well as others, in cities throughout the empire in such a way as to ensure that the populations of many of these cities were mainly Greek and/or Makedonian. So these peoples were more often than not in the majority, replacing the old majorities of indigenous peoples there. And this policy was quickly and energetically put into practice throughout Judea to such a degree that many areas became almost wholly Greek.

Alexander himself had planted colonies of Greeks and allies at Samaria, Skythopolis (Bet-She'an), on the east of the plain of Esdraelon, and at Neapolis (Schechem). The Ptolemies who ruled that part of the empire following Alexander's death went even further than that, essentially surrounding the Judean plateau with cities populated by Greeks and her allies. Within a century these cities had become semi-independent city-states, creating a wall of Hellenistic culture around Judea (Bentwich 45-46). Skythopolis (Σκυθόπολις), or "City of the Skythians", was so re-named because Alexander is said to have mainly populated this new city with Skythian settlers. In so many words, his Skythian mercenaries were given this city for themselves and their families, along with some Makedonians, all of whom became the majority there.

In the mean time, the Jews were not, at first, actually being coerced into converting from their faith and were not actually persecuted until the time of Antiokhos (Antiochus) IV Epiphanes (175-163 BCE). They were until then completely free to practice their religion and live by their own Mosaic Law (*Torah*) without fear. Therefore, most Jews continued to practice their ancestral religion. Still, many of the upper classes, having a desire to assimilate and "fit in" with the prevailing culture, did so, living according to the dictates of the surrounding Hellenized culture.

By initiating the process of Hellenization Alexander and his successors mistakenly set into motion forces that began the slow process of the disintegration of pure Hellenic (Greek) culture itself. He had the desire to transplant this pure culture throughout his empire but, instead, Hellenism began to incorporate ideas from other cultures to such an extent that it became less and less recognizable in its pure form over time. So, that which was, on the surface, a great idea, had the unintended consequence of actually weakening Hellenism itself.

Hellenization Dominates

Inevitably, then, the Hellenistic culture that existed within Alexander's Empire and its successors was much different from the Hellenic culture of Greece. "The outward show of the life of the city-state would be reproduced. . . . But the ideal spirit of struggle for human perfection . . . was lacking in the imitation, and the defect deprived it of the old ennobling influence" (Bentwich 54).

Hellenic culture was, therefore transforming into Hellenistic culture, even in Greece. The pure religion, philosophy and ideals of the Greek city-state, and the culture as a whole, was being transformed due to the new influence of eastern ideas, creating a bastardization. The conquest of the Achaemenid Empire had brought western Greek civilization into direct, continuous contact with eastern Persian civilization. The "natural" and intended outcome of this encounter was an intermixing of cultures and ideas. This mixture, however, was actually a lower, motley, creation as compared with the Hellenic civilization which Alexander had known and this transformation was effected rather quickly. And perhaps the speed of this transformation was the main reason that Hellenistic culture lacked the most important positive attributes of Hellenic civilization as a whole.

Now, the truth of the matter is that, as a result of this process of Hellenization the philosophical trends of this period in history tended to run counter to the strongly intellectual systems which had been developed by the likes of Platon and Aristoteles. Philosophy, along with religion, became decadent, focusing on mystical speculation rather than intellectual discipline. So "[t]he decay of philosophy runs parallel with the degeneration of Hellenic religion" (Bentwich 66). Thus, both philosophy and religion decayed at once together. Philosophers of this time period began to see themselves as "citizens of the world" and to advocate for a fusion of cultures rather than for the old Hellenic exclusiveness. So both religion and philosophy were utilized in an effort to create this social amalgam. Only the Jews tended to hold out for their own separate national way of life to any degree (Bentwich 71).

> The philosophy which was hawked around was as poor an image of the thought of the genuine Hellas as the Hellenic cults which were set up in the cities of Egypt and Syria were a poor reflection of the national religion of Athens and Sparta (Bentwich 83).

Indeed, there was little left within the philosophy of the time which Platon or Aristoteles would have recognized. The influence of eastern thought - contemplations concerning the soul, good and evil as abstract or unearthly values, and life after death - were essentially foreign to Hellenic philosophy. But the philosophy of the ancients was used with great ingenuity, especially by Philo, to give support for the thought of the East. Western philosophy, then, essentially became the slave of eastern speculation. These are the philosophical trends that the apostle Paul would later label "vain philosophies", for he had no real concept of the old pure Hellenic philosophy.

Also, during this same time period, beginning in about 100 BCE, the Jews began an aggressive, entirely pacifistic, proselytization campaign in the Diaspora partially as a result of the translation of their Scriptures into Greek as well as their Maccabean victory over the Seleucids. This effort was largely successful with many converting to Judaism. So, with the decay of Hellenism, Hellenization and Greek philosophy came a zealous force of Jewish proselytization which was largely effective, even though Judaism still remained a distinct minority religion throughout the Mediterranean. This proselytization effort continued into Roman times and lasted into at least the early fifth century CE. All of this also resulted in an increase in popular wishes for a messiah who would rule Israel forever and subjugate the Gentiles.

"Persecution" by Antiokhos (Antiochus)

And soon the Hellenistic civilization, the remnants of Alexander's empire, already fragmented into a handful of large states, including the Seleucid Empire, would face a threat which they would not be able to withstand. The Romans were on the horizon and gaining strength with each new conquest. Eventually the Hellenistic civilizations created out of the empire of Alexander would fall either to the Romans or to the revived Persians. And, at this crucial time in history, the Jews would face what was, perhaps, their first great test, at least since the time when they were conquered by the Babylonians.

The Seleucid Empire, at that time ruled by Antiokhos IV Epiphanes, was having great difficulty standing up to the blows being inflicted upon it by the advancing Romans. So Antiokhos decided to strengthen his empire by attempting to increase its homogeneity. Judea was the one area of his empire which had resisted assimilation to Hellenistic culture to any great degree and their territory was on the edge of his empire. He came to consider it necessary to make them conform. In so many words, Antiokhos, seeing that the proposed assimilation was basically working everywhere better than it was in Judea, decided to force his hand there and to *make* it work there also, if he could. But, in his effort Antiokhos made a crucial error. He misunderstood the mechanics of assimilation and by forcing Hellenization upon a people, who, for the most part, did not want it, he succeeded only in creating the opposite of his desire, *resistance*. Because of his efforts many Jews became suddenly and almost completely adverse to the process which Alexander had put into place and many who had previously embraced it, at least to a point, now totally rejected it. This conflict culminated in the revolt, led by Judas Maccabaeus, in which the Jewish people were ultimately victorious, gaining their independence from the Seleucids, lasting about one-hundred years until the conquest of Judea by the Roman General, Pompeius Magnus (Pompey the Great).

But this is not really a complete picture of that which was taking place, for in addition to the efforts of Antiokhos, competing efforts by more than one Jewish faction were also at play. See, the Jews who had more or less accepted Hellenization were one faction and they wanted to expand their influence. Those who had not accepted Hellenization resisted these efforts. Thus, a civil war among the Jews began to ensue at about the same time that Antiokhos moved to achieve greater synchronization throughout his empire. All of this led to heinous atrocities on all sides as the various factions and their armies fought one another and at the same time perpetrated mass executions of one population or another, mainly by crucifixion. And in 168 BCE Antiokhos captured Jerusalem and desecrated the temple there by sacrificing swine to Zeus Olympias, whose statue he also placed within the temple. This resulted in full-scale revolt against him which was ultimately successful and the temple thereafter purified (Friedman 364). In the mean time many Jews refused to submit in any way and willingly died as martyrs in various horrific ways. There are many stories about these martyrs, some of which are taken from the books of *I Maccabees* and *II Maccabees*. Eventually, the Hasmonians (the most conservative faction of all) were victorious against the forces of Hellenization and of Antiokhos. They created a state of their own which endured for just over one-hundred years until an alliance with the Romans sealed their fate. Capernaum, a city which is very important in the canonical gospels, was established during the Hasmonean period in about the second century BCE.

One very important thing should be noted here. It was during the time of the Maccabean Revolt and later Hasmonean rule that the genre of literature that we refer to as "apocalyptic" first came into existence. Scholars are in general agreement that the book of *Daniel* was actually written during this time period, *not* as early as it is purported to have been written. And it is certain that no other known apocalyptic book was written prior to this period in time. What this tells us is that it was the "persecution" of Antiokhos that essentially caused this form of literature to come into existence. Whereas there had been minor apocalyptic references in patriarchal monotheistic religion prior to this time, now the concept of the apocalyptic truly began to take shape and to grow wildly as many, many apocalyptic books were written and circulated among the folk. Without the apocalyptic expectation of a messiah, Jewish Gnosticism would never have produced Christianity but would have simply remained within the realm of Neoplatonic philosophy. The result of the apocalyptic, frankly, has been disastrous for history.

The Jewish Temples

Now, contrary to popular belief today, the temple in Jerusalem, with its three phases of building and destruction, was not the only "Jewish" temple in the ancient world. Still, the one in Jerusalem was the most important one overall even though the others sometimes rivaled it. First, Shiloh had been holy ever since the Israelites initially invaded Canaan and it remained so even after Jerusalem was captured and made the capitol. At Shiloh, the tabernacle had first existed, but was apparently later made into a temple. Archaeologists have found the remains of a temple there which appears to have replaced an older Canaanite temple. It was a two-story structure with great columns. But the time-frame in which it existed does not seem to be certainly known.

There also existed a temple of the Samaritans on Mount Gerizim, not far from Shiloh, which the Jewish historian, Titus Flavius Josephus (Yosef ben Matityahu), wrote was built during the time of King Manasseh (although this is disputed). He stated that Manasseh's father-in-law obtained permission from Cyrus the Great to build a temple there after a split ensued between the two Jewish factions in Jerusalem. Indeed, a schism did in fact take place as the intolerant faction led by people such as Ezra and Nehemiah rejected any unity with the Samaritan people, especially with reference to religion. No compromise could be made here, so people (who knows how many) along with some disaffected priests left Jerusalem and formed their own sect of the Hebrew religion and built their own temple. This temple, believed today to have been built about 450 BCE, may instead have been built during the reign of Artaxerxes II Mnemon (405-358 BCE) and is known to have been rededicated to Zeus Xenios in 166 BCE by the Samaritans after Antiokhos IV Epiphanes rose to power. In any case, it was destroyed first in about 200 BCE, then rebuilt and later destroyed again in about 108/9 BCE by the Maccabean forces of John Anhydrous once he took Samaria. So it didn't last long, physically, in either phase of its existence. But it has lasted in the memories of the Samaritan people. And, by the way, there also existed a temple to Serapis-Isis in Samaria during this time period, which was destroyed by John Hyrkanos (Hyrcanus) in about 125 BCE (Parrot 96 & 110).

The Jews of Egypt now become our next focus. It is they who developed the system of thought (Gnosticism) which evolved into a religion that changed the entire world. Alexandria is the place where the largest number of Jews resided outside of Judea. In Egypt, Alexandria became the center of Jewish existence as Alexandria became the second Jewish city in the world, second to Jerusalem. In addition, there were considerable Jewish settlements along the Nile (Bentwich 36). They still recognized that their deity, Yahu, had been a chthonic deity and, thus, like all chthonic deities, he was eventually seen as requiring a mediator between himself and humankind. The concept of a mediator eventually developed into the concept of the celestial savior-messiah.

Thus, there were considerable Jewish settlements of importance not only in Palestine and in Alexandria, but also elsewhere in the Mediterranean world. There was the famous Jewish temple to YHW located on the Egyptian island of Elephantiné. The Jewish community there, along with its sister colony from Aramea located nearby at Syene (modern Aswan), are believed to have been founded as military garrisons about 650 BCE during the reign of King Manasseh, and therefore existing during the time of Ezra and Nehemiah, sent there to assist Pharaoh Psammetichus I during his Nubian campaign, which included both Jews *and* Samaritans who, amazingly, appear to have gotten along quite well there. Thereafter they remained to guard that frontier and, since these colonies were founded under Persian rule, they spoke Aramaic, the common language of the Achaemenid Empire. This temple at Elephantiné existed in close proximity with the temple of the Egyptian god Khnum, the Egyptian ram-headed deity and, although conflicts did sometimes arise between the two groups, the overall situation there appears to have been one of mutual toleration, at least. But this mutual tolerance did not last forever, as letters from both locations attest, one in particular written to the then rulers in Judea requesting that the Persian King, Darius II (423-404 BCE), issue an order that the temple be rebuilt after the Egyptians demolished the Jewish temple there. History, and these letters, actually provide us with the reasoning behind the temple's destruction by the Egyptians, for when the Persians invaded and conquered Egypt, they destroyed several Egyptian temples, but spared this Jewish temple. In so many words, the monotheist (or dualistic) Zoroastrian Persians spared the temple of the monotheist (or dualistic) Jewish population, obviously seeing it in a favorable way. The Egyptians resented this and eventually struck back against the Persians in the only way they could, by destroying this Jewish temple.

Interestingly, Khnum is one of the earliest of Egyptian deities. He was deity of rebirth, creation, and the evening sun. He had a consort, Satis, who was seen alternately as a war goddess and as a fertility goddess. They together had a daughter, Anuket. They are called the Elephantiné Triad. More interesting than this, however, are the manuscripts, etc. found by archaeologists known as the *Elephantiné Papyri*. These are Jewish manuscripts written in Aramaic dating from the fifth century BCE. They were penned by the community at Elephantiné and document that community during Persian rule (495-399 BCE). The religious practices there are said to have been virtually identical to Iron Age II Judaic religious practices (Noll 248). Most interesting of all, the papyri also show that they worshipped Anat-Yahu (Yahu and his consort, Anat).

In addition to these temples, and the ones of the Samaritans at Shiloh and on Mount Gerizim (where, although the temple has been long destroyed, the Samaritans still today perform ancient rituals, including the offering of the Paschal Lamb), it is said that there existed yet another Jewish temple which was located ". . . near Carthage, at the coast town of Boricum . . . [which was still] standing in the reign of Justinian, which was said to have been founded by King Solomon" (Bentwich

38), although I have not been able to confirm this. The worship which existed in the temple at Boricum must surely also have been somewhat different from that found in Jerusalem, but little seems to be known about it today.

So it seems that we have six other Jewish or Jewish-type temples located at strategic points around the Mediterranean, but, interestingly, *not* in Europe; all of which differed slightly and which would have provided a place for Jews to worship, more or less, locally so that they all would not have to travel to Jerusalem. And this was partially the result of Jewish proselytization and was definitely a result of the Jewish Diaspora.

The temple at Jerusalem, by the way, was linked with the concept of *mountain*, it seems, in order to portray the temple as the embodiment of the *cosmic mountain* (Mt. Parwan?), since mountains were considered sacred over much of the Mediterranean world (Friedman 363). However, less well-known is the fact that there was also another ancient Israelite religions center, located at what is now called Kuntillet Ajrud, in the Egyptian Sinai close to the modern Israeli border. This center operated at least during the seventh to the ninth centuries BCE, existing during the time of the prophet Jeremiah. There, archaeologists have found pot shards which depict animals and humans, contrary to Torah, and which indicate that the Hebrew god there, referred to there as YHWH of Sharon or Tiamat, had a consort, the goddess Asherah, who was associated with trees and serpents. Both are depicted as having large ears like those of bulls/cows and, it appears, also tails.

Now, Jeremiah, the prophet who, when the Babylonians approached Jerusalem - Jeremiah who knew exactly what was coming and how cruel the Babylonians could be - is known to have fled to Egypt! There he lived out the rest of his life. But, for Jeremiah, was not every other refuge of Judaism full of idolatry? After all, even the closest place, Kuntillet Ajrud, which was even then in Egyptian territory, was a sanctuary to YHWH and his consort, Asherah. So one has to wonder just where in Egypt Jeremiah made his abode. That, unfortunately, is a question yet to be answered by any evidence. But if he had gone to Kuntillet Ajrud or to Elephantiné, he would have met with exactly the same thing in both places, an impure, objectionable (to him), dualistic monotheism at best.

The Gnostics and the Birth of the Son of Man

Again, a fusion of cultures, philosophies and religions, including Judaism, is what Hellenization was attempting to create. This is readily seen in the intentional assimilation or syncretism of the deities of each culture with those of all other cultures. The most readily recognized example being the syncretism of Greek and Egyptian deities, one example being the combination of Zeus and Osiris/Apis resulting in Zeus-Serapis. This process of syncretism was one of the main products of Hellenization and the fusion of philosophical thinking was its other main product. And why not, since both religion and philosophy led to enlightenment according to Greek thought?

Now, one of the main ideas to come out of this fusion of Hellenism and Judaism (also incorporating elements of the Persian Zoroastrianism), which was most prevalent in Alexandria, was the concept of the *Divine Man*. The Jewish Gnostics there began to euphemistically substitute the word "man" for "god." Thus, god was seen, essentially, as a man. This led to the concept of the "Son of Man" which we find repeated so often within the Christian gospels. Redemption was the key in this thought process since the Son of Man was envisioned as a mediator between god and humankind, sort of like Akhenaten. Gnosticism (a fusion of religion and philosophy), then, became the form of enlightenment that led to salvation.

That Jesus, in the gospels, is portrayed as repeatedly calling himself "Son of Man" is a direct allusion to this Jewish Gnostic thought which literally had its roots in Alexandria, Egypt and which predated Christianity by up to two-hundred years. And Jesus is also portrayed as the celestial messiah in Christian literature, especially in the *Apocalypse of John*, who would return to rule a "kingdom of heaven" and who would serve as the eternal mediator between god and humankind. In fact, the term "Son of Man" in every respect *meant* "messiah". The "philosophers" in Egypt, especially the Neoplatonists, thus developed *all* of the notions which would later be integral parts of the Christian religion. Their fusion of religion and philosophy warped both, but also preserved both.

Egypt [by this time heavily influenced by Zoroastrianism] is the hearth of... notions of the immaculate conception, the divine incarnation . . . and Hellenistic theology is marked by a gradual surrender of Greek to Egyptian thought. . . . At Alexandria, then, and throughout the Hellenistic kingdoms, Greek religion lost its ideal element, and became a mixture of universal skepticism and empty show, of gross superstitious beliefs in magic and astrology, and of Oriental mysticism and human abasement (Bentwich 66).

The Jewish Gnostic and Neoplatonic models from Egypt, then, were the beginning of the mystical and apocalyptic movements which combined into the sect of the Essenes and others, that eventually coalesced into what we now call Christianity. That the Christianity we know today retains little of its original Gnostic/Neoplatonic flavor is mainly due to later historical influences. Regardless, it was the Essenes (who were actually surviving Atenists) who best incorporated these trends.

Josephus tells us that the Essenes had been excluded from the temple services in Jerusalem and that they also possessed secret books of their own. And we now know this to be true since the Dead Sea Scrolls have been found. These Essenes are also likely those referred to in the ancient Jewish *Talmud* as "the saints who waste the world". In the *Talmud* it is indicated that they practiced austerities so severely that they neglected to take part in the normal expected duties of social life. The Essenes are known to have reached the apex of their development during the first century BCE. At that time a preacher of singular piety is said to have emanated from their midst. This preacher was none other than John the Baptizer. Thus they still had a great influence upon the later Christian church, the Ebionites (Jewish Christians) essentially being their successors in Judea and adjacent areas (Bentwich 105 & 109).

So, it becomes clear that Christianity was born from the influence of the Alexandrian Neoplatonists and Gnostic Jews and the Atenist Essenes through John the Baptizer and Jesus, one of John's disciples. This religion incorporated elements of both Hellenism and Judaism

(Hellenization) along with some elements of Zoroastrianism in a mystical apocalyptic syncretism which was, essentially, the natural culmination of the thought of the time.

As already noted, the Essene Jewish temple at Elephantiné had been destroyed long before, in about 420 BCE, as part of the expansion of the temple of Khnum. Some of the priests from the temple at Elephantiné, however, managed to become accepted within the temple in Jerusalem about that time, but were then forced back out in 175 BCE. Thereafter they returned to Egypt where they were granted sanctuary and where they built yet another Essene Jewish temple at Leontopolis in the Egyptian Nome of Heliopolis "where, at the time of the Seleucid persecution, the exiled [high] priest Onias [IV] obtained permission [from Ptolemy Philometer III] to erect a temple [which was] to be a new center of Jewish worship. This temple, which had its special ritual, outlived the sanctuary at Jerusalem by three years, but it never obtained a position to rival the authority of the central shrine" (Bentwich 36). Rabbinic sources mention this shrine several times, some advocating the worship there, others calling it heretical. Undoubtedly, the same mystical influences which were present in Jewish worship and thought found in Alexandria, which was close-by, existed also at Leontopolis. Later, some from this Jewish community eventually returned to Judea and established the Qumran community in 153 BCE. This community stood in strong opposition to the temple activities in Jerusalem. These are known facts.

Then Cometh the Romans

The Roman General, Pompey the Great, captured Jerusalem in 63 BCE, thus ending its independence. When his armies gained access to the temple there they entered it and even went into the Holy of Holies, but they took nothing with them as they left (Perowne 50). No doubt they were not just "looking around". Indeed, they were, true to form, likely looking for the conquered Jewish god so that they could take him back with them to Roma as a symbol of Roman conquest. Certainly, if there had been so much as a rock within the sanctuary, they would have taken it, but they left empty-handed. Finding no image there must have astonished them greatly!

Herod the Idumean was made ruler over Judea by the Romans in 37 BCE. He set about to accomplish what no one before him had been able to do, to radically change Judea into a "model Hellenistic culture" (Friedman 364). But, following a brief revolt in 6 CE and because of it, Judea became a province of the Roman Empire, governed by a Roman procurator.

"By the time of the reign of Caesar Augustus, a quarter of one million inhabitants of Alexandria were Jews" (Cantor 62). Under the rule of the Ptolemies the Jews who resided in Egypt, especially in Alexandria, were considered an integral part of society. They enjoyed exceptions from certain laws there and had certain privileges in keeping with their unique religious sensibilities. However, under Roman rule, this privileged situation deteriorated as some of these exceptions were rescinded. This occurred not only in Alexandria, but elsewhere in the Diaspora, and the tension between Jews and Greeks became so great that more than one massacre of Jewish populations occurred within the empire. One of the privileges that the Jews still enjoyed, however, was that they were exempt from performing "expressions of loyalty" to the empire and to its ruler. Everyone else had to comply. This would become pivotal during the early centuries of Christianity as the early Christians (once they separated from Judaism) expected exactly the same privilege, but did not receive it. Of course, they didn't ask for it either.

But the most egregious example of intolerance and attempted submission of the Jews by the Romans was when the imperator, Gaius Caligula (reigned 37-41 CE), demanded that he be worshiped by *all* inhabitants of the empire with *no* exception for the Jews. Caligula "ordered Petronius, the legate of Syria, to set up a statue of himself as Zeus in the temple at Jerusalem, by force, if necessary". Thus, Caligula attempted to repeat what Antiokhos had done before him, but with his own likeness incorporated into that of Zeus. But Petronius avoided an all-out revolt over this in Galilee and Judea by delaying the implementation of this order. When Caligula and most of his family were assassinated, Petronius was able to ignore the order altogether, thus averting a catastrophe (Sinnigen & Boak 288). Then, in 41 CE, a settlement was reached under the imperator Tiberius Claudius Germanicus (Claudius) reaffirming the rights of the Jews to be exempt from such requirements. But Jews were still excluded from the gymnasium, thus depriving them of the secondary education which they needed in order to become full citizens or to enter Greek social society. Claudius also forbade Jews from further emigration from Judea to Alexandria since it was believed that extremists from Judea had caused the Jews in Alexandria to riot in the first place (Perowne 138).

Conclusions

The overall failure of Hellenization was not in it's conception nor in its lofty goal of uniting humanity religiously and philosophically. These goals were worthy and philosophically valid and, in some respects, actually worked. Its failure was singular because it was based upon a false premise. That premise was that polytheism and monotheism could actually coexist together in some sort of syncretism. The truth was that this was simply not possible. Monotheism and polytheism were never meant to exist together in such a way. Conflict was inevitable.

This is the one and only reason that Hellenization did not work; could not work, in my view. It was fundamentally flawed because it was based upon this false premise. But, Hellenization "succeeded" in that it did produce two offspring, as it were. These offspring were Jewish Gnosticism and Neoplatonism, with Christianity emanating from both. These offspring originated in the one place where Hellenization happened to take hold the best, Alexandria, Egypt. All repudiated the Jewish Torah and all compromised the monotheism of Hebraic tradition. But, as we have seen, all also compromised pure Hellenism and pure Hellenic (Greek) philosophy. So, in so many words, monotheism and polytheism were forced into a wretched semblance of each. The combination totally lacked whatever beauty may have existed of the separate entities.

Yet, as time unfolded, Neoplatonism, while degenerate and weak as compared to original Platonism, was still the best philosophy of the time, outside of Stoicism, and was, in a way, a rival to Christianity.

In fact, it is the main reason why the Christians were able to accept Aristoteles more easily than they could Platon, in my view. Platon and his philosophy took all the sting away from death; left people with no fear of death. This was simply unacceptable for the Christians, who needed to fear death if there were to be a reason to seek salvation and the absolution of sins. How could they gain converts if the people did not fear death? And how could people accept the concepts of reward or punishment after death if they did not accept a creator and physical resurrection? As Pierre Chuvin puts it:

> The Neoplatonists would have entirely agreed that God, in his many manifestations, is one. But what is unique about the God of the Jews and the Christians is that he is the creator of the universe, which pagans regarded as not created (Chuvin 108; Zacharias, *Life of Severus*, pp. 20-22).

The struggle of beliefs and philosophies which eventually culminated in the development of Christianity out of the roots of Gnostic Judaism and Neoplatonism, and the regrouping of Judaism as a means of survival is complex, but important to trace. That Christianity developed from these movements which were prevalent in Egypt, especially Alexandria, just prior to the Common Era through its introduction in Judea by the Essenes can hardly be doubted by serious students of religious history today even though the Essenes have essentially been written out of the *Bible*. The mechanism was put into place, not for the so-called "natural development" of Christianity, but for the transformation of the religions and philosophies of the ancient world into a coherent, functional religious system which could, and did, overtake most of the world. Indeed, the total transformation of the whole western world, and much of the rest of it as well, was the inevitable, but not the intended, outcome of Hellenization.

Now, one can readily fault Antiokhos IV Epiphanes for being short-sighted enough to conclude that the Jews needed to be forced to fully assimilate and integrate into overall society. He, rightly or wrongly, perceived their resistance and obstinance as a danger to the stability of his empire and sought to correct it. But his effort resulted in much more destabilization than it corrected. In fact, his effort likely corrected nothing. So, it could be said that this was a case of religious intolerance perpetrated by a polytheist against monotheists. Indeed, if Antiokhos could have had it his way, Judaism surely would have been wiped out entirely. He was certainly a persecutor who inflicted horrific punishments upon the Jews and he is not to be excused for this.

Conversely, it should also be made clear that Hellenization was *not* primarily about the export of Greek (Hellenic) religion, per se. It was actually primarily about the export of the Greek way - their way of government and of their social and societal values and systems along with their architecture, etc. But their philosophy and their religion, naturally, could not be separated from the rest of it. So this was not some overt effort to *change* the religion of certain areas of the Empire of Alexander so much as it was an effort to improve society in general by utilizing the Greek model as a basis for a new overall society. It was supposed to be a mixture with key elements of Greekness inserted where most appropriate. It was not an effort to destroy anything, but to improve.

So one still has to recognize one difference between Antiokhos and the monotheist persecutors. In his case, the effort *was* meant to change a sub-culture within his empire so that it might conform to a specific standard, religiously and philosophically. But it was not, as with the monotheist, an effort to convert and subjugate the entire world. Surely that does not make it any better. But this key difference still remains and should be recognized for the fact that it is. Because of his deeds with reference to the Jews he has, therefore, been vilified as a monster in the historical record. Judging from the heinous and ferocious acts that he and his armies perpetrated, this label is justified. But I submit that, since it is justified, then several others in the historical record should succumb to the same fate, most notably figures such as Akhenaten, Constantine I, Constantius II, and so on; the latter two being considered by many today as Christian "saints" and the first being considered by many today as, somehow, misunderstood in his day (some would make him into a saint too if they could also somehow make him into a Christian - some actually going so far as to make of him some kind of proto-Christian).

For our present interest here, the most important thing is not the conflict between the Greeks and the Jews with reference to the Maccabean Revolt, although that is indeed important to the story. That is the very reason it is not detailed in this work. The most important thing is the means by which Christianity was created by people who took Hellenization to heart, made out of it a religious system we call Gnosticism and a philosophical system called Neoplatonism, and adding to both apocalyptic and eschatological overtones. And the Essenes, who were already monotheistic Atenists, were among these people. In fact, this is the era (the last two-hundred years or so BCE) from which apocalyptic literature emerged. Atenism had just a touch of the apocalyptic in that some expected Akhenaten to return to complete his religious reforms. But Atenism produced no literature to that effect directly. Zoroastrianism, by comparison, had at least some literature to that effect in that they expected a savior to appear at the proper time and defeat the evil force and its adherents, initiating the end of the world and the salvation of humankind. Jewish Gnosticism, as we will see, incorporated elements from both within itself as did Christianity by way of the Essenes. Thus, apocalyptic thought became the most important precursor in the creation of Christianity.

3

THE REAL JOHN AND THE REAL JESUS - THE APOCALYPTIC BAPTIZER AND THE REVOLUTIONARY SON OF MAN

The Reality of the Egyptian Connection

In 9 BCE the Roman imperator Gaius Octavius "Augustus" Caesar had his *Ara Pacis Augustae*, located in the Campus Martius of Roma, consecrated. It was an open-air altar, surrounded by a walled enclosure, which exhibited, in part, personified images of Terra Mater (Mother Earth) and Roma, shown on the west wall, Terra Mater being the dominant symbol of Augustan peace depicted there. On that frieze, the central figure was a seated, draped female figure representing Terra Mater along with two other draped female figures (one with a swan, the other with a dragon). Terra Mater was seen as representing Augustan peace over the *entire* earth, not just in Roma or even the Roman Empire; the earth being seen as "returning to fertility and security, taken back from the male warrior and restored to the female mother" (Crossan 32-33). This structure was erected and consecrated mere years before the birth of Jesus/Iesous (Ἰησοῦς). For Pagans of the time, the symbolism on this structure, with its portrayal of Augustan peace, was virtually perfect in its conception. But for others, it held little direct meaning. Those others included the Jews, especially the Essenes, who prayed for a messiah to save them from Roman subjugation. They yearned for this final messianic war in which their enemies would be completely vanquished. Approximately one-hundred and three years of freedom and self-rule, and now subjugation to the Romans! And history had taught them that the only answer was war.

Just who really was Jesus; born into such a climate? That has been the burning question that many have asked for centuries. People want to know who he was. They want to know who it was that died on the cross for their sins. They want to know what he and his disciples were really like. Most will say that Jesus was the "Son of God". On this they will stand firm. But few will say that he was the "Son of Man". Why would this be, since he referred to himself in this way constantly in the gospels? The answer to this question lies in the development of subsequent history.

The *Psalms of Solomon*, which was written by an unknown Jewish group in Egypt, probably between 63 and 48 BCE, are quite detailed as to Jewish messianic expectations during this period in time. In fact, the expectations found here have "more substance" with reference to the expected messiah than any other extant Jewish writing of the time. In it, the messiah *must* be a son of David who would establish *the Kingdom of God* **on earth** which is to remain *forever* (Crossan 284-85). Their messiah would not use violence and would also be sinless, all virtuous and, by his word alone, able restore Israel, which would then rule over the entire earth (Crossan 107), in most ways a direct replacement for Terra Mater. And it does seem that Jesus actually fulfilled most of this, if one accepts the gospels and other New Testament accounts.

But, interestingly, there is not one word about biblical prophecies with reference to this messiah. As we will see, this is significant. And there is nothing here about any *Son of God* who would die in a humiliating execution for the people's sins and physically rise again to rule a **heavenly** kingdom. That is the twist that made Jesus different from all others who purported to be the messiah, and there were several. The latter is the way that the followers of Jesus portrayed him *after* his death. But this does not seem to be the way he portrayed himself during his lifetime regardless of what the gospels say. He seems to have portrayed himself much more like the former, rather than the latter. It would seem that Jesus fully intended, at least at first, to establish the

Kingdom of God *upon this earth* without having to resort to direct violence against others himself. But he later succumbed to the reality that violence was the only way that this could be accomplished and paid the price for it. He tried the way of peace and, when that failed, he resorted to revolution.

Frankly, there are many myths and traditions concerning Jesus and his life, some of which have been misconstrued as *real* history even by modern authors. One of these myths, to begin with, is the so-called "massacre of the innocents". The actual facts are simple here. There is absolutely *no* evidence that such an event *ever* occurred. Popular protests in Judea and other parts of what would later be called "Palestine" often did result in retaliation by Roman authorities, such as one incident which occurred in 4 BCE when the protests resulted in what is known as the Passover Massacre (Crossan 128-29). This event *is* documented in actual records, in this case, from the writings of the Jewish historian, Titus Flavius Josephus, in his *The Jewish War*. Now, if history recalls events like this, there is no reason why history would not recall events like the so-called "massacre of the innocents" if it had really ever happened. But history does *not* mention this event *at all*. Total silence, except from the gospels which all will agree were written well after Jesus' death. Frankly, this was an effort to make Jesus like Moses.

What, then, does this mean for Christianity? If the "holy family" did not flee from Judea into Egypt (a reversal of the Moses story) because Herod was after the baby Jesus, as some gospels tell us, then we are left with two questions; (1) Did they actually go to Egypt and, if so, (2) Why did they *really* go to Egypt? Frankly, one has to eventually admit that the gospel writers did not write much at all about Jesus' early life exactly because *they did not know anything about it* and, what they did write, was from other sources which had become tradition by the time the gospels were written. Enough time and history had passed so that, not only did they not know, but there was no one left to ask. They did not really know where he was born - Nazareth - so he could be called a Nazoreans; Bethlehem - to connect him to the Davidic line…. Both are likely incorrect. The fact of the matter is that *no one knows* where Jesus was born. Also, if Jesus ever went to Galilee, it was likely just after the death of John the Baptizer due to fear of authorities in Judea.

But he could just as well have gone to Qumran. Qumran, after all, was closer although, perhaps, a bit more difficult to get to. So, the belief that Jesus had very much of a Galilean ministry may not be correct either, as will be shown.

We also must question the portrait painted in the gospels of John the Baptizer. Did John also have ties to Egypt somehow? After all, he was supposedly about the same age as Jesus and, therefore, one would think that, if the "holy family" had to flee into Egypt, then John and his parents would also have had to do the same. I mean, what Roman soldier would have taken it upon himself to have been really careful about the age of the infant he was about to slaughter anyway? No soldier who would perpetrate such an atrocious act in the first place would have cared whether the child was really the right age or not! It's not like anyone would have sued him or anything and neither John nor Jesus had a birth certificate to consult.

And, John the Baptizer was the son of a priest, according to the gospels, but since he did not act in a priestly manner, he seems to have been showing the people that the priestly order was coming to an end. So he appears even in the gospels to have rejected the Levitical priesthood and the temple in Jerusalem. But why? And no one seems willing to ask why leadership in the Jerusalem church became hereditary with James, the brother of Jesus, becoming the leader there following Jesus' death. But it actually seems obvious that it was meant to be so. After all, did not Jesus follow his cousin, John?

John, The True Messiah

The Mandaeans, whom we will get to later, are right. John had a lengthy ministry and is called "messiah" by them. Jesus had a practically infinitesimal ministry which may or may not have even took place in any part of Galilee at all, but he gets practically all of the credit. Also, Paul had, perhaps, a greater overall ministry than any other apostle and is known for certain to have died for the faith, so he is also referred to as "messiah" by the Mandaeans. So why do these Mandaeans call both John and Paul "messiah", but not Jesus? Exactly because Jesus succumbed to violent rebellion rather than peace (and they also reject Moses because he resorted to violence in the form of striking the rock and, thus, was not allowed to enter the promised land). In addition, Paul, who had previously been a Pharisee, following Stephen's death went to Damascus, an Essene stronghold. Thus, he clearly converted to a more Essene point of view even though, as we will see, he still remained more strongly influenced by Zoroastrianism.

Both John and Paul held to peace and gave their lives for the faith. Jesus died as a criminal. Whatever the truth of Paul's conversion, he met up with other Essenes, followers of John, at Damascus and had to convince them that he was their friend. Then Paul proceeded to create his own Jesus. Later the Christians in Jerusalem turned Paul over to the Romans. And to absolve themselves of any guilt for this, they began to claim that the Jews had done it, a clever reversal. This is surely the main reason that the Mandaeans call Paul "messiah" and consider Jesus to be a false prophet. Paul really was turned in by his own and was then executed, dying for the faith. But Jesus never actually went through the trial described in the gospels because it was illegal under Roman law to hold a trial at night. So the Jerusalem church was actually more a descendant of John, the true founder, than of Jesus.

To make all of this more clear, it is all too obvious that John and Jesus were Gnostic Atenist Essenes. That has been suggested by more than one scholar already. In fact, according to modern-day tradition among the Mandaeans (or, as they refer to themselves, the *Nazorāyā*, the Arabs calling them the *Sūbbā's*, or Baptizers), the only known survivors of ancient Gnosticism, John (again, the true messiah) was actually a Gnostic who, obviously, believing in gnōsis (*Mandā*) as the way to salvation and who also rejecting Torah, was very much misunderstood by the Jews in Judea who in return rejected him and drove his community out of the area (Mead 2 & 16). And the Mandaeans, again, reject Jesus, whom they call *Yahyā*, as the "deceiver-messiah" (Mead 27). Their rejection of Jesus should not be surprising for those who have studied Jewish Gnosticism from its beginnings since Jesus, even being a Gnostic, in no way fulfilled what they expected of their anticipated messiah. He "appeared" at first to fulfill, but ultimately did not (because he turned to violence), thus the deception, in their view.

The Mandaean religious literature (for of secular literature there is none) supplies us with the richest direct sources of any phase of ancient Gnosticism which we possess; these documents are also all the more valuable because they are purely Oriental without any Hellenistic immixture. Indeed our only other considerable direct sources, that is sources not contaminated or rendered suspect by transmission through hostile hands, are the Trismegistic literature, the Coptic Gnostic documents [in Egypt] and the recent Manichaean finds in Tūrfan (Mead 30).

In any case, the Mandaean literature does cause Jesus, or *Yahyā*, to say one particularly interesting thing for our purposes here. In the Mandaean *Letter of Truth* he says, when questioned by John about the nature of the soul: "Firmly developed has the soul been brought into the vain body. If the soul has kept herself perfect, she ascends in a garment of glory" (Mead 60). This is of interest for two reasons; (1) the concept that the soul existed prior to entry into the individual human body and (2) the concept of the soul as feminine, a very Gnostic concept and that which the Gnostics also attributed to the *holy spirit*. In other words, for the Gnostics, the holy spirit (a concept which they invented themselves) was not masculine, but was *feminine*. Obviously this is a Gnostic concept which was modified by later Christians.

And They Were Gnostic Essenes Influenced by Zoroastrianism

It seems obvious, then, that Jesus was brought up in Egypt in an Essene (*Εσσήνοι/Εσσαίοι*) community there, and that he later became a part of the Essene community at Qumran, which John the Baptizer was obviously already also a part of. And there is a direct correlation between the Essenes and the Gnostics as evidenced by their writings as well as a location. What is this location? *Egypt*. Again, Jesus repeatedly called himself "Son of Man" which was, contrary to popular opinion, a concept developed in Alexandria, Egypt from Jewish Gnostics/Essenes who had begun to substitute the word "man" for "god", effectively calling the Jewish *god* "man". Thus, Jesus called himself "Son of Man" and by doing so equated himself with this Gnostic/Essene concept. This "Son of Man" was already envisioned, as pointed out earlier, as a mediator between god and humankind with reference to salvation. This was because over time it came to be believed that one could not approach god directly for salvation; a mediator or mediators was/were needed (as in Atenism). And, as it turns out, by his death, Jesus became the eternal mediator between god and humankind in the minds of his followers (like Akhenaten and Moses?). So it was due to Jewish Gnostic/Essene apocryphal and apocalyptic literature that the messiah came to be seen more as a celestial being than an earthly king; more as the former rather than the latter; more as a mediator than a victor. This is who Jesus was *supposed* to be.

The fact that, in the Aramaic language which Jesus likely spoke, the phrase that is translated as "Son of Man" is the same as for "a person" is irrelevant. After all, what significance could be attached to Jesus running around calling himself "person"? That Jesus repeatedly used that phrase "Son of Man", however, *is* relevant. The Gnostics/Essenes believed that a divine ingredient existed within themselves - all humans - which they referred to as the "divine-self". This can easily be equated with Platon's concept of the immortal soul, something that was essentially missing from Jewish thought and belief until about the first century BCE. It was the realization of this fact by the individual, that he or she incorporated this "divine ingredient", that brought the enlightenment of "self-knowledge" and, thus, salvation. Yes, for them, as in Platonic philosophy, *salvation* came through *Knowledge*.

Again, it can clearly be seen even from the gospels that Jesus had some direct connection to Egypt. This is not in dispute by anyone, as far as I know. And he had a connection with magicians from the East, from Persia, by way of the Magi (the "wise men"), who were, in fact, priests of the Zoroastrian religion (something glossed over by most Christians). Egypt, for its part, had recently been an opponent of Roma until the Romans invaded and took it over during the reign of Kleopatra VII Philopator (Cleopatra). And Persia, in whatever form it took at any given time, was and would continue to be Roma's arch enemy. Even after all of the centuries that had passed and even with the influence of the fragmented empire of Alexander the Great and his institution of Hellenization, the Persians, among others in the East, remained obstinate opponents of practically anything western, especially with reference to religion, philosophy and education (something we are still dealing with today).

In any case, that Jesus worked miracles, like the Zoroastrian Magi, is a major tenet of Christianity, although modern Christians tend to shy away from the many references to him casting out demons. But no one seems to want to acknowledge that Jesus "inherited" anything from Egypt during his stay there (just as they refuse to acknowledge that the Hebrews inherited anything from the Egyptians). So, the question actually becomes just how long did Jesus and his family remain in Egypt? It seems obvious that the two families, that of Jesus and that of John the Baptizer, both journeyed to Egypt, as suggested earlier, about 6 CE during or after the rebellion of Judas the Galilean and Zadok the Pharisee, which eventually resulted, in part, in the rebellion of 66-74 CE (Josephus A J 18,.1, 1). As Josephus puts it:

> All sorts of misfortunes sprang from these men, and the nation was infected with this doctrine [i.e., that God would assist armed Jewish rebellion and allow the Jews to be victorious] to an incredible degree; one violent war came upon us after another . . . [so that] the very temple of God was burnt down by their enemy's fire (Modrzejewski 90).

The gospels tell us that Jesus and his family returned to Judea or Galilee while Jesus was still a young child. But there are other still extant references which state that Jesus, and I think also, John, did not return until young adulthood. After all, both of their appearances in Judea and the beginnings of their ministries there are shown even in the gospels as having been initiated *suddenly* so that people actually seem to have wondered where they had come from. And even in *Acts* 21: 37-38 we have an indication of this when Paul was asked by a Roman official . . . "Do you know Greek? Then you are not the Egyptian who some time ago stirred up a revolt and led the four thousand men of the Assassins out into the wilderness?" Certainly this Roman official tells us directly that the Essenes at Qumran were recognized as being Egyptians.

Later Pagan writers would try to explain Jesus' origins. The Greek philosopher, Kelsos (Celsus), for example, writing in about 177 CE:

> adopts the position that Jesus is a magician and sorcerer. Repeating the story that Jesus was brought to Egypt by his mother to escape the shame of an illegitimate birth, Celsus says that in Egypt Jesus learned the magic arts, and finding himself successful in the use of sorcery *returned to Palestine* 'full of conceit because of these powers' (Sanders, E. P. 117, Jewish and Christian Self-Definition/*CCI*.28.).

Now, Kelsos, unless he had a source we know not of (and he actually may have, as we will see), didn't know any more than the next person why Jesus and his family went to Egypt or anything else about his early years. But the above reference can serve to illustrate just the kind of hateful response that early Christians could elicit from Pagans during this time period. They truly *loathed* the Christians that they knew of! And this, most likely, because these Christians set themselves apart and insisted that they were the *only* ones with the keys to salvation. And how could Pagans see Christians as loving or good when they read or heard biblical passages such as *Luke* 12: 49-51, which reads "I have come to cast fire upon the earth; and how I wish it were already kindled! But I have a baptism to undergo, and how distressed I am until it is accomplished! Do you suppose that I came to grant peace on earth? I tell you, no, but rather division. . . ." Or *Matthew* 10: 34 "Do not think I came to bring peace on earth; I did not come to bring peace, but a sword". And it appeared that this was exactly what Christians were indeed bringing upon humankind - war and family division as opposed to peace and family unity. Thus, Tacitus calls Christians "a class of men loathed for their vices" and he called Christianity a "pernicious superstition" (*Ann.* XV.44.2-4.). Suetonius also stated that Christianity was "a new and mischievous superstition" (*Nero*, 16.). Finally, Pliny the Elder stated that Christianity was nothing more than a "depraved and excessive superstition" (*Ep.* 10.96.) (Sanders, E. P., Jewish and Christian Self-Definition 104-05). In fact, the word *superstition* became the favorite term among Romans for Christianity, next to the term *atheist*.

But the key point in the preceding quote from Kelsos is that he indicates that it was some time before Jesus returned to Judea from Egypt. He shows that Jesus did not return as a young child, but as an adult. This is the type of thing that would be more easy for someone like Kelsos to confirm as a historical fact, regardless of the other details. And, according to *Luke* 3: 1-3, John began his ministry "[i]n the fifteenth year of the reign of Tiberius Caesar". *Mark* 1: 4 further states "John the baptizer [*suddenly*, for how can one not read the word "suddenly" here] appeared in the wilderness".

The Qumran Connection

That both John and Jesus amassed large followings can scarcely be doubted since the gospels attest well to that and no one disputes it. Their large followings certainly would have been enough to arouse the suspicion of the governing authorities, religious as well as political. That John especially, like the Essenes at Qumran, preached an apocalyptic message with victory for the Jewish people at the end is clear by his reference to "the wrath to come" found in the gospels. That John, again, like the Essenes at Qumran, did not favor the religious authorities in Jerusalem is evidenced by his retort to them "But when he saw many of the Pharisees and Sadducees coming for baptism, he said to them, 'You brood of vipers, who warned you to flee from the wrath to come?'" (*Matt.* 3: 7). But, interestingly, the writer of *Luke* changes this and states that John said that to *everyone*, not just the religious authorities (*Luke* 3: 7); this ever so subtle change obviously made in order to shift the focus from religious authorities to *everyone* in general, i.e., from Jewish authorities to *all* Jews; the *Gospel According to Luke* obviously having been written last among the canonical gospels, as we will see.

Now, also according to the writer of the *Gospel According to Luke* (*Luke* 3: 23) Jesus was about thirty years of age when he began his independent ministry, having previously been a disciple of John. And we know that at this time Herod's temple was still not yet complete and that, from its foundation to its destruction was a time period of forty-six years. In fact, Herod's temple was not actually completed in all its detail until 64 CE, only six years prior to its total destruction by order of the Roman general, Titus Flavius Caesar Vespasianus (better known as Titus). And *John* 3: 24 states that "for John had not yet been thrown into prison". Finally, *Matthew* 4: 12-17 states that Jesus began his ministry once he heard that John had been imprisoned and he had had time to withdraw into Galilee. So, if we could ascertain exactly what year John the Baptizer was imprisoned, we would presumably know what year Jesus began his ministry, if he really had a ministry at all. That is, unless we are reading the *Gospel According to John*, which seems to indicate that Jesus would not have actually had much of a ministry after all and would have been executed soon after beginning said ministry, given the time-frame presented. Regardless, however, of when Jesus began his presumed ministry, it seems clear that John's entire ministry was in Judea and that Jesus had intended to follow suit until John's arrest, at which point Jesus changed plans.

But, again, did Jesus really have much of a ministry? If one reads the *Gospel According to John*, one tends to feel that if he did, it didn't last long before he was captured and executed. What does seem obvious here is that Jesus did not take the leadership role of whatever was taking place, whether it be ministry or insurrection, until *after* John's arrest. Certainly Jesus knew, just as everyone else did, that once John was arrested he would by no means ever be freed. Even this seems obvious from the gospels because otherwise Jesus would have been quite presumptuous to have taken over leadership on his own immediately after John's arrest. And, frankly, one cannot reasonably posit that John had been nothing more than a simple preacher and that, once John was arrested, Jesus simply decided to fill that vacuum by also becoming nothing more than a simple preacher. If that were true, how could one really explain that both were arrested and later executed? The Romans did not arrest and execute simple preachers for no reason. Jesus, at least, must have been fomenting rebellion. Once John was arrested someone did indeed have to fill the vacuum in order to keep the momentum going, not as a preacher, but as the leader of an insurgent movement bent upon driving the Romans out of Judea at the very least. John perpetuated no violence himself, but Jesus, having previously been non-violent, was, perhaps, forced into this role by circumstance.

And one must indeed ask, if Jesus were truly a Galilean peasant, a son of a carpenter, then exactly in what way would he have ever been exposed to this concept of "Son of Man" from Alexandria, Egypt? EVEN IF the family had fled to Egypt when Jesus was an infant, they would supposedly have returned only a short couple of years later, to Galilee, according to the gospels. So there would have been no opportunity for Jesus to have been exposed to this concept unless his parents instilled it in him, which is certainly doubtful if they were Galileans. Certainly, one cannot claim that if Jesus was simply using the term which could mean both "Son of Man" and simply "person" in Aramaic and that it was, therefore, an innocuous statement, that one cannot also turn around and assert that Jesus was not making a messianic claim because he used that particular term. To make such an assertion, as has actually been done (*Bible Secrets Revealed. The Real Jesus*, Dec. 4, 2013), one is tacitly admitting that there *is* a connection between the term "Son of Man" and messiahship. And, in fact, such a connection does indeed exist. See, to the Egyptian Jewish Gnostics the concept of the "Son of Man" and the concept of the messiah were *one and the same*. Their messiah *was* to be the "Son of Man"; they were seen as one and the same, *exactly*. So the idea that, in Aramaic, the phrase "Son of Man" is equivalent to the word "person" is, again, irrelevant. The *fact* is that Jesus used the term "Son of Man" when referring to himself and that is clear from the Greek. And it is also clear that Jesus was making a messianic claim thereby and was recognized by others as doing so. It would be a bizarre translation indeed if one were to substitute all reference to "Son of Man" with the word "person"!

Also, there is, in fact, no real basis for the prevailing theory that there existed a "messianic secret." This theory is based on the multitude of "Son of Man" statements found throughout the gospels and the idea that Jesus wanted this kept secret. The truth, again, is that the "Son of Man" statements in each of the gospels are of Jewish *Gnostic* origin. Among Jewish Gnostics in Egypt, again, the term "man" was used in place of the term "god." So, "Son of Man" literally means "Son of God". And the commonly held belief that the "Son of Man" statements are characteristic of the *Gospel According to Mark* and to a lesser degree the *Gospel According to John* is not quite accurate either. Such statements are made in each of the four canonical gospels (but interestingly never in the very Gnostic *Gospel of Thomas*, for example) so frequently as to rule out any special emphasis in one gospel as opposed to another. Regardless, it is perfectly obvious, because of these multiple references, that Jesus *did*, in fact, refer to himself as "Son of Man" (the Mandaeans simply referring to him as "Man"), a reference which must have infuriated Jewish authorities in Jerusalem because they well knew that such references originated in Egypt among their rivals, the Essenes! And they would also have known that this was a reference to messiahship.

Jesus and the Temple

Now, the event which is referred to as the "overturning of the tables of the money-changers" or the "cleansing of the temple" is very significant when examining who Jesus really was, or became, at least. Why? First, because all four canonical gospels refer to it. And because it was the major event that precipitated the end of Jesus' life. In fact, this is *THE* pivotal event. But why? Why, while portraying Jesus as a pacifistic teacher, the "Son of Man", would each of the canonical gospel writers suddenly portray him in violent, aggressive terms? It would seem that the answer would most likely be that this particular event is one that we *must* accept as authentic. This event *really* happened. Thus it is found in all four canonical gospels and also portrays Jesus differently than in other instances. The only question is exactly why it happened. After all, it is actually inconceivable to believe that this was Jesus' very first visit to the temple during Passover celebrations. Certainly he had seen the money-changers, etc. before. No, there had to have been something more here that the gospel writers simply do not allude to. It is simply preposterous to suggest that Jesus had never seen the money-changers in the temple before and that he suddenly became righteously angry at their presence. So there had to have been some other motive behind this event.

Let us first dispense with the notion that when this scene occurred the Romans went after Jesus because he was interrupting the flow of money to Roma from the temple. Some pseudo-historians in recent times have proposed this idea as the reason for the capture and eventual execution of Jesus. But, *nothing* could be further from the truth. Nothing! The real fact of the matter is that the Romans did not collect any revenue through or from the temple in Jerusalem at all. NONE! In fact, it was among the privileges that Jews had throughout the empire that part of the money they were taxed would go toward the maintenance of this very temple. So, instead of the horrible Romans profiting from the proceeds of the temple, they actually provided for its maintenance, just like both Cyrus the Great and Darius the Great of Persia had done centuries earlier.

So, as surprising as this may sound, I submit that Jesus made a scene in the Jewish temple in Jerusalem by overturning the tables of the money-changers, at least in part, as a cover for his Essene allies to be able to steal temple "treasures". He (presumably along with his disciples) was creating a distraction. This is probably really why the authorities were so mad at him and brought him to trial, not because he broke some religious law! See, the Copper Scroll found at Qumran tells of the very treasure they likely sought. In other words, they were not after physical treasure that would have been housed within the temple as no treasure was there. They were after *this* very scroll, which they knew to be in the temple, so that they could go find the treasure. Of course, they might have taken the opportunity to grab some money during this chaotic situation as well. It is fascinating to note that most of the numbers on this scroll are written in *Egyptian*, not Hebrew. There are also fourteen Greek letters scattered throughout the text and the first few appear, amazingly enough, to spell the name *Akhenaten*!

And, after all, we know that the temple in Jerusalem was not good enough for the Essenes. They rejected it. But with such treasure, the Essenes could conceivably have purchased weapons and still had enough left over so that, if they were successful, they could destroy the temple and presumably build a new one. Perhaps, then, the echo of Jesus stating that the temple would be destroyed can now be heard properly as, if he ever said such a thing, he may well have shouted it as part of the distraction. And, after all, did Jesus not instruct his disciples to buy swords, etc.? (*Luke* 22: 36).

Indeed, there is an inconsistency with all of this and the scripture in which Jesus tells his disciples that they would judge the twelve tribes of Israel (*Matt.* 19: 28). *The twelve tribes of Israel*? Who actually thought in those terms anymore since ten of those tribes were supposedly the hated Samaritans?! It would seem that this is a passage that was clearly made-up by later gospel writers in order to cover up and modify what really happened. It seems much more likely that the twelve disciples were supposed to have been twelve commanders leading their own sections of Jesus' army. Yes, it seems that he was initiating a coup.

In any case, whether Jesus and his disciples were actually planning a coup or not, it is a fact that *the* way for any invading army to enter Jerusalem in ancient times was *only* from the north by way of the Mount of Olives, where they had gathered. There is no way that the Roman or Jewish authorities could have dismissed this gathering, following the incident in the temple, as simply harmless, especially if Josephus is correct in that about 150 disciples were with him on the Mount of Olives. Surely Jesus and his disciples would have known this. They knew that, at the very least, they were provoking the authorities simply by being there, gathering at night. If they were discovered, they would be arrested. And that is exactly what happened, to Jesus, at least.

In the Gnostic *First Apocalypse of James* (25:7-9) Jesus is depicted as telling James, "They will arrest me the day after tomorrow, but my deliverance will be near" (Evans & Hagner 282). What did the writer, presumably James, know about that was to take place? The likelihood is that Jesus and his disciples were planning to do something, for why else would they perform two openly provocative actions in quick succession - the incident in the temple and then gathering on the Mount of Olives. They probably expected the Qumranites to join them and when the authorities arrived, believing that they were Qumranites, they were taken by surprise. But, of course, the Qumranites never arrived, leaving Jesus to his destiny.

Also, according to the former Roman Catholic Priest, John Dominic Crossan, when Jesus overturned the tables of the money-changers, this was symbolic of the destruction of the temple just as the destruction of the fig tree was. The temple was to be destroyed utterly and *never* rebuilt (contrary to the beliefs of those who today misread the *Apocalypse of John*). It seems clear here, then, that the fact that the temple does not physically exist on earth anymore can be equated with the fact that Jesus himself does not physically exist on earth anymore, according to Crossan. Crossan further states, "[t]he Temple and the Magician were one of the characteristic antinomies of late antique religions life; the tension between them contributed much to its extraordinary creativity and vitality. . . . No matter, therefore, what Jesus thought, said, or did about the Temple, he was its functional opponent, alternative, substitute; his relationship with it does not depend, at its deepest level, on this or that saying, this or that action" (Crossan 355). Because Jesus (supposedly), according to the gospels uttered a statement about the destruction of the temple, it seems that Jesus was showing the authorities that he understood his role concerning his enmity with the temple in Jerusalem. According to *Luke*, Jesus wasn't even asked about this. But in each of the canonical gospels he does directly answer the question as to whether he was the King of the Jews, *but answers differently in each gospel.*

All well and good - except that Jesus probably never uttered any statements relating to the temple's destruction in the first place unless, as I have suggested, it was as a cover for what they were really doing. And, if he did, the only reason they are found in the gospels is because the temple had been destroyed *before* any of the gospels were even written, as I will show. Note that there is no reference either that the Essenes wanted the temple to be destroyed exactly because the Essenes were written out of the gospel history altogether. Thus, the connection between John, Jesus, and the Essenes is erased.

In addition to these two things, the supposed raising of Lazarus from the dead would have been deeply provocative to the authorities, whether such a thing could have really happened or not, especially as they paraded him around for all to see. The fact that Jesus and/or his followers would even claim to have done this would have been a deliberate provocation to them. When Asklepios mythically raised a man from the dead, he had gone too far, had defied nature, and Zeus killed him with a thunderbolt (i.e., his labyris). Raising someone from the dead was a thing that was deeply unacceptable for mere mortals to do, both in Greek *and* Jewish society. In fact, in Greek thought, it was also totally unacceptable for a deity to do because it went against the very principles of nature and natural law and was therefore sinful. But Asklepios was deified following his death, becoming a Greek hero in the truest sense, because Zeus forgave him. And he rose from the status of hero, to demi-god, to a god over time. Similarly, it wasn't long after Jesus was said to have brought a man back from the dead that he himself was executed and later called the "Son of God" (without the nuance of "Son of Man"). And his status also became that of god, eventually. There is a correlation here.

The Coming Apocalyptic Kingdom

Now, according to the Jewish historian, Flavius Josephus, the great invention of John the Baptizer was the creation of a new religion that was inexpensive, was offered to all, was divinely sanctioned, and which offered the remission of one's sins through the simple act of baptism (which John got from the Essenes). Jesus and/or the early Christian church adopted baptism from John as an initiation rite for the same purpose. Part of the reason John first did this was because the only other way available was through animal sacrifice at the temple by way of the Levitical priesthood in Jerusalem and this was expensive, so few could afford it. That left a lot of people out of salvation. And, after all, John as an Essene, rejected this method - that of animal sacrifice, at least within the temple in Jerusalem which, as we have seen, he would have rejected as an Essene in any event. In so many words, again, this method of animal sacrifice left many people, essentially, out of salvation - outside of the coming kingdom, because they could not afford to sacrifice. So with John the average person could accept baptism and, thereby, become prepared for this coming kingdom (Crossan 231). Therefore, "King no longer needed to refer to the actual king of a city or kingdom. 'King' became an abstract representation of ανθρωπος ("human being") at the 'highest' level imaginable, whether of endowment, achievement, ethical excellence, or mythical ideal" (Crossan 287).

So, if people were being initiated into the kingdom through baptism and that kingdom was not of this world, it was no great leap to envision the coming messiah as being the king of this extra-worldly kingdom. And, again, this is exactly what the Jewish Gnostics expected of their messiah. Still, according to Crossan, Josephus left out the most important thing concerning the work of John the Baptizer. When he baptized people he used the act of baptism in a way that seemed to threaten Roman authority. Specifically that:

> ... people cross over into the desert and are baptized in the Jordan as they return to the Promised Land. And that is dangerously close to certain millennial [apocalyptic] prophets, well known to Josephus ... who in the period before 44 and 62 C.E., invoked the desert and the Jordan to imagine a new and transcendental conquest of the Promised Land [like that under the leadership of Joshua ben Nun]. Whatever John's intentions may have been, Antipas was not paranoid to consider a conjunction of prophet and crowds, desert and Jordan, dangerously volatile (Crossan 232).

In so many words, even if the coming kingdom was not of this world, the effort toward it still had to be made *in this world*. And that is what John was demonstrating. If Jesus were to have incited a rebellion, as the authorities apparently feared, then he would have had to have been seen as a ruler who liberated the people not only from the Romans, but also from the temple system, including the Levitical priesthood. He was liberating it, if one takes the book of *Hebrews* into account, for the legitimate priesthood - that descended from Melchizedek. And, again, it is well-known that the Essenes wanted the temple in Jerusalem to be destroyed so that a new one could be built which would have included a new priesthood. So, whereas the Samaritan temple had been unacceptable to fanatics like John Hyrkanos, even the Jewish temple in Jerusalem was unacceptable to the fanatical Essenes. It seems to me, then, that Jesus was the impetus that eventually *caused* the destruction of the temple in Jerusalem after all even though he probably did *not* say that *he himself* would destroy it. Thus the connection of the revolt of 6 CE with that of 66-74 CE by way of John the Baptizer and Jesus.

So, one must ask the question here of whether anyone could truly be so blind as to assume that, after the incident in the temple, the authorities would not have been looking for Jesus. And can anyone truly believe that Jesus would not have known that? Why, then, does he seem so taken by surprise when the temple authorities arrived? It was not because he already knew his destiny but because his "supporters" did not rally to him as he had expected them to. The Qumranites never arrived, but the temple authorities, whom he may have mistaken for his supporters, did.

Now, again, the Mandaeans today believe that John the Baptizer was a Gnostic and that the Jews did not understand his message (Mead 2). John also seems to have followed closely the restrictions appropriate for a Nazir or Nazirite, who was to be holy before god from the day of his birth and, therefore, could not allow his hair to be cut nor could he drink wine (Mead 7). And, again, some people believed that the expected messiah would be a Nazir, like Sampson who freed Israel from domination by the Philistines. In addition, the passage concerning the "sprout" found in *Isaiah* 11 which would spring from the root of Jesse was applied to many characteristics expected of the messiah. The Hebrew word for sprout is *neser* or *nezer*. This expectation led to the speculation in which many believed that the messiah must, therefore, be a Nazaraian (Heb. *Noscri*). Others believed that the messiah was to be a carpenter, from the Aramaic word *bar nasar*. Samaritan midrash carried this one step further in expecting the messiah to be a carpenter since, as a second Noah, he would spiritually construct a new ark for the salvation of humankind (Mead 8). And, of course, the gospels claim that he was from the town of Nazareth.

Interestingly, both John and Jesus baptized in the Jordan River (one has to assume, after all, that Jesus did perform this rite for those who were to enter his kingdom such as certain disciples who had not previously been baptized by John) even though it was deemed unfit by other religious authorities for this purpose. The reason seems to be that John believed that this was a way of fulfilling a vision contained in *Ezekiel* 47 in which Ezekiel himself is addressed as "Son of Man". It was expected that a stream of holy water would flow down from the temple mount into the Jordan River and heal said waters when the time of the arrival of the messiah was at hand (Mead 9). Still, this was not to be taken literally, but allegorically, so that the water was seen as the "Word of God" or the outpouring of the holy spirit (like the birth flow from the female womb?), which was to occur in the last days. And in both cases, that of John and of Jesus, the rite of baptism had to be preceded by a cleansing of the soul through the fulfillment of a person's duty to his or her neighbor and to god (Mead 4). Contrary to the misreading of Jesus' various injunctions over the ages, Jesus never told anyone that they could enter the Kingdom without first performing their neighborly and religious duties in a pure manner. Only the truly righteous who loved neighbor were to enter just as, in most of the ancient Greek Sacred Mysteries, only the virtuous were to enter. Jesus repeated over and over "You *must* be born again. . . ."

The Mandaeans also often mention "Sun-day" in their ancient literature, indicating its religious importance in Gnostic circles. For the Gnostic Mandaeans it was a way of venerating the day of light as a symbol of the true Light, or Knowledge. Meade states that "The same puzzle occurs with the prayer-custom of the Essenes [at Qumran], who turned to the rising sun [like the worshippers of Aten] in their morning orisons. The problem we have here to face is the existence of a pre-Christian Sun-day as rigidly observed as the Jews and others kept the Sabbath, and not a 'pagan' holy-day" (Mead 41). In other words, this is not something that the Christians incorporated from Paganism, as they did in so many other instances. The incorporation of Sunday as the worship/holy day of each week proves a strong connection between Jewish Gnostics/Essenes and the beginnings of Christianity even though the adoption of Sunday as the Christian worship day is otherwise explained as the day Jesus was resurrected.

The Mandaean book *The Letter of Truth* refers to Jesus as "the carpenter" and also as "Yeshu messiah, son of Miryam" and also confirms that John did indeed baptize Jesus. Interestingly, again, it also even refers to the apostle Paul as "messiah". This is interesting since more modern-day Mandaeans, again, reject Jesus as the messiah and believe that he and his disciples were actually evil (perhaps in part a reference to his connection with the Gnostic demiurge as well as the ideas with strong apocalyptic expectations, all of which centered on the appearance of a messianic figure called the "Son of Man". The only other possibility seems to be that they might have actually been brought up in Samaria, which is another idea that no one seems willing to entertain although they both seem obviously to have had connections to Samaria.

Also, some survivors of Jerusalem Christianity, other than the Mandaeans, could very well have included the Sampsaeans of the Transjordan area. This Gnostic sect had such striking similarities to Christianity that Eusebius of Caesarea, in *History of the Church*, 2.17, citing Philo Judaeus (c30 BCE-45 CE), who was a Hellenistic Jewish philosopher and theologian and the leader of a large Jewish community in Alexandria, Egypt, along with some other early church fathers, stated that the Therapeutae were some strange sect within Christianity, and, although they were, obviously, in his view, heretical, he compared these Therapeutae with the Sampsaeans (Allegro 60-61). The Therapeutae, according to Philo, were virtuous people who, in contrast to the Essenes, pursued a life of contemplation (*De vita contemplative/On the Contemplative Life*). Obviously, these Therapeutae existed prior to Christianity. The reason that Philo contrasts the Therapeutae with the Essenes is that he saw the Essenes as pursuing a life of activity (worldly action), not contemplation. These Therapeutae were Jewish mystics and ascetics who resided close to Alexandria, near Lake Mareotis.

Did Eusebius slip here, showing us a connection to pre-Christian Gnostic sects? It does seem that this is likely, for Philo also states that the Therapeutae desired, above all, to have a vision of the true Being with an intensity such as Philo compares with the Greek Bacchoi/ Bacchai or the Korybantes. And their celebrations, especially of the Exodus, were much like those of the Greek Sacred Mysteries (Meyer 229-30). And, if the connection with Egyptian Jewish Gnosticism had not already sufficiently been made:

> The discovery of the Nag Hammadi Library casts new light on the questions of definition and Gnostic origins. Indeed, while the library presents new source material, it also raises new questions at almost every level of

research into the relationship between Gnosticism and early Christianity. In the light of this phenomenal archaeological discovery, an entire generation of scholarship will have to be rethought (Hedrick & Hodgson 5).

But we will return to these manuscripts at a later point. For now let us understand that in recent years it has become relatively well-accepted that John the Baptizer was likely at least influenced by the Essenes at Qumran and may even have been a member of that community, as I have already pointed out. Also, Mead states that, according to Josephus, Herod was afraid that John's movement would culminate into a messianic revolt against Roma. Again, by this time in Jewish thought and history various things were expected of the messiah by such sectarian groups, the foremost of these expectations being the reestablishment of the Davidic kingship over Israel, necessitating a revolt and subsequent defeat of Roma in Judea. These people also, again, believed that this messiah would be a Nazir, like Sampson, who had freed Israel from Philistinian domination.

That John the Baptizer preached an apocalyptic message is obvious from the biblical texts concerning him. One can easily see, then, that Jesus, as a follower of John, also preached an apocalyptic message and that these two prophets were connected ideologically to other apocalyptic communities, such as that at Qumran. One relevant passage comes from *Matthew* 3:6-7, as mentioned already, follows:

> and they were being baptized by him in the Jordan River, and they confessed their sins. But when he saw many of the Pharisees and Sadducees coming for baptism, he said to them, "You brood of vipers, who warned you to flee from the wrath to come?"

"Who warned *you* to flee from the wrath to come?" *The wrath to come* obviously refers to an apocalyptic scenario. It suggests that there is some oracle which warns people to flee from some event which will soon happen. But, flee from where, and when? Later, the disciples were also warned by Jesus to leave Jerusalem when they saw the destruction in the form of Roman armies approaching. Indeed, it seems all too clear that the above passage, then, was *not* meant for everyone, as the writer of *Luke* would have us believe

> Now when he heard that John had been taken into custody, He withdrew into Galilee; and leaving Nazareth, He came and settled in Capernaum. . . . From that time Jesus began to preach and say, "Repent, for the kingdom of heaven is at hand" (*Matt.* 4:12-17).

The Kingdom of Heaven that Jesus was referring to here is obviously an apocalyptic, messianic kingdom which was *at hand*. When John was arrested, then, Jesus appears to have expected the conflict to begin. Jesus here was preaching rebellion. He was preaching apocalyptic holy war against the Romans! No question about it. And the Romans knew that.

> "For those days will be a *time of* tribulation such as has not occurred since the beginning of the creation which God created until now, and never will. Unless the Lord had shortened *those* days, no life would have been saved. . . ." (*Mark* 13: 19-20). "For the coming of the Son of Man will be just like the days of Noah" (*Matt.* 24: 37).] "Whoever is on the housetop must not go down to get the things out that are in his house. Whoever is in the field must not turn back to get his cloak" (*Matt.* 24: 17-18).

Here, Jesus' apocalyptic message is somewhat more refined than was that of John. He tells his followers what it will be like and what to do when it happens. Clearly he is speaking of a catastrophe which was to occur within the lifetimes of his hearers. Likening the coming cataclysm to the days of Noah is probably a back door reference to the Samaritan belief, already mentioned, that the messiah would be a second Noah. And that he is referred to as "Son of Man" is, again, a Jewish Gnostic reference relating to messiahship.

Conclusions

Some scholars, such as Albert Schweitzer, among others, have stated that we all in each generation see Jesus as we want him to be, based upon our own preconceptions of who he was and who he is supposed to be for us. But I do not present Jesus, or John, for that matter, in some form of "how I wish him/them to be". If I had it my way, Jesus would indeed have been at the very least the Jewish messiah who, although he neither ruled nor saved them from supposed Roman tyranny, would still have been an impressive teacher who said things and wrote things no one had ever thought of before and who somehow was still the savior of *all* humankind who could not reasonably be discounted by anyone; who had followers who were able to spread his message of love (for if he actually had a message, that was it) *without* resorting to force and hate. That Jesus, however, *never existed*. And the real Jesus, no matter how hard others have tried to make him into who they want him to be, apparently had little if anything to do with Galilee in his lifetime - probably never even went there, was not brought up there, did not get his first disciples from there - but was only connected with Judea, specifically Jerusalem and Qumran (and maybe also Samaria), as well as with Egypt. After all, if he and his disciples did minister in Galilee at all, then his ministry there can be seen as nothing other than an abject failure, as we will see.

The person detailed here is the Jesus that I have come to believe in because this is where the *actual evidence* leads. That is a fact. There is actually *no* evidence that he had any real or lasting impact whatsoever upon Galilee. Because, if he had, then surely he would have had large followings there by the time he died and there would be archaeological evidence of Christians residing there prior to 70 CE. The glaring absence of such evidence, as we shall see, really tells it all. There was no "Jesus movement" in those areas either during his lifetime or even within forty years of his death. It just didn't happen.

Once it is understood that there were either no, or very few, Christians in Galilee prior to the first major Jewish revolt against Roma (66-74 CE), then we have to admit that Christianity might have originated elsewhere after all as well as the fact that Jesus apparently had no real ministry there. Logically, one might expect to find traces of their origins some other place, then. And that is *exactly* what we find - *in Egypt*. Places such as the supposed house of Peter are nothing other than pious frauds - in that case a home owned by someone who lived later who apparently happened to be a Christian. Actually, some of the disciples, for their part, could have been from Galilee, especially Peter. But we don't need to find his supposed house to prove this to ourselves. If a person's faith is so weak that they require this, then they have no faith at all. And, in fact, whether it is the house of Peter simply can't be proven. Also, even if, by chance, the supposed bones of Peter at the Vatican were to be DNA tested (something that the Vatican is unlikely to ever allow, for good reason, in my view) that would prove nothing other than whether the bones belonged to, perhaps, someone who was of Hebrew descent or not. Such knowledge would ultimately be meaningless. But, there are and have always been those who would go to any length to prove their beliefs rather than simply believing the truth as elucidated by *facts*.

So, frankly, all of the available evidence, which is actually substantial, points to connections with Qumran and Egypt with Jerusalem in-between. *This* was the world of Jesus. He probably spent a lot more time actually *in* Jerusalem than we tend to imagine. He wasn't just some peasant who barely knew Jerusalem, but was probably well-acquainted with her. As for Qumran, at least he had the indirect connection through John the Baptizer who most certainly was a Qumranite. Did Jesus travel to Qumran at all? It seems that the answer must be "yes" if one accepts the story of the temptation in the wilderness. After all, where in the wilderness might he have gone? Certainly not outside of Roman territory into unsafe Arabic lands! No, logically, it could well have been Qumran.

And, after all, where did the disciples establish the very first church and Christian community even after Jesus' death? Jerusalem. How very brave of them to establish a church in the very city where their master had just been executed! And so, the movement essentially, except for Paul and certain others, remained right there until the advance of the Roman legions under Titus Flavius Caesar Vespasianus (Vespasian) and his son, the afore mentioned Titus made it clear that moving on

Apocalypse and Armageddon, The Secret Origins of Christianity:

was necessary. Some still stayed anyway - and were killed or enslaved by the Romans. The others fled before the Romans arrived, and lived.

Many Christians and Muslims also believe that, when Jesus returns, he will first appear upon the Mount of Olives and, from there, prosecute the final war against evil and retake Jerusalem. These people have no earthly idea how close they are to telling exactly why the Mount of Olives was so important in ancient times and how it was, from here, that Jesus had likely planned to begin an assault on Jerusalem. But this fact has been all but lost to history. Still, a hint of it, as already mentioned, is found in the writings of Josephus in which he states that Jesus had gathered there about 150 *disciples* (plus, it would seem, an unknown number of others). For those who do not know much about ancient military structures, this number was nearly the equivalent of two Roman Centuries, which consisted of 80 men each, totaling 160 men. So, is it any wonder that those in authority might have seen Jesus as dangerous?

In addition, the Jews called Cyrus the Great of Persia, a Zoroastrian, the *messiah*. That is really why Jesus had to be connected in the gospels to the Zoroastrians. The Magi were a way to show that the torch had been passed from them to Jesus - it was their recognition of this. And if Cyrus could be called "messiah", so could Jesus, in their view.

This is not the Jesus that I would prefer to see. This is not the Jesus that I grew up believing in. But this *is* the real Jesus. He was briefly a pacifistic preacher who, after the arrest of John the Baptizer, became a brigand who fomented rebellion, was caught, arrested, and executed. And the Romans did not execute those they *suspected* of committing crimes. They executed those *convicted* of criminal activity. Jesus appears to have at first incorporated within himself the Greco-Roman vision of the peaceful *priest-king* as evidenced by his, mostly, pacifistic stance, his life of poverty and of freedom just as the Gnostic "Son of Man" was to do. Also, the idea contained in Greek philosophy that philosophers and priests and poets were virtually synonymous would allow others to call Jesus a *philosopher-king*. Such evidence comes from Roman philosophy via Musonius Rufus, a Roman Stoic philosopher, who believed, like the Greek philosopher, Platon, that all rulers should study philosophy like the philosopher-king of Platon's perfect society. The idea, then, was that a true king should also be a philosopher and, conversely, a true philosopher *was*, therefore, a king. Therefore, everyone could be a king, in a sense, but only those who ruled themselves could be said to be truly royal and free in a kingdom of freedom (Crossan 77).

But, appearances being what they are in the gospels, this picture of Jesus is actually little more than an effort by the gospel writers to portray Jesus as being like Sokrates (Σωκράτης), as I will show. To begin with, one of the main reasons why we still today sometimes question whether Jesus was really real or not is because he left us no writings. That is exactly why some scholars state that his existence cannot be proven. The same goes for the disciples. Even though writings are attributed to them, it is quite questionable whether any of them (except, perhaps, Matthew, Thomas, James and John) actually ever wrote anything at all, other than, perhaps, a few notes. That is, with the glaring exception of Paul. Frankly, the same also goes for Moses, who almost certainly wrote at least some of what is attributed to him, or at least had a scribe write it for him.

No one really disputes whether John the Baptizer lived and few question whether Jesus actually lived. But finding the shroud of Jesus or the finger of John the Baptizer proves absolutely nothing other than the fact that they lived and died. After all, it is a foregone conclusion that they died, isn't it, since everyone dies. Right? So if the Shroud of Turin was ever to be proven to have wrapped the body of Jesus it would only prove that he died. Period. The same would be said concerning the bones of John the Baptizer. Obviously, he died. Period. There is no dispute here, and only faith would make anything more of it. But one does have to question why such relics wound up in Europe. Is it because Europeans needed such relics to truly believe when the evidence was overwhelmingly against such belief and logic would suggest that such belief was absurd?

In any case, no doubt, Jesus *could* read and write if he was anything like the person portrayed in the New Testament. So one has to ask just why he didn't, apparently, write anything. Wouldn't some writing by/ from Jesus himself go further than anything else toward influencing people? Why would god or the son of god or, for that matter, an ordinary yet educated human being neglect to do the one thing that would surely have made the most difference? The answer has to be that either Jesus was not a real person after all or that he simply did not know how to read and/or write. Or he was, in fact, fomenting rebellion and uninterested in writing. Either way, he could not have been god or the son of god if he *was* unable to read and/or write. And he was NOT creating a new religion.

Further, it is known that some stories that are found in the present versions of the gospels were simply not in the earliest extant versions. For example, the story of the woman caught in the act of adultery in the *Gospel According to John*. This story was simply added later, for reasons unknown, according to scholars. But it seems to me that it was added in an effort to make Jesus appear more like Sokrates because in both stories the main figure, Sokrates (in his case, explaining reincarnation) or Jesus, writes on the ground. This probably seemed necessary to someone because Jesus, apparently, never wrote anything himself that has survived. Well, neither did Sokrates, and no one supposes that Sokrates simply could not read and/or write. So, to help explain why Jesus apparently never wrote anything, the story was created to show that Jesus, like Sokrates, could indeed write, but did not. Both just drew on the ground in their separate instances. The ancients would have understood this. But the propensity of the early Christians to compare Jesus with Sokrates really has the opposite effect of what they intended. They wished, in this way, to elevate Jesus to the standard of Sokrates, but they actually succeeded in making Jesus no better than the very human Sokrates. Thus, it is really Sokrates who is elevated. That Asklepios (assuming that he was once a real man), for example, also did not write anything as far as we know is also not an argument in favor of Jesus being who he was purported to have been because we, frankly, don't know that he didn't. With all of the deliberate destruction of ancient manuscripts, who is to say what may have been lost here? His writings, if he wrote anything, could well have been destroyed, but those of Jesus, if he wrote any, could *not* have been, for his followers would have preserved them.

In the canonical book, *The Letter to the Hebrews*, it states that Jesus is a high priest "after the order of Melchizedek" (*Hebrews* 5: 6). The writer paints Melchizedek (using the book of *Genesis* as his source) as being a priest who blessed Abraham. But, if one accepts this, then one must conclude that organized monotheism existed in Canaan prior to the advent of the Hebrew invasions, essentially during the time in which Egypt ruled the area, or Abraham could not have accepted blessings from this high priest. The only way that this could likely have been possible would have been if Melchizedek was a follower of Akhenaten's monotheistic religion of the Aten or if he were a Zoroastrian Magus. And, frankly, the former is more likely. That is, if Melchizedek was real at all, which is doubtful.

Clearly, then, Judaism is a combination, in part, of the Egyptian religion, mainly that of Akhenaten, and of Zoroastrianism. In fact, they clearly did *not* worship ONLY one god until, during, and after their sojourn in Babylon. And some of the Hebrew prophets seem to have been heavily influenced by Zoroastrianism. The direct link, then, is from Atenism (with a little Zoroastrian influence) to Jesus by way of the Hebrew prophets, according to the writer of *Hebrews* himself. Thus, Jesus was likely not influenced by Zoroastrianism from Persia very much at all, but *was* likely influenced by Atenism from Egypt by way of the Essenes much more so. The writer of Hebrews, in effect, tries to subtly show that Jesus was an Atenist.

So, even though Jesus was a monotheist himself, he was actually not the same type of monotheist that most of the other Jews in Judea were, especially the Pharisees, who were very much influenced by Zoroastrianism. Does not the New Testament make that clear over and over again? So he, due to his Egyptian connections, followed Aten, calling the Aten "Father" just as Akhenaten had done over a thousand years before. When Jesus read in the synagogue he read from the book of *Isaiah*, from "the Prophets". Ordinarily one would have read from the *Torah*, but this is not what Jesus did. He followed the religion of Aten, not Ahura-Mazda. The Jewish religious authorities recognized this and worked to suppress his movement. This along with Jesus' later aggressive tendencies resulted in his death. But through his general pacifism, Jesus actually brought war upon the earth because of the intolerant attitude of later Christians as they took more after the Essenes of Qumran.

In the end, the real Jesus must have been that person who said and did things that can be attributed to no one else. At any point at which he can be compared to someone else, such as Sokrates, we can not see the real Jesus - he is *not* there. In those instances, he is a creation from the mind of someone else. When Jesus speaks of the workers who waited all day before being selected to work, he is likely among them. When Jesus tells a parable, he is probably somewhere within that parable himself. When Jesus tells us to love our neighbors, he is surely there. And when Jesus is portrayed as speaking in Aramaic (using magical phrases in the language of the Magi), no doubt, he is there. But, when he wrote on the ground when the woman taken in adultery was brought before him, he is Sokrates and not really Jesus. Where he presses people to think in ways they had not before, he is Sokrates, not Jesus. His debates with Pharisees and Sadducees are not him. When he "cleansed" the temple; that *was* him. But even the criticisms of Jesus - ". . . Behold, a gluttonous man and a drunkard. . . ." (*Matthew* 19) - this is not really Jesus; this is Sokrates. When Jesus cast out demons and performed other miracles, he was merely doing what all of the other charlatans of the time, some of whom also claimed to be the messiah, were also doing. As he said, otherwise no one would have listened to him. But why couldn't the son of god have said something so profound that he would not have needed miracles? This, the gospel writers do not explain.

In addition, it seems that few, if any, ever actually ask the question as to exactly why the Jews anointed the bodies of the deceased with embalming substances, which they knew would not preserve the bodies after all in the climate of Judea, unless it was a carry-over from Egypt. And why do the gospels make such an issue of telling us all about the fact that his body was to be anointed if it were not a subtle way to show his connection to Egypt?

Also, and this is very important, when Jesus rode a donkey into Jerusalem he was symbolically treading upon Roman victory because the donkey was treading upon palm branches (as stated in the *Gospel According to John*), which symbolized victory for both the Greeks and the Romans. Scholars seem to overlook this point. The people were hailing him as a conqueror by spreading the palm branches onto the roadway before him. Their intent was that he would trample the palm branches underneath him. This was a clear symbolic provocation to the Romans, which the Jewish leaders would well have understood too. The Romans saw it for what it was and went after Jesus. That is just it. He had finally gone too far. Add to this the so-called "cleansing of the temple" and the gathering on the Mount of Olives and there really was no turning back. *This* was the real Jesus.

Also, we have *no* documents from the temple in Jerusalem *unless* they are found at Qumran. I am not the first to suggest this, but I do find this suggestion to be valid. It seems quite clear, however it was done, that some of the documents found at Qumran actually originated within the temple in Jerusalem. How and when, then, did this transportation happen? The "cleansing" of the temple is the key. And the Romans somehow knew that the Copper Scroll, with directions to find the hidden treasure listed upon it, was at Qumran and this, I submit, is part of the reason that they diverted to Qumran first before they laid full siege to Jerusalem, a historical fact seldom noted. They wanted that scroll! But, as we know, they never obtained it. If the Romans had obtained it they likely would have destroyed it after looking for the treasure themselves, thus destroying the very last extant trace of Akhenaten prior to modern archaeology.

Indeed, it seems obvious, as will be shown, that if one really wants to find and see the real Jesus, one has to read the *Gospel According to John* primarily. Although it deals only with, at most, the last few weeks of Jesus' life, in my view it must be taken as more authoritative than the other canonical gospels, as will be explained. Even so, having Jesus walk around pronouncing his own demise, somehow knowing ahead of time that he would be executed and accepting his fate was also a way to make him look more like Sokrates, who accepted his fate, which was execution, without remorse, although he was actually innocent of any crime. And this effort began with the very first gospel, as we shall see, the *Gospel According to John*. This is by no means a historically correct portrait of Jesus, but one that was created to make him not only like Sokrates, but also more "European". It was done deliberately by Europeans like Constantine I as well as his followers and successors, as we will see. After all, all of the gospels and other canonical writings (as well as the non-canonical writings) were originally written in Greek, a European language, not Aramaic, the language of the Persians and, presumably, Jesus himself. Scholars will state that the gospels and other writings were written in Greek because Greek was the dominant language of the East at that time. So why, then, did Jesus not also speak in Greek if his mission was to reach the world? After all, Jews in the Diaspora spoke Greek and that is the reason that the Septuagint was made, so that they could read their holy scriptures. And it is well-known that the gospel writers quote exclusively from the Septuagint. They didn't even know any other version to quote from. But surely Jesus would have learned enough Greek to have been able to speak it even *if* he had been brought up in Galilee. It really doesn't make good sense.

In any case, it is obvious that events like the "triumphal entry" of Jesus into Jerusalem are events that really were Jesus himself, for neither Sokrates or anyone else in history did anything like this. But that he walked around pronouncing his own demise is not Jesus. And, contrary to modern Christian theology, this was not Jesus simply fulfilling a prophecy. The real part is actually the fact that, although this is not found in any prophecy, the populace went about laying palm branches upon the road before him so that his donkey could trample them. Such a detail as this could not have been simply made-up by later followers. And this would certainly not have been made up by those who later wanted to absolve the Romans of Jesus' death. But they couldn't really leave out the whole story if they wanted to remember him at all (and only the *Gospel According to John* mentions palm branches specifically. The others only allude to this indirectly), so they combined this event with a prophecy appropriated to make the event *seem* like destiny. After all, the gospel writers might, by the time they wrote, have forgotten the full significance of palm branches for the Romans and they might not have fully realized anymore that if Jesus had trampled upon palm branches it would have been a very obvious and deliberate affront to the Romans as in trading upon their victory over the Jews. Oh, yes, this event *really* happened all right!

Another dimension of the creation of Jesus the "messiah savior king" is the reversal of circumstance found in at least two important situations within the gospels. The first has to do with the episode in which Jesus institutes the practice of foot-washing (*John* 13: 3-10). Now, realistically, foot-washing was necessary in that part of the world when people generally wore sandals or went barefoot, so there was little or no religious connotation to it in the wider society. And, according to the gospels, the disciples were surprised that Jesus would presume to wash *their* feet since he was the greatest among them. This was a reversal in and of itself of societal norms. In addition, a comparison can be made with the cathartic rites provided to the deceased by the ancient Greeks. The washing of the deceased's body, etc. was very important to the Greeks, especially in Classical times. But, perhaps more important than that was the fact that it was customary for relatives of the deceased to *take a bath* following return home from the funeral (Garland 43-44). And, yes, this was understood, in part, as a matter of hygiene. But the fact that Jesus was "bathing", for all practical purposes, his disciples (after all, did he not state that once the feet are clean nothing more is needed?) not long prior to his death is a direct, though twisted, reference to this practice of bathing following the funeral of the deceased. The institution of foot-washing, therefore, is a form of ritual magic, a *reversal* of the Greek way of death and the care of the deceased, but in this case with reference to the soon-to-be deceased.

The second has to do with the meal shared between Jesus and his disciples during Passover prior to his execution and death (*Matt.* 26:17-30). Indeed, one would expect that they would naturally have shared such a seder meal during this time since it was customary to do so for Jewish religious reasons. But what one would not expect and, therefore, does not readily see, is the fact that this is also similar to the meal that the Classical Greeks would have shared among family members of a deceased person. This is referred to as the "tomb feast" and it was the principal way in which the deceased was honored and "delighting his ghost" (Garland 110). That the "tomb feast" was provided to the deceased in the cemetery at the grave site does not negate this comparison even though it is not certain that the family members who provided said meal to the deceased also shared in it. Frankly, it is probable that they did. The point is that Jesus and his disciples shared such a seder meal prior to the death of Jesus whereas such a meal was characteristically provided to the deceased, in Classical times, following death. Thus, another reversal. And, in any event, this also holds Gnostic overtones for those who can see it in that the Gnostics would have said that Jesus was a ghost all along in any case. Thus, he was already a ghost when he was sharing this meal with his disciples. Of course, for them, this also meant that he never really died either because he could not die. In any case, this is that which became the Christian "love feasts" honoring Jesus, who had died and, supposedly, rose again. So the comparison is solid and this meal was indeed a reversal of this "tomb feast". This was indeed ritual magic and was later rightfully recognized by Roman authorities as such.

Also, another connection with Classical Greece is shown when Jesus said ". . . YOU SHALL NOT PUT THE LORD YOUR GOD TO THE TEST" (*Matt.* 4:7) because he was actually paraphrasing a Delphic Oracle, which is recorded by Herodotos, wherein one Glaukos, who had been entrusted with a large sum of money to keep in trust for a friend who had traveled abroad, upon his friend's return denied that he had ever received said trust. His friend challenged him to maintain what he was saying by oath and, delaying a reply, Glaukos went to consult the Delphic Oracle as to whether he could be allowed to swear in an effort to keep his gain. The Pythia answered:

"Glaucus, son of Epicydes, for the moment the gain is more thus to conquer with an oath and plunder the money. Swear then, for death awaits even the man whose oaths are true. But the child of an oath has no name and it has no hands or feet. Yet it is swift to pursue until it seize a whole family together and all the house. But the family of the man whose oaths are true is better hereafter."

Glaukos, who was shocked by the Pythia's response, begged for forgiveness. But the Pythia did not console him at all, but retorted instead saying that *to tempt the god to countenance his deed was as equally heinous as Glaukos having committed the act himself.* The point was that having merely thought to commit such an act, and having thought to make the deity culpable in it, was *every bit as heinous* as actually committing said act. In so many words, no subsequent advantage could justify an unjust act (Parke & Wormell, The Delphic Oracle I 380-81). One should keep exactly this in mind when insisting or even assuming that some deity sanctions one's actions or even one's beliefs.

Also, one parable relates how a Magnesian of great wealth arrived at Delphoi bringing a hecatomb (one-hundred) of sacrificial victims to Apollon. He asked the Pythia who it was that was the best and most enthusiastic of men in honoring the god, making the most pleasing offerings, fully expecting the be named as that person. But the Pythia surprised him by naming someone else, one Klearkhos of Methydrium in Arkadia. The Magnesian then searched for this person and on a tiny farm found him. He asked Klearkhos about this and his reply was that, although he was very poor, he always paid all of his obligations to the gods scrupulously. The moral here being that the gods preferred those who were able only to make the simplest offerings, as long as they meant it with all their hearts, rather than ordinate gifts easy for a rich person to afford. This is comparable to the parable of the "widow's mite" (*Mark* 12: 41-44; *Luke* 21: 1-4).

Indeed, another variant on the "widow's mite" is found in the gospels, based upon an oracle written long before said gospels, in which the Pythia answers a wealthy enquirer who is very arrogant that Apollon preferred the poor man of Hermione, who had just offered him a handful of barley from his wallet. Upon hearing this the poor man was so impressed by this response that he emptied the remaining contents of his wallet upon the altar, thinking that this would cause the god to prefer him even more. At this the Pythia replied that by his act he himself had become *twice as hateful* as he had been loved previously! It was not the value of that which was offered, but the ostentation with which it had been offered (Parke & Wormell, The Delphic Oracle I 384). Ostentation equaled hubris! These oracular statements can also adequately be compared with the gospel parable of the important man praying in the Jewish temple who justified himself before god. Thus, Jesus is made into the Oracle of the Jerusalem temple by the gospel writers.

And just a few other examples from the gospels need be cited to show the revisionist hand who made the effort to absolve the Romans from the death of Jesus. One of these is the incident in which Jesus is asked whether the Jews should pay taxes to Roma. Aside from the editor's apparent ignorance of Roman tax law on the matter, when Jesus is presented with a Roman coin and he states "Render to Caesar" (*Matt. 22: 17-21; Mark 12: 14-17*) it is actually obvious that Jesus is being made to paraphrase that which Paul had already written when he enjoined Christians to obey Roman law. Any effort to make it appear that the earliest Christians were not subversives who stood against Roma and hoped that their messiah would release them from Roman domination would be employed by redactors, as it was here. For, certainly, if Jesus were even attempting to appear like the promised messiah, he would have had a very different answer, especially as an Essene. In this passage, however, Jesus was clearly indicating that he would not fight the Romans at all. With such an answer, no one would have expected him to function as the promised messiah. And in the gospels the only people that Jesus came into any kind of conflict with were the Jews and Jewish authorities. That was certainly not supposed to be the position of the messiah! He showed *no* desire whatsoever to have any sort of conflict at all with Greeks or Romans.

Now, it is true that, as an Essene (and, again, the Essenes are completely absent from the gospels; deliberately so), he would naturally have been in conflict with Jewish religious authorities, especially the priesthood. But an Essene would also have been in conflict with the Roman authorities. So this story is an obvious fiction created by later Christians who did not want conflict with the Romans. Frankly, all of this butting-heads between Jesus and the Jewish authorities is not Jesus at all, but is Sokrates. Why? Because there was no thought among any Jewish sects that the messiah would do such things and because it provides a reason to believe that he was the son of god rather than a man. The messiah would never have argued with Jewish authorities because said authorities would have recognized him as messiah. But it is easy to see a "son of god" as arguing with, well, any human authority at all.

Still, the very fact that people even presumed to argue with Jesus in the first place shows that the things he presumably said and did were not very profound as compared with the things that other "mere humans" had already said and done. After all, why didn't the "son of god" say anything that had not been said and heard by others before and that would, then, have stopped all argument? Why could he not have said things so profound that no one would have been able to argue with him? And why, of all the miracles that he is purported to have performed, did he only perform only rather pathetic ones that anyone might be able to explain away (until he raised Lazarus from the dead) rather than miracles that might have proven who he was? If the folk were seduced by the miracles that he is purported to have performed, then they were very stupid indeed! Even Zoroastrian Magi could presumably have performed such so-called miracles. Frankly, the gospel writers failed in their efforts to elevate Jesus to the status of a philosopher, but the world has been so changed that the folk have become entirely gullible and now believe all of it as literal truth.

And no one can really point to the raising of Lazarus, which was certainly only a falsification by the gospel writers, as are his "physician" statements, placed in the gospels to make him seem like Asklepios, just as the changing of water into wine was an effort to make him seem like Dionysos (both of whom are closely connected with Apollon). All of this is a hoax perpetrated by the gospel writers, whoever they really were. And Asklepios was (mythically) rightly punished for what he did and his story is meant to teach that such a thing is unnatural and against the will of the deities. But the Christians perverted it, twisting it around to make physical resurrection seem like a good thing (this is where they began to depart from the Jewish Gnostics and become more like Neoplatonists). And how about poor Lazarus anyway, who would have had to twice taste death? Are we really supposed to believe that Jesus did him some kind of a favor by raising him? And why would god's son become emotionally overwrought over death anyway, especially one particular person's death, when all must taste of it? Only if death were bad - an evil - could this make any sort of sense. Thus the Christians hated Platon who showed that death was a good rather than an evil.

Whoever Jesus really was, Christianity was a complete *reversal* and became, thereby, a complete perversion of everything that the Greco-Roman world was and had always stood for. And this, I submit, was deliberate. This was their way of destroying the world that they so hated. From the Greco-Roman point of view, no one had ever risen nor ever really been raised from the dead - ever! The story of Asklepios was an allegory meant to teach a lesson, not a story meant to be literally believed. Therefore, even if a god were to raise a person from the dead he would be punished for that transgression of natural law. That is what was meant to be understood. The Christians could call that a miracle all they wanted to, but for the educated Greeks and Romans it was a horrifying perversion of natural and societal norms. It upset the universal balance with a new, unwanted, equation which was necessarily incorrect and, therefore, false. And, therefore, this perversion could not be accepted other than allegorically, which some attempted to do. But, in the end, the literalists would not let that pass.

Here is another interesting point that, as far as I can tell, literally everyone has missed. If Jesus taught using parables and even stated that it was necessary to teach using parables, why did none of his disciples apparently *ever* utilize this method of teaching? Did they not learn from their master how to teach others using parables? Were they not around him enough so that he could have taught them how to do so? Did they even *really* know him after all? A student of philosophy was expected to learn from the philosopher, his master, and to be able to expound wisdom and knowledge like his master at a certain point. Why were the disciples evidently not expected to do the same? Not one of them seem to have even tried. This leads to one almost inescapable conclusion - that the parables found in the gospels were later inventions, part of the tradition that had grown up around the figure and memory of Jesus. But it was unreal. They were creations by the gospel authors who wrote long after Jesus had died with the intent to make Jesus seem like Apollon or Sokrates, etc. So Jesus runs around telling parables just as the Pythia had uttered oracular responses difficult to decipher.

And, after all, was not the disciple Thomas also called "Didymus"? Yes, these names both mean "twin", but the explanation given in the gospels that his name simply means "twin" and further explanations later given by others that he was the twin of Jesus are preposterous! No, the canonical gospel writers did indeed know something about this Thomas, but it wasn't that. It was that Thomas (or his disciple) had written down "Secret Sayings" of Jesus (today known as the *Gospel of Thomas*) which they had utilized to formulate their gospels! See, an Oracle of Apollon known as the *Didymaion* was located in the city of

Didyma and it also provided oracular statements for those who posed questions to it, just like at Delphoi. Thus, the very name "Didymus/Didymos" ties directly to ancient Didyma and its Oracle. And the statements in the *Gospel of Thomas* (which are *not* parables, by the way) can be seen as nothing less than oracular statements of Jesus which are probably more authentic than those actually found in the canonical gospels, this gospel having been written during the late first century, probably predating all others. No one in ancient times could have missed this if they had known of this book of secret sayings. But most did not and it was lost to time until found in Egypt in 1945 CE among the other Nag Hammadi manuscripts.

Thus, I have sadly had to conclude, after many years of research, that the Jesus who was real was really not very much like the person who is presented in the canonical gospels. He was certainly not born of a virgin and was most likely not born anywhere near Nazareth. He did not return from Egypt as a child, but did so as an adult. He did not minister, at least not much, in Galilee. He did not really perform miracles or cast out demons. He did not speak in parables nor even deliver his wisdom in a Sokratic/Platonic manner. He did not raise anyone from the dead and he himself did not rise from the dead. And he certainly did not appear and disappear as some ghost and then ascend into heaven following his death. He was just an ordinary man who probably intended to start a revolt, whether he saw himself as messiah or not, which he probably did. But he was rightly executed for this by the Romans according to their law, *not* Jewish law. And his religious movement only succeeded some 300+ years later because of brute force, harassment, persecution, and other told and untold atrocities perpetrated by those who followed him, or that person whom he had been made into. ". . . 'Peace, peace,' But there is no peace" (*Jeremiah* 6:14) - probably the only biblical prophetic statement that has certainly come true. Oh how *this one* has come to fulfillment!

Finally, the Jewish Gnosticism from which Christianity sprang contained three important elements - (1) a celestial messiah and mediator (Son of Man), (2) a holy spirit (although theirs was feminine), and (3) the concept of salvation (through knowledge for them) of the soul from the sins of the fleshly body; the flesh and the creator of it both being

Apocalypse and Armageddon, The Secret Origins of Christianity:

seen as evil once Neoplatonism is combined with the rest. See, it is also from Neoplatonism that we get the concept that if creation (flesh) is evil, then the creator must also, by default, be evil. In this way they and the Gnostics found a way to acknowledge a creator - a concept foreign to the thinking of ancient Pagans in the European West - and called him the "demiurge". Therefore, if Platon was right and the soul was uncreated and immortal and, by default, good, then the body it was housed in, which was created by this evil demiurge, must be evil. This was literally the only way that the western Pagan mind could accept the concept of a creator such as that posited by the Jews (regardless of their creation myths) and the only way that Judaism and Hellenism could be combined. So *this* was the result of the attempted fusion of Judaism with Hellenism, religiously and philosophically.

Frankly, Gnosticism and Neoplatonism messed it up by creating the demiurge. This because before, if the soul was uncreated, then the universe was also uncreated. The uncreated soul was good by default, but so was the universe. All was seen as good even though the flesh and matter were understood to be corruptible and uncreated according to Platonism. But it was *not* seen as ***corrupt***. So it could be redeemed by fire, i.e., by cremation. But, once the demiurge was created by the Neoplatonists in an effort to combine Judaism with Paganism, this was all changed. Then the material universe came to be seen as created by him and, since it was corruptible, both it and he "became" evil. But the soul continued to be seen as uncreated and, therefore, good. Thus the soul only had to escape from the flesh in order to be saved through Knowledge. But, ultimately the entire universe, and especially this world, had to be destroyed and recreated in order for the soul to truly be saved, as in Zoroastrianism. Thus, the creation of apocalyptic literature.

So they created a dichotomy or at least a dualism (sort of like in Zoroastrianism) with the soul being good and the flesh being evil. Nothing could have been further from the Platonic Pagan mind. So, the whole reason that Christians believe the flesh to be evil is not really because of Paul, but because of Jewish Gnosticism and Neoplatonism, both of which emanated from Hellenization. Therefore, when Jesus, who had existed previously as a spirit, "became flesh", he was literally taking evil onto himself and that evil (flesh) had to be crucified - to suffer as an atonement for humanity's sins. The "lamb of god" would take on the "sins of the world". But, according to the Gnostics, Jesus' soul was not harmed by this since it could not be. Still, this was this very concept that led also to the belief that the entire creation had to be made anew, because it was evil since it was created by the demiurge. So apocalyptic literature incorporated this concept and added the concept of the end of time and a final judgment from Zoroastrianism. And all of this, in the end, led to the practice of asceticism among early Christians, especially monks, in an effort to mortify the flesh, which was seen as evil, so that their souls would indeed be saved. It was a sick perversion of original Platonism at best.

The Neoplatonists went too far in their emphasis that it was the soul that mattered and not the body. Instead of instilling the understanding that the body was a seed, they emphasized the idea that it was an evil prison *because* of the combination of Hellenism with Judaism. That makes little sense to us, but it made perfect sense to them. The demiurge had to be evil because his creation was obviously evil. So much for the Hebrew god stating that his creation was "good".

This is all to say that Christianity did not emerge from nor exist in a vacuum. Christianity literally grew out of the soup that was Hellenization and emanated directly from the one place where Hellenization had taken hold the best - Alexandria, Egypt. In so many words, it is obvious that Christianity is a direct result of Hellenization and that it could never have formed if not for Hellenization. So the Neoplatonists and, by default, the earliest Jewish Gnostics, just took it all too far, combining it with apocalyptic literature, etc. Thus, the mix ultimately didn't work. Neither Hellenization, nor Neoplatonism, nor Gnosticism actually *worked* and their various combinations didn't work either. But they did produce the one by-product that ultimately did "work" once force was employed to ensure that it did. And that was the religion that became Christianity.

Both John and Jesus were Gnostic Jewish Essenes with connections to Egypt as well as Qumran and the apocalyptic world-view found there. Period. Jesus did not create, nor did he intend to create, a new religion centered on him. Far from it, for if he had why would Christianity have remained a Jewish sect for so many years after his death? No, it was the gospel writers who skillfully created a religion centered on Jesus that was at odds with Judaism. This is probably the real reason that Jesus never wrote anything down himself, at least that remains extant. For if he had intended to create a new religion surely he would have written at least *something* himself. It is not that Jesus and his disciples used and quoted from the Septuagint that matters; it is that the gospel writers did so. It would be illogical for Jesus and his disciples to have used this source if they had really grown up in Judea and Galilee and spoke Aramaic. No, it had to have been the gospel writers who quoted from it even if Jesus was brought up in Egypt because, again, apparently Jesus never wrote anything himself. Thus, the gospel writers must have been brought up in the Diaspora, except for Luke, who is believed to have been a Greek. They didn't even know Aramaic, much less Hebrew, but did quote a few words in Aramaic that Jesus had used when performing "miracles". The gospels, then, were clearly written for audiences who spoke only Greek.

If one understands that no one has ever actually been resurrected physically from the dead (modern medical "miracles" aside) then one has, by default, to understand that Jesus, therefore, was also not resurrected. If, then, that is true, it stands to reason that the story of the resurrection was made-up and, therefore, cannot be true. Indeed, this may be the real reason why the *Gospel According to Mark* leaves it out entirely (in the oldest extant manuscripts), not, as some suppose, because the end of that gospel account somehow went missing. The writer of this gospel evidently either had not heard any traditions of the resurrection or did not accept them, but had no explanation of his own that is extant today (if there was indeed more to his gospel). But I digress here.

The fact of the matter appears, then, to be that the idea that someone might return from the dead was fairly widespread, at least in the eastern Mediterranean area. For it seems to have been here (perhaps in Anatolia) that the idea that Nero might return from death was actually hatched. And already the Jews were expecting Moses or Elijah to somehow return, although how and in what form was not quite explained. Thus, it became all too easy for Christians to make up the scenario that Elijah had indeed returned in the form of John the Baptizer and that Jesus had simply risen from the dead, but perhaps not at the first. Still, this was all in perfect keeping with already prevalent apocalyptic literature of the time. It was probably not until the situation in Jerusalem became almost completely dire, during the revolt which began in 66 CE, that the idea probably began to really circulate that Jesus had been resurrected because, otherwise, how could he return and function as the messiah who was supposed to free the Jews from Roman domination? So they began to expect him to return in an apocalyptic fashion, but he didn't. After all, it seems obvious that, although the pseudo-Zoroastrian Pharisee, Paul, had written and preached about this very thing, the concept did not truly take hold among the pseudo-Atenists in Jerusalem until close to the time of the revolt and even closer to the time of the destruction of Jerusalem in 70 CE. It seems that this was one of the teachings of Paul which the disciples in Jerusalem had rejected, along with rejecting Paul himself. They, the pseudo-Atenist Essenes, knew that it was an influence from Zoroastrianism and they were going to have none of it! But, we are getting a bit ahead of the story here also since the disciples and Paul have not even been introduced yet and the case has not yet been made for Paul having been strongly influenced by Zoroastrianism, let alone the disciples having been influenced by Atenism, although the latter has been briefly touched on with reference to Jesus himself. So let us proceed. If the point has not quite been proven here yet, there is more, because it is a bit more complicated even than this.

4

THE REAL CHRISTIANITY AND WHAT ACTUALLY HAPPENED TO THE DISCIPLES

A Confused Christianity

> ... nothing remained once this hate-inspired counterfeiter realized what alone he could use. *Not* the reality, *not* the historical truth! ... the ... great crime against history - he simply crossed out the yesterday of Christianity and its day before yesterday; *he invented his own history of earliest Christianity.* Still *further*: he falsified the history of Israel once more so that it might appear as the prehistory of *his* deed: all the prophets spoke of *his* 'redeemer.' Later the church even falsified the history of mankind into the prehistory of Christianity.
>
> Fredrick Nietzsche
> (Kaufmann 617; Nietzsche *The Antichrist*)

Thus Fredrick Nietzsche wrote of the apostle Paul, although it would have fit better with Constantine I or his biographer, Eusebius of Caesarea. But why on earth would anyone, even Nietzsche, say such things about the beloved apostle Paul? It was because Nietzsche, and some others, had come to believe that Paul had deliberately falsified early Christian history. And, in fact, he was partially right. Christian history - all of history, has indeed been falsified by those who wish for everyone else to believe that things unfolded in a certain way. In short, they lied. Robin Lane Fox stated in her book, Pagans and Christians, "No generation can afford to ignore whether Christianity is true and, if it is not, why has it spread and persisted and what is the proper response to it. Historians have a particular contribution to make to these inquiries" (Fox 8). Indeed, they do, and they have been.

To begin with, a simple premise that most scholars and historians seem to ignore, perhaps deliberately in some cases, is that, in order for the history of the first century CE to make sense the Romans had to have had a more complex reason for the barbarous destruction of Jerusalem and the temple there than is commonly understood to have been the case. While it is true that the Jews had revolted and Roma's patience with them in general was likely wearing a bit thin, a detailed analysis of the situation of the time, especially in terms of religion, reveals something more to be seen. Indeed, there is a question as to just what the Christians in and around Jerusalem may have had to do with this situation. After all, Christianity was actually gaining ground in that area during the first century following the death of Jesus and they were gaining converts in Jerusalem. This is something that is seldom noted by historians even though it seems quite obvious by use of only a little investigation. So, one has to ask; what part did Christians (who were still just a Jewish sect) actually play in the events which culminated in the destruction of Jerusalem and Jewish hopes for a new independent state?

The fact of the matter is that Christianity actually did NOT originate in Galilee or Judea or even Samaria, but instead originated in, and can successfully be traced to, *Egypt*, and to its true origins within the Jewish Gnosticism of Alexandria, as already shown. Gnosticism was widely diverse, but still held some core beliefs in common. Indeed the early church father, Ignatius, himself argued that the earliest form of Christianity, even at Antiokheia (Antioch), *was* actually a form of Gnostic syncretism (*Orthodoxy and Heresy*, 63-67). And more than one Church father traced Gnosticism directly, though incorrectly, to Simon Magus, showing that it was an early form of Christianity, not simply a second-century heresy, as many modern historians would have us believe. And, in fact, both Jesus and John the Baptizer were probably

Apocalypse and Armageddon, The Secret Origins of Christianity:

actually born in Egypt, *not* in Judea. And they certainly were Essenes, as has been shown.

Once one understands these things it is almost fiat that one will see the connection between Gnostic Jewish Christians in the first century CE and the destruction of Jerusalem and the temple. So, Christianity, although not the Christianity that we know today, is a religion that originated about the first century BCE or slightly earlier, *which came to eventually be seen* by early church fathers simply as a Gnostic heresy which had, at all costs, to be stamped out. So, the earliest origins of Christianity are actually about a religion, a sect within Judaism, which flourished in Egypt and which produced at least two major prophets who literally changed the world. Christianity, then, did not originate with "Jesus of Nazareth" after all, but with John and Jesus of Leontopolis or Alexandria, and Qumran! Jesus himself, and John the Baptizer, were actually Jewish prophets, probably from Egypt, who undertook the impossible task of converting the peoples of Judea and, *perhaps*, Samaria and Galilee, to a form of Jewish belief which was a thorough mixture of Neoplatonism and Gnostic Judaism with apocalyptic overtones.

Now, to begin with, the crucifixion of Jesus, it is generally agreed, took place in either 30 or 33 CE. But, actually, Jesus' crucifixion could easily have taken place as early as 29 CE. In my mind, according to the best sources (the reader can consult the sources listed in the bibliography if desired as such detail is too much for the purpose of this book), the stoning of Stephen would have taken place in about 31 CE and the conversion of Saul of Tarsus would have followed in about 32 CE. Now if Saul had been singling out those of "The Way", as it was then called, for arrest, etc., prior to his conversion, then this was indeed a persecution. But how widespread the scope of this persecution actually was can no longer be known by using extant evidence. It does seem to have encompassed the territory of Judea, Samaria and Galilee according to *Acts* 9:31. Still, if Saul was the main persecutor and it had mainly taken place in and around Jerusalem, perhaps barely reaching Damascus (a seldom noted Essene power-base), then it was not very widespread and did not affect a great number of people. Later, about the year 34 CE, would have occurred Peter's encounter with the Roman Centurion Cornelius after which he began to accept Gentile converts as part of his ministry. But, the caveat to this was that the Gentile converts who would be accepted were those who adhered to *Torah*, or the Law of Moses. There was absolutely *no* move whatsoever to accept those who would not adhere to Torah at this point. Period. That is, except for the efforts of Paul. What a contradiction for a faith that, it seems, placed the Prophets above the Law! This was their very first real compromise and it was one much like their predecessors, the ancient Hebrews/Israelites, had had to make, as detailed previously.

> Further, it is evident that from the beginning there was antagonism between these two bodies of Christians and that it continued to be accentuated by the liberalizing policy adopted by the one and the reaction thereto of the other, which at first condemned, and then later sought to control, the resulting admission of Gentiles into the Church (Brandon 129)

In the mean time, Barnabas sought out Saul, who, following his conversion, had gone back to his home city of Tarsus and had, by this time, changed his name to Paul/Paulos (Παῦλος), and they went to Antiokheia and taught for a year. And the Roman imperator Tiberius died about this time, in 37 CE. What happens during the next few years is fuzzy at best as the writer of *Acts* refers to little during this time period.

The "revelation" of the prophet Agabus, mentioned in *Acts*, probably took place in 43 CE, setting in motion events which led to the Jerusalem famine relief effort made by Paul and Barnabas. At this time, the Jerusalem church was facing persecution, according to *Acts*. Indeed, it is very possible that this persecution may have started because the Jewish Christians, or *Nazoreans*, in Jerusalem were being blamed for the famine. It is certain that Herod Agrippa I was instrumental in initiating this persecution in any case. During this time, the apostle James, the brother of the apostle John, was executed and the apostle Peter was imprisoned, awaiting execution. Interestingly, there is no direct mention of the apostle John in *Acts* at this time although he had figured prominently, along with Peter, prior to this. So it would seem that John had moved on elsewhere.

Paul and Barnabas went to Jerusalem during this pivotal time, bringing with them relief provisions, and then returned to Antiokheia after completing their mission. They obviously would not have wanted to remain in Jerusalem long while persecution was taking place. Peter also somehow escaped from prison and fled, probably to Antiokheia, where other members of the faith would take him in and protect him. One has to wonder here whether Paul and Barnabas might have had some hand in Peter's escape from prison since they were all there at the same time and all, apparently, went to Antiokheia afterward. I submit that this is exactly what happened; Paul and Barnabas helped Peter to escape from prison and all three then fled to Antiokheia! But, because Peter did not wish to draw attention to himself there, he gradually withdrew from table fellowship with converted Gentiles. Because of this, Paul disputed with him openly. Then, when King Herod died in 44 CE, the persecution ended. So, I think, although a rift had taken place there between Paul and Peter, the fact that Paul had been instrumental in saving him made a great difference later, as will be seen. And the division of the early church is clearly seen here.

Then Paul and Barnabas, along with John Mark, begin their first missionary journey, probably in 44 CE. The sect at this time was clearly still referred to as "The Way", so those who followed it were *not yet* calling themselves *Christians*. During this missionary journey they went to places such as the island of Kyprus (Cyprus) as well as Pisidian Antiokheia. At the latter place Paul preached in the synagogues against Torah. Some Jews opposed this, so Paul promised to go only to Gentiles from that point forward. But, as the writer of *Acts* tells it, as they move on they still continued to go to Jewish synagogues rather than directly to the Gentiles. Their travels took them to places such as Ikonion, Lykaonia and Attalia, totally bypassing Ephesos (Ephesus) and the cities in the provinces of Phrygia and Galatia, and then, by sea, back to Antiokheia. They probably arrived back in Antiokheia about 46 CE.

Now, why would Paul swear to go only to Gentiles and then immediately go to yet another Jewish synagogue? It would seem that here, as in other places, the writer of *Acts* is fudging the facts a bit. It seems more logical to conclude that it was not Paul who said that he would go only to Gentiles from that time forward, since he did not follow through with this, but that it was instead the members of these Jewish synagogues who, in driving him out from their midst, told him that they did not want to hear what he had to say and that he should henceforth go only to Gentiles, who might listen to him, since he was not welcome in their synagogues. In their anger, they had cast Paul out and hoped that he would no longer trouble them. But, this would prove not to be the case.

Then, in about that same year, according to *Acts*, "men from Judea" (apparently sent by James "the Just", the brother of Jesus who was the church leader in Jerusalem) went to Antiokheia and stirred up Gentile converts there by insisting that they were to be circumcised and follow Torah. Now, frankly, even according to *Acts*, this was not novel. After all, this is exactly what had been previously agreed to, however Paul, when writing the *Epistle to the Galatians* at about this time, chooses to twist this situation according to his own viewpoint. But new converts to The Way *were* at this time still expected to follow Torah, circumcision and all. Period. And this was already some sixteen or so years *after* the crucifixion. Could the party of Judaizers mentioned by Paul in *Galatians*, who are said to have "troubled" the Galatian church and who clearly were intent upon bringing the new converts fully into Jewish proselyte status, have originated in the Jerusalem church, although the writer of *Acts* strenuously denies this? And were they a part of a delegation sent by James "The Just", the brother of Jesus (as most scholars believe), into Paul's territory by way of Antiokheia?

That such a Jerusalem delegation did go to Antiokheia and that it was probably sent by James can hardly be disputed, so the possibility does exist (Longenecker 73). And, if one takes the internal evidence of the epistle of *James* as it stands, it appears obvious that this book was actually written during *this* time period. So it appears that James, the brother of Jesus, the leader of the church in Jerusalem, was at this time opposing Paul and his position that Gentile converts did not have to follow Torah and was emphasizing his authority both as the brother of Jesus and as the duly elected representative of the church. So here we see a Jerusalem church that was both rigid in its insistence that Torah be practiced and was also hereditary where leadership was concerned (In today's climate can one even help but see the comparison with the Sunni faction of Islam, which bases its lineage on heredity from Muhammad's relatives and adherence to strict Sharia law?).

One only has to look at *Galatians* 2:1-14, for example, to see that there was a rather severe disconnect between Pauline Christianity and Jerusalem Christianity within the early church. Here Paul claims superiority over the other apostles, which is certainly *not* the way those in Jerusalem would have seen things. All of this is another indicator that the apostle John (by now along with Peter) was elsewhere, most likely already at or near Ephesos. The fact that the book of *Acts* is little more than a biography of Paul with little mention of the evangelistic contributions of others provokes a question as to exactly why the writer chose to write in this way. After all, it is certain that others were instrumental in carrying the gospel to the wider world too, especially to Alexandria and to Roma (Brandon 130). But *practically all* were in opposition to Paul's teaching concerning Torah. And it is also known that Jewish Christians at this time still referred to themselves both as "those of the Way" and as "The Poor", i.e. "The Poor among the Saints in Jewish Christianity and *Qumran*" and the Ebionites, or "poor ones", were one branch of these Jewish Christians (Longenecker 59), as well as the Nazoreans.

In any case, because of this controversy, Paul and Barnabas, along with Timothy, went to Jerusalem again (Paul's *third* trip as a believer), supposedly in an effort to resolve this conflict. However, contrary to popular belief, it is more likely that they were actually being *summoned* to Jerusalem to answer for their position. Paul, in *Galatians*, twists this meeting into a win for his position, but the writer of *Acts*, although claiming to have been an associate of Paul's, shows things just a little differently. According to *Acts* it was agreed, basically, that Gentile converts were to abstain from fornication, from (female menstrual) blood, from things strangled, and from meat offered to idols. That is all. These aspects of Torah were considered most important for them to adhere to.

Now, Hans Cozelmann believed that this Jerusalem Council (if that is what it should really be called) took place about 48 CE. But the fourteen years that Paul mentions in Galatians need not be seen exactly as fourteen full years. And there must be more time between the Jerusalem Council and the end of the second missionary journey. It must also be added that most scholars appear to believe that the council occurred in 49 CE. However, that is very unlikely because of the fact that a revolt took place in Jerusalem in that year and at the same time Paul was in Kórinthos (*Κόρινθος*, Corinth). So the *latest* that this council could have taken place would have been 48 CE, just as Cozelmann believed, but it would seem, as indicated, that it would have had to have taken place just a little bit earlier even than that. There is really no doubt that it had to have taken place prior to the revolt of 49, which lasted about one year. So the date of the council cannot be placed in 49 CE just because, for some, it looks nice and corresponds to what they *want* to believe. History cannot be written in a vacuum, although some have endeavored to do just that. In any case, after the Jerusalem Council Paul and his companions returned to Antiokheia with a letter stating what had been determined, after whence the second missionary journey began.

Nothing more is said of Peter in *Acts* after this point. From this it is completely reasonable to infer that he had proceeded on his own missionary journey, which is not something that the writer of *Acts* may have known about and, if he did, he did not write about it. It is perfectly reasonable to posit that, at this time, Peter, having had time to consider and accept Paul's version of The Way (and remembering how Paul and Barnabas had rescued him), having first assisted John in Asia, went to Roma and established the church there, basically in Pauline form. Both missionary journeys, then, would have taken place about the year 47 CE. That would provide time for a church to actually be established in Roma to which Paul would have later written. So the Council would have taken place in either 46 or 47 CE, no later.

As for Paul, he and Barnabas, sadly, went their separate ways this time due to a disagreement. The writer of *Acts* does not state what exactly this disagreement was about, but it seems obvious that it had to do with the emissaries from the Jerusalem church, led by James, and the only major thing that they might have disagreed on would have been how strenuously Gentile converts had to adhere to Torah. Paul, of course, provides his own, different, explanation in *Galatians*. So Barnabas went to Kyprus. Paul took John Mark with him and went elsewhere, first to Anatolia, again bypassing the provinces of Phrygia and Galatia where we, I think, can no longer doubt, the apostle John (who did *not* accept Pauline Christianity) was already working. In Anatolia they mainly went to "Troas" (the Troad) and from there into the Roman province of Macedonia, where they went to the cities of Philippoi and Thessalonike. Then they, according to *Acts*, proceeded to Berea and then to Athenai (Athens). Their reception, while good at Berea, was not very good at Athenai. And, although churches were established at Philippoi, Thessalonike and Berea, the same cannot be said for Athenai.

It is intriguing and, perhaps, important to note some things about this purported visit to Athenai. In *Acts* 17:16 it is stated "Now while Paul was waiting for them at Athens, his spirit was being provoked within him as he was observing the city full of idols". This is the only description we have of ancient Athenai from the pages of the *Bible* at all, scanty as it is. Paul must have actually been greatly impressed by the things he saw, if he really ever went there.

Here it is said that Paul famously proclaimed the "Unknown God" to the Athenians. And, most interestingly, during his speech Paul (*Acts* 17:28) said "for in Him we live and move and exist, as even some of your own poets have said, 'For we also are His children.'" The interesting things about just this small quote from Paul's speech are these; (1) that this is a direct quote of Aratos of Soloi from about 300 BCE, and (2) that the Greek word for "poet", ποιητων, is used to describe Aratos. Now, I am not going to get into whether Paul actually said these words or not because it is perfectly plausible that he *could* have. Whether he actually did is irrelevant here. But calling Aratos a poet was exactly the same as calling him a *prophet* according to Greek usage. So, essentially, Paul and/or the writer of *Acts* acknowledged not only that the ancient Greeks had prophets who actually said useful things, but that Aratos himself had been such a prophet. The implications of this are usually totally glossed over by those who utilize this passage.

That Paul's speech was something less than a success, even though they apparently wanted to hear him speak again later, is shown by *Acts* 17:32 where it states "Now when they heard of the resurrection of the dead, some *began* to sneer, but others said, 'We shall hear you again concerning this'". Why Paul did not return is an open question. But it does seem obvious here that the author of *Acts* is indicating that not only had the Athenians rejected the message of Sokrates centuries earlier, they also rejected the message of Jesus through Paul. Frankly, this in and of itself throws suspicion upon Paul's visit there altogether (even though Paul mentions this visit in *1 Thessalonians* 3:1). This, then, may be one place where Paul actually did *not* visit (or where the writer of *Acts* took certain liberties with the facts). And there is just too much evidence of a potential later interpolator here.

According to *Acts*, Paul and his companions almost immediately left Athenai and proceeded to Kórinthos, where they were able to establish a church and where Paul remained for about eighteen months, staying with a man named Titus. It is interesting to note here that the writer of *Acts* makes no mention that anything within the city of Kórinthos provoked Paul even though it was widely known to have once possessed at least one of the greatest of all temples to Aphrodite from which ritual prostitution was continually practiced (and which continued even though the temple had ceased to function). This is another indication that Paul may not have visited Athenai - that that part may be made up to show how Paul must have got to Kórinthos and how the Athenians rejected Christianity.

We know about when Paul and his companions arrived at Kórinthos because the writer of *Acts* notes that Paul meets Jews who had been expelled from Roma because of an edict of the Roman imperator Tiberius Claudius Caesar Augustus Germanicus (Claudius). Historically, we *know* that this edict was promulgated about 49 CE. This is one date that, so far, *is* fixed. Since it had recently taken place, Paul could not have arrived in Kórinthos any later than 49-50 CE. But here, again, Paul runs afoul of Jewish synagogue leaders and again, supposedly, swears to go only to Gentiles afterward. It is also from here that Paul writes, first, *1 Corinthians*, then *Romans* along with *1 Thessalonians*, most likely in that order. It seems reasonable to assume that Paul would not have presumed to write a letter to the Roman church *if* Peter were still alive. So it would appear that Peter died in Roma about 49 CE (although Paul did not know that when he wrote *1 Corinthians*). It is important to note that, in *1 Thessalonians* 2:15-16, Paul writes, in part:

> ... who both killed the Lord Jesus and the prophets, and drove us out. They are not pleasing to God, but hostile to all men, hindering us from speaking to the Gentiles so that they may be saved; with the result that they always fill up the measure of their sins. But wrath has come upon them to the utmost.

But who is it that Paul is talking about? It is generally accepted that he is referring to the Jews who have not accepted Christ. But, I contend that he is talking about more than just those Jews. He is also talking about Judaizing Christians who still remained in Jerusalem. Paul was clearly upset with those who opposed his teaching of grace through faith only, whether they be mainstream Jews or Judaizing Christians. And, as Donald A. Hagner has pointed out (Evans & Hagner 134, *Paul's Quarrel with Judaism*), this was the polemic of an in-house debate and does not reflect hatred toward Jews or Judaism. And, as he further points out, Paul uses similar language and polemic in other passages, such as *Gal.* 5:12; *Phil.* 3:2, 18-19; *2 Cor.* 11:13-15; *Rom.* 11:8-10 and 16:18. And he also maintains that the first two of these is definitely directed against Judaizing Christians (Evans & Hagner 136).

Revolution and Hysteria

Now, again, it is also historically known that a revolt took place in Jerusalem, beginning in 49 CE, Paul, again, already being in Kórinthos by this time. It is by no means difficult to see that a sudden influx of Jews from Roma to Jerusalem could have helped to stir things up and trigger the revolt which began in about 49 CE, the year that Claudius expelled Jews from Roma. And, if such is true in this particular case, could it have also been true during a later period in time under similar circumstances? And could some of these Jews have been Christians? The answer here seems to be obvious. Now, of course, as in all situations, some Jews did remain in Roma anyway and, as long as they caused no trouble, they were not harassed. This would also have been true of those of the Christian sect, to whom Paul would later write.

Interestingly, it should be noted that neither the book of *Acts* nor any other New Testament source refers directly to this revolt as having taken place at all. What? Did the writer of *Acts* not know about the revolt that took place in Jerusalem? Certainly he did know. Just like the writers of the gospels knew that Jerusalem and the temple had already been destroyed (as we shall see), the writer of *Acts* knew of the revolt of 49 CE, but none directly referred to either of these events. The reason it is left out, I submit, is because this revolt failed and no one wanted to remember that.

Now, as Craig A. Evans astutely points out in the book <u>Anti-Semitism And Early Christianity</u>, it is erroneous to believe that early Christianity during the first century opposed Judaism because, for that to have been the case, there would have had to have been a clearly defined Christianity separate from Judaism, as well as a clearly defined Judaism. Instead, Judaism was pluralistic and diverse and still included Christianity, although they were clearly beginning to reject Christianity little by little. And the early Christians saw themselves as being a part of Israel, not opposed to it (Evans & Hagner 12). Indeed, as Bruce Chilton also points out (Evans & Hagner 42; *Jesus and the Question of Anti-Semitism*), if Jesus had intended to create a religious system distinct from Judaism then it is quite remarkable that there exists such a lack of uniformity of thought, especially as an alternative to Judaism, within the New Testament. So it is more plausible to suggest that Jesus and his movement were, at first, Judaic and Torah-abiding for all practical purposes but that this changed over time and that it is reflected predominantly within the Pauline writings.

Still, by the second century CE the Rabbis (while Christianity was dealing with a resurgence of Gnosticism, as we will see) had begun to more clearly see the threat that Christianity and other heresies formed and they took steps to prevent further erosion of their Jewish way of life. They did the only logical thing they could do to ensure the survival of their people and their religion. They began to suppress the teachings which had led to the situation in which they found themselves. The Rabbis refused to sanction the apocalyptic and pseudepigraphic books which tended to have their origins among the Greek-speaking communities of the Diaspora. They came to be considered as having little or no value and as being mischievous. And following the loss of their national independence, the leadership of the Jewish schools attempted to preserve mainstream Judaism intact and, perceiving the danger of these writings, not only rejected them as part of their corpus of Scripture but even forbade the study of it (Bentwich 109-10). However, this literature was preserved by the Christians of that era, being regarded with great veneration by the church fathers and the monks, for exactly the reason that the Rabbis had sought to eliminate it - because they recognized that it contained the very germs of Christian origins (Bentwich 197-98). So it is here that Judaism decidedly changed by rejecting the apocalyptic.

Rabbi Yohanan ben Zakkai, who escaped from Jerusalem during the siege of 70 CE, was allowed to establish a school at Yavneh (Jamnia), where the Hebrew Canon was finally codified about 100 CE. He became instrumental in holding the people who survived together through the agency of this school and through reforming Judaism. This resulted in a rebirth of Jewish learning which produced some of Judaism's greatest intellectual figures. By the end of the second century CE the Jews had come to terms with the fact that they would spend their lives in exile. But they retained the hope that a messiah would still appear and deliver them (Bentwich 297) while continuing to reject the apocalyptic. Indications are that the Jews who resided in Sardeis (Sardis), for example, took an active part in the life of the city as a whole while retaining an awareness of their own identity. But the situation in Roma was quite different as illustrated by this quote by Thomas Kraabel:

> In the first century A.D. many Jews in Rome were slaves, products of successful campaigns in Palestine by Roman armies. Jews in Sardis were more prosperous and had a less direct tie with Jerusalem: their community had not come from the Holy Land but had been founded by Jews from Babylonia and Mesopotamia two centuries earlier (Walters 24; *"The Roman Diaspora: Six Questionable Assumptions." The Journal of Jewish Studies, Vol 33*, p. 457).

It Started in Roma

It is not known when Jews first arrived in Roma nor what prompted their arrival. But large numbers did inhabit the imperial city by the time of the late Republic. Jews were first mentioned as being present in Roma in the *Valerius Maximus* text in which it states that they were expelled for proselytizing. They may also have been dabbling in astrology since the expulsion of astrologers is also mentioned within the same text. This text states that they were "compelled to 'return to their homes'" in Judea and elsewhere (Walters 28). This text was written about 31 CE. Interestingly, this is the same year during which the stoning of Stephen in Jerusalem may well have taken place. And the future apostle, Saul (Paul/Paulos), supposedly, was present.

It would seem that the main influx of Jews into Roma must have occurred after Pompey the Great captured Jerusalem in 63 BCE, during which the Romans took many Jewish prisoners, making them slaves and returning with them. Philo Judaeus stated that Jews resided mainly beyond the Tiber River (the Transtiber or Trastevere) and that they were mainly Roman freedmen (former slaves). Tacitus stated that "four thousand descendants of enfranchised [Jewish] slaves" were expelled from Roma in 19 CE by order of Tiberius Claudius Nero (Tiberius). And Marcus Tullius Cicero (Cicero), in his *defense of Flaccus*, written only four years after Pompey returned from the Judean campaign, made reference to Jews as a large group of people who had a great deal of influence in public affairs (Walters 29-31). So it would seem that Jews first arrived in Roma mainly after Jerusalem was captured by the Romans and that many quickly gained their freedom and became loyal residents of the city. But it also seems that they were often disruptive and expelled from the city for one reason or another, perhaps, only to return later in some cases.

Cicero in his *defense of Flaccus* "accuses them of practicing sacred rites that are 'at variance with the glory of our empire, the dignity of our name, the customs of our ancestors'". And this type of charge would also later be brought against the Christians. So the Jews were accused of contaminating Roman customs, according to the *Valerius Maximus* text (Walters 37-38). Finally, and most importantly for this work, Gaius

Suetonius Tranquillus (Suetonius) stated that the Roman imperator Claudius expelled the Jews from Roma in 49 CE "at the instigation of one *Chrestus*" and due to constant disturbances among them (Walters 49). *All* Jews were commanded to leave by Claudius' edict (Walters 51) although, again, some probably stayed and kept a low-profile or returned soon after leaving.

Now, there was a Gaius Iulius Chrestus who was a Roman citizen serving in the mounted guard of the provincial governor (legatus) and also of the quaestor of Germanicus, Publius Suillius Rufus. Publius himself "stood only a single person away from the innermost circles of the imperial family" during a time period which is "consistent with that Claudian expulsion of Rome's Jewish population. . . ." (Slingerland 219). It is believed by some that this Chrestus had been a Jewish slave who had obtained his freedom and had worked his way into an important position in Roman society. Publius Rufus was Chrestus' patron and was also a friend of the imperator Claudius. Now, it is also thought by some that it is exactly this man, Gaius Iulius Chrestus, who was the same *Chrestus* who was the impulsor through whom the decision was made to expel Jews from Roma under Claudius (Slingerland 235). The aim of this expulsion was to get rid of the Jewish "superstition" from the city.

A more common view of this expulsion is that it occurred because of instigation from the propaganda of Christianity which caused disturbances similar to those found elsewhere as related in the book of *Acts*. However, in fairness, Slingerland points out that ". . . unless *Chrestus* may mean *Christus*, there exists no basis whatsoever for the attempt to associate *Claudius* 25.4 with any aspect of Christianity." Also, it is from the fifth century writings of Paulus Orosius that we first get the implication that the name Chrestus may be linked with Christus (Christ). Still, as Slingerland points out ". . . he was sometimes untrustworthy in these matters, especially since this is not the only occasion revealing a tendency [by him] towards the Christianization of happenings within Jewish history" (Slingerland 203). In other words, he tended to falsify things at times to his liking.

The problem here is that if Suetonius meant *Christus*, he obviously misspelled it. James Walters makes a good case that such mistakes were common since Chrestus was a very common proper name and

Christus was unknown as a proper name. He believes that a simple error in spelling did indeed occur and goes on to point out that Tertullian complained that *Chrisitianus* was often mispronounced by enemies of the gospel as *Chrestianus*, adding "you do not even know accurately the name you hate". Lactantius also points out that the "ignorant" (and the early church fathers and apologists never missed an opportunity to paint Pagans as ignorant in their writings just as the writer of the book of *Acts* had done) often made the mistake of spelling *Christus* as *Chrestus* (Walters 52).

The other problem, as pointed out by Walters, is that it seems implied in the statement by Suetonius that this Chrestus was "present in Rome, instigating the disturbances". He states his belief that Suetonius may have believed that Chrestus was present in Roma at that time due to limited information or "simple misunderstanding of the Christian claim that Jesus was still alive" (Walters 52). And I concur with this.

So, while it is true that these words/names were sometimes confused, a misspelling does not initially seem to be likely because in *Nero* 16.2 Suetonius writes that "punishment was inflicted on the *Christiani*, a class of men given to a new and mischievous superstition". There is no error here. He is here *obviously* referring to Christians. "As a result, the claim of confusion seems to apply poorly to *Claudius* 25.4. Moreover, *Nero* 16.2 reads as if it was the first time that Suetonius referred to the new religion." Suetonius, it would seem, would surely have spelled the word in question correctly in both instances (Slingerland 204). However, I can personally attest to the fact that I have often spelled the very same word in different ways within the same text, whether because I was in some hurry or because I had simply forgotten how to spell it properly. So, positing that Suetonius was always perfect in his spelling is also problematic.

The above quote adds that "*Christus*, the founder of this new superstition, had been put to death during the reign of Tiberius after he was sentenced to death by the procurator Pontius Pilatus. It must be emphasized again here that "our earliest witness to the text of Suetonius is the fifth-century Orosius, who cites the manuscript of Suetonius before him as registering Christus instead of Chrestus" (Slingerland 205). Still, Suetonius really seems to mention *Chrestus* in one writing and *Christus* in another. In each he is writing about two separate imperators, Claudius and Nero. He is concentrating on them, *not* on the Christians. He is *not* writing a "Christian" history. So it seems most likely, taking all available evidence into account, that this event was indeed precipitated due to conflict between Torah-abiding Jews and followers of "The Way" in Roma who, by this time, appear to actually be calling themselves *Christiani* (Christians). So, it is entirely plausible that the name "Christian" began to be used by members of the sect in Roma this early, and first, but that the writer of *Acts* did not know this.

The simple fact from known history, in any case, is that, for whatever reason, Jews were expelled from Roma by Claudius in about 49 CE. That these Jews were likely of more than one faction, as they were in all other places, can hardly be disputed. That one of these factions may have been that of the Christians must be accepted as a distinct probability. That, if this is so, the reason for the expulsion was mainly due to infighting between those who followed Christ and those who did not, then, seems obvious, regardless of this other fellow named Gaius Iulius Chrestus. Frankly, trying to find this *Chrestus* in any individual other than Jesus is like grasping for straws. There is really no reason to do it other than to try to disprove that the Christian faction existed among the Jews in Roma at that time. And that would indeed be illogical.

The Jews in Roma were stirred up over one *"Christus"* - that is it. And this situation became so bad that Claudius decided that they needed to be expelled from the city. So, where did they go? Mainly to Jerusalem where they fomented rebellion against the Romans. This is a known fact. So, if a sudden influx of Jews from elsewhere in this event could have, and did, prompt a revolt in Jerusalem, who is to say that a similar event around 66 CE might not have also triggered *that* revolt? To ignore such a possibility, which is exactly what has happened for the last several centuries, is tantamount to foolishness!

Regardless, approximately nineteen years prior to the writing of Paul's letter to the Roman Christians we find here a great deal of fear in the capitol concerning easterners, particularly the Jews, and an expulsion of the Jews, probably in part due to the attempted propagation of Christianity among the Jewish population in Roma, which resulted in riots, in 49 CE. So the very type of situation which could have precipitated the expulsion of Jews from Roma in 49 CE may also have influenced Paul to write his letter to the Roman church in about 50/51 CE after that short-lived Jerusalem revolt was over.

> It is one of this minority's achievements that there are so many histories of the Christians' expansion and mission, but hardly a note of the people who tried being Christians, could not bear it and gave it up. Christians have made their history into a one-way avenue, with the further implication that "paganism" and Judaism were so gross that nobody would have wished to return to them.... We do not hear of anyone who left Christianity for simple paganism without any accompanying philosophy: perhaps this silence is significant and a lapse from Christianity did always lead to a favor for some systematic belief. Much the most attractive belief was full-fledged Judaism. We hear very little of Jews who became Christians after the Apostolic age, but much more of Christians who flirted with Jewish teaching.... Nevertheless, Christians spread and increased: no other cult in the Empire grew at anything like the same speed (Fox, Robin Lane 270-71).

The Demise of Paul

After Paul's sojourn at Kórinthos he and his companions sailed to the Roman province of Syria, first stopping at Ephesos briefly (his first visit there). He arrived at Caesarea in Syria and from there returned again to Antiokheia. Here, it must be noted, it seems obvious that Paul would not have dared enter the territory of the apostle, John, if John had still been there. So, it seems that by 50-52 CE, John had already been arrested and, presumably, sent to Patmos. The field appeared to be opening up wide for Paul, as he even indicates in *1 Corinthians* 16:9. With both Peter and John out of the way, he could go virtually anywhere he wished. His only true rival now was James, the brother of Jesus, in Jerusalem.

Then, by 52-53 Paul had embarked on his third missionary journey. On this journey, for the very first time, Paul went through the provinces of Phrygia and Galatia and also to Ephesos itself. At Ephesos, according to *Acts*, while Paul was there, *the first known deliberate popular book burning in all of history* took place in which all sorts of Pagan books were destroyed *forever* (*Acts* 19: 19). This would have taken place in probably 54 CE and set the precedent for widespread destruction of Pagan books, libraries, etc. in the future. But Paul found that he was not entirely welcome at Ephesos (even though John was not there anymore), so he went on to nearby Tyrannus where he is said to have remained for two years. And it was either at Ephesos or Tyrannus that Paul penned *2 Corinthians*.

It was in the year 54 CE that Nero Claudius Augustus Germanicus (Nero) became imperator. His ascension occurring either just prior to or at about the same time as the book-burning at Ephesos - Nero must have taken note of it and must have enquired as to just who might have caused it. He would have been told that Jews, particularly the sect of Christians, had caused it. So Nero would have been on the alert concerning the Jewish sect of Christians from the very start. This event, then, would soon prove problematic for Christians in Roma. They had by this time caused trouble in Roma, Jerusalem and Ephesos.

Now, it appears that, following his sojourn at Tyrannus, Paul went back into the Roman province of Macedonia and through the province of Achaia (Greece) once again and from there back into Anatolia. At that time he returned to Ephesos and it was at this time, about 55 CE, that the famous incident concerning the temple of Artemis (Diana) took place during which Paul was nearly killed (*Acts* 19: 23-20: 1). But there he was, stirring up trouble in Ephesos yet again! If Nero had not taken note of the previous book-burning, he surely would have noted *this* incident. So Paul soon left as authorities were probably seeking him.

And someone else, I submit, also took note of the events taking place in Ephesos. That person was the writer of the *Apocalypse of John*, whether he was the apostle or an associate. This book was likely written in response to Paul's meddling in John's territory as well as in response to recent provocative actions by the Romans. The writer apocalyptically prophesied the downfall of Roma and the destruction of those who were not "true Jews". And the true Jews, of course, were Christians, but only those who adhered to Torah. It seems reasonable to assume that, not long after this, the apostle John, whether he was the actual author or not, must have died.

Perhaps, due to these incidents and the writing of this book, which they would soon have obtained from John, Paul was even less welcome at Ephesos. For, whatever the reason, Paul moved on again into the province of Macedonia, then on to Greece, then to Macedonia again for three months. It's almost as if he was being chased around. Then he visited several places by sea on his way, hurrying, according to *Acts* to Jerusalem. Apparently warned not to go there by various people, he proceeded anyway. At Caesarea, in about the year 56 CE, the prophet, Agabus, enters the picture again and further prophesies that Paul would meet disaster if he went to Jerusalem; so states the writer of *Acts*. Certainly a hotbed of dislike for Paul existed in Jerusalem because the Christians there would have strongly disagreed with the position Paul had taken concerning Torah and would have known about him stirring up trouble everywhere he went. And some there were probably aware of the fact that Paul was on his way. So they might have been waiting for him.

Now, the writer of *Acts* states that the first thing Paul did was to go see James and the other disciples/apostles. This does seem to be a likely scenario because, even though they disagreed on some points, to whom else would Paul go? He almost had to commune with other Jewish Christians, whatever their differences may have been. But, whether he had known ahead of time or not, he went straight into the lion's den, so to speak.

> It is in this record of this last visit that Luke again gives ground for very serious doubt about the true nature of the transactions which he purports to relate, and the impression which he gives is that of one who has awkward facts to recount, but does his best, without too overt distortion, to maintain the edifying theme of his work (Brandon 133).

The writer of *Acts* never says exactly why Paul made this last visit to Jerusalem. He portrays Paul as wanting to go and journeying with all haste even against the direction of the holy spirit. The real truth here becomes obvious to those who are willing to read between the lines. Paul claimed to be "bound in the spirit" to go to Jerusalem. But, it becomes obvious that Paul was finally submitting to authority (and may well have been in chains, having been captured) and heeding the very first Christian "Papal Bull", as it were. And he knew what he would be facing, as the writer of *Acts* repeatedly alludes to. He was *summoned* to Jerusalem to the very first Christian *inquisition* in history! And there he was examined or, as *Acts* states, he gave his report to James, his arch rival in the presence of the elders of the church (*Acts* 21: 18-19). Paul was questioned by James concerning his orthodox standards, or lack thereof, James *still* indicating that adherence to Torah was important for converts (*Acts* 21: 20-22). Perhaps Paul's answer to this inquiry was less than acceptable, but at least plausible. So James proposed a test for Paul which Paul agreed to, the test being one of complying with a quaint and expensive Jewish ritual which would prove his orthodoxy to everyone (*Acts* 21: 23-24).

> For Paul the dilemma was inescapable. For all his gospel of the sufficiency of faith in Christ, he had illogically continued to recognize the claims of Judaism upon the Jew, and now that he was faced with the consequences of this fatal weakness in his logic, he obviously felt that he could not formally repudiate his national faith and accordingly submitted to his opponent's astute demand (Brandon 151).

But he was discovered while in the temple by Jewish Christians from the province of Asia, according to *Acts*, and arrested very soon after his arrival. He was then quickly spirited off to Caesarea, where he was imprisoned for about two years. So he was there for some time until his hearing in about 58-59 CE. James had effectively eliminated his greatest competitor! Or, at least, so he thought.

During that hearing Paul presented his case before Felix and, in part, stated (*Acts* 24:14) "But this I admit to you, that according to The Way which they call a sect I do serve the God of our fathers, believing everything that is in accordance with the Law and that is written in the Prophets". So Paul was obviously telling Felix that he was a good Jew and, by the way, never called himself a "Christian". During his hearing, Paul is said to have appealed to Caesar, who happened to still be Nero. Because of this he was sent to Roma. The writer of *Acts* states that Paul spent two full years at Roma under house arrest. So, presuming that Paul arrived in the year 60 CE, at the latest, he would have remained there until at least 62 CE, the year that James is believed to have been killed in Jerusalem, immediately succeeded by his cousin Symeon, according to Hegesippus, with no break; an easy transition, thus fully establishing the concept of dynastic succession (from John to Jesus to James to Symeon, but never to Peter) within the Jerusalem church (Brandon 152). During that time it is generally accepted that Paul wrote the books of *Ephesians*, *Philippians*, *Colossians* and *2 Timothy*, and this is the only scenario that makes sense.

However, some do posit that, according to tradition, Paul was released and traveled again and was then re-arrested and sent again to Roma, where he was finally executed. One of the main reasons that this is done is that there is an obvious problem with the books *1 Timothy* and *Titus*. *1 Timothy* and *Titus* seem to indicate such a scenario. But, frankly, there is no evidence at all to back such a scenario up and if one eliminates *1 Timothy* and *Titus* from the writings actually penned by Paul, as many scholars do, then there is no need to believe anything other than the *probability* that Paul was *never* released from prison at all. Whether the writer of *Acts* did not know exactly what had happened to Paul or did not want to inform his readers is an open question. But it is most likely that, as with the other apostles, John and Peter, this writer simply did not know. And, not knowing, this writer had the integrity not to engage in perpetuating whatever gossip or tradition that might have been gong around by this time concerning these leaders of the movement. Thus, instead of potentially telling a lie or two, he simply left these things as open questions. So, although the writer of the *Gospel According to Luke*, presumably one and the same person, does engage in perpetuating tradition concerning the life of Jesus, he refrains from trying to answer any questions he does not have knowledge of about the apostle's deaths in *Acts*.

It is interesting to note here that when Paul is said to have arrived in Roma he met with the Jewish community there in an attempt to explain his situation to them. Their response to Paul was:

> They said to him "We have neither received letters from Judea concerning you, nor have any of the brethren come here and reported or spoken anything bad about you. But we desire to hear from you what your views are; for concerning this sect, it is known to us that it is spoken against everywhere" (*Acts* 28:21-22).

Two things must be pointed out here. The first is that, although it may seem on the surface that the Christian sect was something not directly known (i.e., not yet in Roma) by the Jewish community in Roma, that is not really in the reading. For the Jewish community to state that they had heard about it does not preclude the existence of such a community in Roma. In fact, as we have seen, such a Christian community was probably already in Roma, having likely been established by Peter himself, and it was probably the impetus for the expulsion of 49. But the second and, I think, most important point here is that they stated that the Christian sect was "spoken against everywhere". So already, by about 59 CE, some thirty years or less after the crucifixion, the report that had spread as far as Roma was that this sect was at least greatly disliked. So, when Suetonius and others write about how vile Christianity was, it is obvious that this was the general consensus even before the Great Fire in Roma. Nero didn't just select some pacifistic group of Christians who weren't bothering anyone when he blamed them for the fire. He was probably not the only one who believed that they may well have set that fire. That was probably the common consensus at that moment in time. And, perhaps, it had been a result of another attempted book-burning. So people hated them already and Nero responded in kind. That the executions generally backfired with the Roman people beginning to feel sorry for the Christians, however, is interesting in and of itself. It seems sort of like the Athenian rulers who regretted having Sokrates executed centuries before.

It also has to be stated that one really does have to consider the sad, but unlikely, possibility here that both Paul and Peter *could* have still been alive and still in Roma when Christians were executed by Nero in 64 CE because of the Great Fire there. If so, they would surely have been executed at this time, together. Once again, the writer of *Acts* simply does not tell us. Again, this is less than likely, but it does have to be kept in mind as a remote possibility. In any case, no one really disputes that Paul was arrested during the reign of Nero and, thus, once brought to Roma, Nero finally had the instigator he had sought for so long. No appeal would have worked. Nero would have by no means whatsoever been persuaded to let him go.

The final question here is that of just when the book of *Acts* may have been written. Certainly it was written after Paul had spent at least two years in Roma, which would place its writing in about 62 CE at the earliest. But, if it was written after the *Gospel According to Luke* and if that gospel, like the rest, must have been written after the fall of Jerusalem and the destruction of the temple there, then it could not have been written prior to 70-71 CE. And, if *Luke* is a later gospel, which I and many others contend to be the case, then it was written during the last decade or so of the first century at the earliest. And there can be no doubt that, once it was written, Paul had long been deceased. And it has to also be reasoned that probably all the rest of the apostles were also deceased by the time *Luke* and *Acts* were written. If any were still alive, this writer, I think, did not know about it.

The Roman Response to The Way and Its Results

Now, it is also ironic to note that the lifetime of Jesus coincided with a temporary low-point in the use of Pagan shrines in many places within the Roman Empire. But, following his death, the use of Pagan shrines and performance of Pagan religious practices in these places quickly resumed (Fox, Robin Lane 75). This is what Paul, John and Peter, among others, had to contend with when they journeyed over the empire trying to gain converts. A renewed surge of Pagan faith, if you will, was occurring exactly at the same time that they went out to oppose it.

Still, everything went down-hill from here, so to speak, for the Jewish people and for Apostolic Christianity. Again, as already noted, in 64 CE the Great Fire occurred in Roma, for which Nero blamed the Christians. Many Christians were horribly (but, lawfully) executed; many more certainly fled. They returned to their old homes in places like Antiokheia (calling themselves "Christians") and Jerusalem where they stirred up even more trouble. The first great Jewish revolt against the Romans began in 66 CE. Although slightly caught off-guard at the beginning, the Roman response was as swift as it was brutal. Contrary to the hopes of the writer of the *Apocalypse*, the Romans moved swiftly from north to south, blazing past and decimating Megiddo (Armageddon) almost as if it weren't even there. The resistance there and in other northern areas crumbled! In the mean time, in 68 CE, Nero died.

The Jewish forces regrouped in the one place they should not have, as it turned out - Jerusalem, thus sealing her fate. In 70 CE Jerusalem and the temple were destroyed by the Romans and the expected parousia did not materialize for those who remained there. In 73 CE the new imperator, Vespasianus, ordered that the Jewish temple at Leontopolis also be destroyed, lest it also become a center of rebellion. Finally, in 74 CE the Romans took the last stronghold of Jewish resistance at the fortress of Masada, the defenders of which (except for Josephus, it seems) had all committed suicide rather than face the Romans. All had failed.

It seems obvious today that the Christian sect made absolutely no effort to truly differentiate itself fully from Judaism until it had to - until the destruction of the temple in Jerusalem. Until then, by the account of the writer of *Acts*, they retained their headquarters in Jerusalem teaching in or around the temple area. One can have little doubt that it was after the fall of Jerusalem, then, that the *Gospel According to John* was written. The same must go for the other gospels. *John* was written directly after the fall and the great dislike between Jews and Jewish Christians is clearly evident within this gospel. And the fact that this gospel was placed last among the canonical gospels illustrates one of two things; either (1) that those who made that decision probably did not know when it was written and, thus, did not know that it was written *first*, or, (2) that if they did know, they wanted to hide this fact and make it appear as if this gospel was written last, which is exactly the viewpoint most have unwittingly espoused. Either way, there would have been no need for gospel writings prior to this because they still expected Jesus to return and save them. But, when this did not happen, it was decided that narratives concerning the life of Jesus should be written. Trouble was, there was no one left around who had directly known him. The result is mainly fiction.

Thenceforth, for all practical purposes, the only surviving form of Christianity was Pauline Christianity. This was the type of Christianity that won the day. It was the type that *had* to win, even if the price was the falsification of the historical facts. Pauline Christians emphasized the cross and the death of Jesus while Gnostic Judaizing Christians had de-emphasized the cross and emphasized the final days of Jesus' life. For James, for example, one does not actually need Torah, per se, but one does need to adhere to the ethics which come from the observance of Torah. For Paul, ethics should come without having to observe Torah at all. All other forms of Christianity, where possible, including Gnostic Judaizing Christianity, were eventually simply written out of the historical record (along with the Essenes) and, those that could not be written out in this way, were demonized as heretical. And the Jews as a people continued to pay the ultimate price for Pauline Christianity's success as early church fathers and Christian apologists, such as John Khrisostomos (Chrysostom), wrote vile anti-Semitic diatribes and homilies that would make anything found within the pages of the New Testament look as if it were written by a kindergartner!

That some Jews and "Jewish-Christians" must have escaped from Jerusalem prior to the Roman siege under Vespasianus and Titus and gone to places such as Leontopolis and Alexandria, must simply be accepted since it is the only logical conclusion. *Of course some did.* Probably, in part, because of this Vespasianus had this temple closed and dismantled because of a backlash from there after the destruction of the temple in Jerusalem. Josephus tells of this and states that this temple had existed for 343 years (*Wars of the Jews* VII, 10§4), but that is a mistake. It existed for approximately 243 years instead. But, in any case, it was in this way that Vespasianus prevented a new rebellion from emanating from that temple as well.

But then, somehow, came the resurgence of Gnosticism in the second century CE. Against this newly energized Gnosticism both Pauline Christianity and Judaism competed successfully. Gnosticism was seen as dangerous by both because of its dualism which would permit only one outcome concerning the question of god. Thus came the second-century Gnostics Barnabas and Marcion, both of whom deduced from allegorical interpretation that the Jewish god along with his Torah had been the power of evil which Christ, the good power, had had to struggle against. After all, the Torah had actually been the seduction of Satan (Bentwich 268). That was their Gnostic response to opposition from the other Christians and from Judaism. The internal crisis instigated by this renewed Gnosticism culminated in about the mid-second century CE as it rapidly spread throughout the Diaspora, causing open abandonment of Torah and advocating separation from other forms of Christianity (Bentwich 271). The Gnostics did have some early successes of a sort, but the influence of Gnosticism was to wane because of its inability to attract the masses due to of its emphasis on secret knowledge and salvation of the elect (sort of like the ancient Egyptian and Greek Sacred Mysteries).

The Effect of the Temple's Destruction Upon Judaism

The destruction of the temple in Jerusalem showed once and for all the inherent problem of the attempt of Hellenization to mix Hellenism with Judaism. The heretics, or *Minim*, were rightly seen by later Rabbis as the main instigators of the rebellion which destroyed Jewish civilization as an independent entity until modern times. This rebellion had many causes. But the influence of sects such as the Essenes and Christians cannot be doubted, although their influence is seldom noted by historians. Their messianic and apocalyptic hopes got the better of them and they started something which they were unable to bring to a successful conclusion. There would be no repeat of the Maccabean victory. Roma was an entirely different opponent.

> Some kinds of *Minut* were known before the spread of Christianity. The embryo of the later sects . . . existed in Philo's time (ibid 291). [T]hey [the Theraputae, etc.] were [later] treated as Christian-Gnostic sects; but it is likely that they derived their tenets from Jewish Gnostics who sprang from the heretical hotbed of Alexandria. The Minim began to be prominent in rabbinic literature from the time of the desecration of the temple, and the Midrash contains endless stories of polemical controversy with them. The rise of Christianity, coming at the same time as the shock to the national life inflicted by the destruction of the temple, emphasized the peril of *Minut* (Bentwich 292).

The Sadducees also disappeared as a political force along with the destruction of the temple in Jerusalem. And in later rabbinical writings, the Sadducees were equated with the Gnostics and other heretical groups (Bentwich 104).

Again, after the destruction of Jerusalem and the temple there in 70 CE, Pauline Christianity was destined to play the dominant role. Judaism would fold into itself and renewed Gnosticism would lose its appeal after a brief resurgence in popularity. The world, especially with reference to Judaism, would never be the same. The outcome of Hellenization for the Jews was, thus, disaster, at least in the short run.

> The communities of Alexandria, Cyrene, and Libya never recovered from the decimation which followed the risings against Trajan and Hadrian. . . . Their reduced numbers were little by little won over to Gnostic and Christian ideas. . . . Alexandria . . . what had once been the most productive centre of Hellenistic-Jewish literature gave not a single Jewish record to the world after the second century. Christian scholarship,

on the other hand, soon took up its chief abode in Alexandria. . . . [And later] Cyril, the "most Christian" bishop of Alexandria, expelled all Jews from the city of Alexandria, and persecuted them bitterly when anywhere found in the land of Egypt. Thus the greatest Jewish community of the Hellenistic disapora was finally broken up (Bentwich 301 & 320).

The Egyptian Connection Revealed

Now, again, from biblical texts one can gather enough information, when combined with the accounts of the Jewish historian Flavius Josephus and others, as well as more modern scholarship, to show that Jesus was indeed taken to Egypt as an infant or young boy, but not at the time or in the way that is portrayed in the New Testament gospels. Instead, he, and probably John together, would have been taken to Egypt around the year 6 CE during or after the revolt of the Jews in Judea, Samaria and Galilee which was led by Judas the Galilean and Zadok because of Caesar Augustus' plan to conduct a census there. Jesus, at that time, would have been about ten years of age. This, then, would seem to discredit the possible intent of the authors of the *Gospel According to Mark* and the *Gospel According to Luke* in which some modern scholars suggest that they plainly portray Joseph and Mary as good citizens of the Roman Empire, perfectly willing to be enrolled in Caesar Augustus' census. Instead, they are more likely to have been revolutionaries themselves who had to flee to Egypt once this revolt was crushed by the Romans, and Judas and Zadok were killed. After all, even in *Acts* 5: 37 it states of this Judas that ". . . [h]e too perished, and all those who followed him were scattered." The Jews at Leontopolis or Alexandria would have offered the family of Jesus safe haven.

And, again, as modern scholars also know, there is absolutely *no* reference or allusion in *any* extant historical document to what has become known as "the slaughter of the innocents" in which King Herod I "the Great" is said to have ordered the execution of any male child under a certain age. Herod may have been and done many things which one might consider evil and heartless, but this is one thing which he, apparently, did *not* actually do. And, after all, it is written ". . . Out of Egypt I called My Son" (*Matt.* 2:15). It should also be re-emphasized that:

> From Paul, from Matthew, and from Josephus we learn of a Torah-observant Christianity in Jerusalem that opposed the attempt of Paul (and others) to turn Christianity into a non-Jewish religion - that is, into a religion that would accept gentiles without requiring that those gentiles become proselytes to Judaism. The religious authorities in Jerusalem persecuted both versions of Christianity, the latter for admitting the gentiles on the terms described, and the former for, as far as we can tell, being insufferably self-righteous and condemning the temple cults. . . . From material remains we learn only of a possible small Christian presence in or near Jerusalem (Sanders, Jack T. 39).

Sanders continues that there appears to be no archaeological evidence at all which shows that Christianity even existed at all in Galilee prior to the revolt of 66-74 CE. What an astonishing revelation! He adds that even the book of *Acts* does not actually attest to the presence of Christianity in Galilee. Such a potential presence is only mentioned in 9.31 where it states, "So the church throughout all Judea and Galilee and Samaria enjoyed peace. . . .". Sanders thinks that the mention of Christians in Galilee may be an assumption on the part of the writer. He adds that it is probable that there were some residing there prior to 70 CE, but that *there is no direct extant attestation* of their presence there so early (Sanders, Jack T. 39). I tend to agree with Sanders here. If there were any, they were very few. Still, it does seem evident that both Jews and Jewish Christians did reside there between the wars, as Sanders also points out. But the contact between the two groups was anything but cordial, as conflicts were rather continuous. Christianity, then, likely went north into Galilee mainly *after* the first revolt of 66-74 CE (Sanders, Jack T. 67).

Why, indeed, would Christianity (even Jewish Christians) have not even existed in Galilee if this was the place where Jesus' main mission took place? Why would this be so if Jesus were indeed a Galilean and if his family were from Galilee? The answer does seem to be that Galilee simply was not really where the mission started after all and that Jesus did not grow up there after all. Perhaps Jesus may have been born in Judea, but probably never resided in Galilee. Would this be an assertion based upon silence, i.e., the lack of evidence either way? Perhaps. But if one wants evidence for something and one is determined that the gospels must contain that evidence, then one should at least consult *Luke* 2:21-24 which reads:

> And when eight days had passed, before His circumcision, His name was *then* called Jesus, the name given by the angel before He was conceived in the womb. And when the days for their purification according to the law of Moses [Torah] were completed, they brought Him up to Jerusalem to present Him to the Lord (as it is written in the Law of the Lord, "EVERY *firstborn* MALE THAT OPENS THE WOMB SHALL BE CALLED HOLY TO THE LORD"), and to offer a sacrifice according to what was said in the Law of the Lord, "A PAIR OF TURTLEDOVES OR TWO YOUNG PIGEONS."

Now, I am not sure just how many people would have been willing to travel from Galilee (or even Bethlehem in Judea) to Jerusalem with an eight day old child regardless of what Torah said, but it would not have been an advisable journey for an infant of only eight days not to mention his mother. Be that as it may, it would not have been impossible. But the real point here is that the "holy family" are being portrayed here as completely Torah abiding Jews in every way, even as far as being willing to offer animal sacrifice and they likely didn't travel far to do it. So they followed both Torah *and* Roman law.

This should be no surprise at all since obedience to Torah and animal sacrifice were expected of Jews of this time period. But one truly has to ask whether, if it was expected of the holy family and, in addition,

Jesus was circumcised according to Torah, it should not have been a requirement of Christians - the later followers of Jesus. And that was exactly the crux of the matter which divided earliest Christianity. No doubt, all of Jesus' brothers were circumcised too, including James, who had become the hereditary leader of the church in Jerusalem following Jesus' death; their cousin, Symeon, afterward.

The Egyptian Files

In any case, another literary source, the Nag Hammadi library, is instructive for us here. Scholars who have studied Gnosticism have known virtually from the beginning that the Gnostics de-emphasized the crucifixion of Jesus because, for them, it was not so much the cross that mattered, but the knowledge or gnosis that he imparted as the very way of obtaining salvation. But the Nag Hammadi manuscripts were a bit of a surprise for said scholars when they came to understand that these documents contained several references to the passion story. Here, in these passages, the crucifixion is shown as a reality and is not explained away. Jesus was not portrayed as a ghost. Also, significantly, the Jews are *not* blamed for the death of Jesus. But in some texts said responsibility is levied onto the "archons" - the rulers of the Jews, but still not the Jewish people as a whole (Evans and Hagner 269-70; R. McL. Wilson, *Anti-Semitism in Gnostic Writings*). Wilson illustrates this by citing the Nag Hammadi source, the *Concept of Our Great Power*, thusly:

> The archons raised up their wrath against him. They wanted to hand him over to the ruler of Hades. Then they recognized one of his followers. A fire took hold of his (i.e. Judas') soul. He handed him over, since no one knew him.

The "archons", as Wilson astutely points out, seem to have been "the *archontes tōn Ioudaiōn*, the rulers of the Jews, but this has long been forgotten (Evans & Hagner 285). So, in this passage, the Jewish *people* are not blamed. Instead, only their *rulers* are (much as in the case of Sokrates). This surely evidences an early first century Christian Gnosticism which accepted the passion as well as the Hebrew Bible, *not* one from the second century CE. Marcion changed all of this with *his* Gnostic rejection of the Hebrew Bible and its god (like the Neoplatonists). And, indeed, as Wilson further points out (Evans & Hagner 287), the alleged origins of Gnosticism within Judaism is unchallenged by the facts. And the Nag Hammadi manuscripts support, rather than contradict, this.

So, we can clearly see that in the earliest known references to the passion, the Jews as a people are NOT blamed. This falls perfectly in line with the portrayal of the holy family as being "Torah-abiding" Jews. Thus, one would expect the church to follow suit with this type of Gnosticism. And it did - *in Jerusalem*. Most likely also in all of Judea where it was found and other proximate areas as well as in the Roman province of Asia. Most likely also in Egypt where it spread early, as we will see. But *not* in the areas where Pauline Christianity held sway. Thus, there was conflict.

Now, although the majority of the texts within the Nag Hammadi library do not fit easily within any of the known Gnostic systems described by the early church fathers because they were only acquainted with the second century version, there are a great number of "parallel motifs". This, frankly, is to be expected. And these texts must have been written *prior to* the second century and, therefore, the early church fathers were unacquainted with them. They were only acquainted with the second century version of Gnosticism. And these texts do not appear to have been composed solely for only one religious community, but may have been collected by one particular community over time and utilized by them (Hedrick & Hodgson 8).

The dating of these texts is also instructive. At least two, the *Apocalypse of Adam* and the *Gospel of Thomas*, have been clearly dated to the *first* century CE (Hedrick & Hodgson 9). And some of these texts are distinctively Gnostic and show no signs of having been influenced by later Christianity in any way, including the already mentioned *Apocalypse of Adam* as well as the *Paraphrase of Shem*, the *Three Steles of Seth* and *Eugnostos*. This shows without any doubt that Gnosticism was not simply a second-century Christian heresy, as most of the early church fathers and many later scholars would have us believe. And other Nag Hammadi texts, such as the *Gospel of the Egyptians*, the *Apocryphon of John*, the *Hypostasis of the Archons* and the *Trimorphic Protennoia* were later adopted and changed by second century Christian Gnostics as texts of their own. So, these texts demonstrate that pre-Christian Gnosticism existed in an ideological sense, if not a chronological sense (Hedrick & Hodgson 9).

Also, according to Hedrick and Hodgson, Birger Pearson points out that Jewish intellectuals at Alexandria produced the earliest Gnostic literature as a by-product of their revolt against the Jewish creator god (the demiurge), as already alluded to. And Mandaeism is "the most important enduring example" of those non-Christian forms of Gnosticism that produced some of the works found in the Nag Hammadi Library (Hedrick & Hodgson 16). So there can be little doubt that Gnosticism itself originated within Judaism, probably in Egypt. If not, it was soon transported there by believers (perhaps from Samaria) who settled there and continued to practice their new faith. As Pearson further puts it, these "Jewish intellectuals could, and did, use the materials of their ancient religion . . . in giving expression to a new, anti-cosmic religion of transcendental *gnosis* 'knowledge'" (Hedrick & Hodgson 17-18).

Similarities between these early Egyptian Jewish Gnostics and later Christianity are multiple. John D. Turner in his work Sethian Gnosticism: A Literary History, states that the Sethian Gnostics of Egypt, for example, performed a rite of baptism which they often called the "Five Seals", symbolizing an individual's removal from this world of flesh and a translation into the celestial world of light. This rite also included the invocation of divine personages who were mediators between humankind and the true god. He also points out that Sethianism, which flourished in Egypt during the first two centuries, BCE and CE, practiced this baptismal rite, although it was certainly *not* a Christian sect. This Gnostic movement evolved over time to eventually identify their hero, Seth (or Adam) with the pre-existent Christ (Hedrick & Hodgson 55-56). They also held to the belief in a divine trinity of Father, *Mother* and Son, all of whom were considered

Apocalypse and Armageddon, The Secret Origins of Christianity:

the Savior during different epochs of time (Hedrick & Hodgson 58), like in Zoroastrianism.

The Divided Church

It must, therefore, be emphasized here that it has become obvious to almost anyone, including modern scholars, that there were two main competing versions of "Christianity" in the fist and second centuries CE, contrary to that which we have always been taught by the church itself. The most important proponent of this view, I think, was F. C. Bauer. These competing ideologies within "Christianity" were those represented by Paul on the one hand and the Judaizing Christians, mainly in Jerusalem, on the other hand. And the evidence indicates that the early Christian Gnostics were represented by the original apostles in Jerusalem, but not by Paul.

Bauer further states that the book of *Acts* portrays the earliest church as unified and without conflict, generally, by making whatever conflicts that existed appear to be minor, local and temporary, thus easily resolved (Hedrick & Hodgson 178). However, for me the gospels and the book of *Acts* are actually quite clear concerning the conflict between Paul and the Judaizing Christians in Jerusalem. But the author of *Acts* did play this down somewhat, it seems. So, if the reader is not paying attention, he or she misses this conflict and glosses over it, which is exactly the intent of the writer.

A century later, W. Bauer thoroughly dismembered the orthodox view of Christian history from the first centuries CE. Bauer proved that the traditional claim that orthodoxy preceded heresy either logically or chronologically has *no* historical basis (and yet people still believe that it did). There is no historical basis for the idea that the earliest church was "pure" and without division. This concept of the earliest church was promulgated by the author of *Acts*, by Hegesippus, and, most of all, by Eusebius of Caesarea. So heresy, as defined by the early church fathers, was not some deviation from the original after all - it *was* the original, which the later church wanted to stamp out! Bauer also proved that orthodoxy was actually *not* the majority view during the second century

CE and that it was limited mainly to the churches in Roma, Kórinthos, Antiokheia and western Anatolia, the very churches that Paul had either founded or later nurtured (Hedrick & Hodgson 182).

In addition to this W. Bauer has shown that there is a "curious scarcity of anti-orthodox polemics in the heretical literature. . . . [T]hey appear uninterested in refuting the orthodox position" (Hedrick & Hodgson 184). This should not seem so very strange after all once one realizes that even during the latter centuries of the Roman Empire non-Christian and Pagan historians characteristically omitted any reference to Christianity, for the most part, as if it did not even exist. So it would seem that the Judaizing Christians employed the same tactic. They all must have been under the impression that, if Pauline or orthodox Christianity were to be ignored, then it might simply *fade away*. But they obviously did not understand what they were up against.

Bauer further adds that the absence of anti-orthodox polemics in heretical literature shows that the "heretics" (i.e., the Gnostics) were, in fact, the dominant form of "Christianity" during that time period and felt secure in their large geographical areas. The orthodox churches were outnumbered and relatively isolated, so they were "forced to attack heretics wherever and whenever they could" (Hedrick & Hodgson 184). That is why anti-heretical statements and diatribes are abundant throughout early orthodox writings.

Fredrik Wisse (The Use of Early Christian Literature as Evidence for Inner Diversity and Conflict) adds that during this time period heresy was not defined by a variant teaching itself so much as it was by any type of teaching from someone who had not been authorized to teach by the church leadership or who was somehow deemed unacceptable or unworthy. The converse was that any type of teaching that was promulgated by someone approved by the church leadership was considered orthodox. The reputation and status of the author defined sound doctrine (Hedrick & Hodgson 184-85). And Wisse agrees with W. Bauer that "'heresy' appears to precede 'orthodoxy' in most areas" (Hedrick & Hodgson 187). Finally, Wisse adds that:

> The disappearance of most early Christian writings by the time of Eusebius, even the non-polemical writings

of reputed heresiologists, would be explained if most of these books did not meet the later standards of orthodoxy . . . (Hedrick & Hodgson 190).

In so many words, by the time of Constantine I and Eusebius of Caesarea most early "Christian" writings, even those written by acceptable persons if they contained very much of the unacceptable viewpoints, had already been "lost", re-written or destroyed because of the orthodox church's unrelenting assault upon *any other* viewpoint. Stop long enough to contemplate that.

The True New Covenant

Now, to return to the true origins of what we call Christianity one must look a bit more at the Essene Jewish sect at Qumran. The sectarians at Qumran believed that the Old Covenant, which the Jewish people and their leaders, they said, had desecrated, foreshadowed their *New Covenant*. Certain signs were to accompany this New Covenant, which included references to the desert wilderness, a new circumcision, new vows, a new Sabbath (Sunday), a new way of dressing, and a new calendar complete with new holidays. And, along with the Gnostics, the Qumran Essenes made a concerted effort to "destroy the works of femaleness" (Sheres & Blau 45-46), a theme repeated several times throughout the Gnostic text entitled the *Dialogue of the Savior*.

Indeed, Jesus, according to the gospels, does seem to have been basically against marriage as Paul also was. Jesus was certainly against divorce once married, but he also states that there is no marriage in the soon to come Kingdom of Heaven. Frankly, for Jesus, procreation was unimportant and those who speculate that he might have had a wife and at least one child are basing such proposals on no evidence. The evidence they purport to provide is circumstantial and unproven at best. And certainly the earliest Christians disfavored marriage as they expected the Kingdom to soon arrive and, thus, no need for offspring.

Sheres and Blau further state that "The concept of nazir (Nazirite) is related to neser ('sprout', 'shoot') . . ." (50). And, according to Matthew

Black (Sheres & Blau 165), in his book The Scrolls and Christian Origins: Studies in the Jewish Background of the New Testament:

> When the sectarian [Essene] 'priests' seceded from Jerusalem and the service of the altar, they became virtually and in practice Nazirites. More than that, Qumran was not the only Nazirite-type center" 'a related group had established itself . . . in Egypt - the 'Therapeutae', who, according to Philo, were involved in healing via ritual baths. . . . There may [also] have been other fundamentalist, Nazirite-type sects as well (Sheres & Blau 49).

Here, one begins to see that a secure connection can be made between the Qumran Essene community in Judea and the Essene/Gnostic Jewish communities at Leontopolis and Alexandria, Egypt. Further, at both Elephantiné, before that temple was destroyed, and Qumran, horse breeding was practiced and the messiah figure was already characteristically portrayed as riding on a white horse (as in the *Apocalypse of John*), which became a heavenly symbol of perfection. In addition to this, scholars now believe that both of these communities practiced artificial insemination on horses *and* that human artificial insemination actually took place at Qumran (Sheres & Blau 146-47). In this way, men did not actually have to have physical sexual contact with women. "Once the possibility and probability of artificial insemination are recognized, the mystery of immaculate conception becomes quite mundane" (Sheres & Blau 158).

Sheres and Blau have also been able to show how the various Jewish communities, including those at Elephantiné and Qumran, were actually intricately connected, not remote and far away from one another, other than by time and distance. This helps to bolster the probability that the Qumran community itself had its origins at Elephantiné and Leontopolis in Egypt. And at Qumran the "saints in the desert" intended to join forces with the angelic "Sons of Light" in a forty-year war effort against the "Sons of Darkness", according to their own writings. This war was supposed to take place upon this earth itself and the "Sons of Light" would, of course, be victorious and produce paradise on earth (Sheres & Blau 160).

The Failure of the Qumranites

Is it possible that the revolt that resulted in the destruction of Jerusalem and the Jewish temple there was actually started at Qumran or, at least, because of people from Qumran, rather than by people actually residing in Jerusalem itself? Could this, in fact, be one reason that the Romans, as they approached Jerusalem to put down this rebellion, suddenly diverted from Jerusalem, first going to Qumran and destroying that community, only then returning to Jerusalem to complete the job? Why else would they bother to attack and destroy some rather remote and isolated community? It *had* to be, at least in part, because the Qumran community had actually instigated this rebellion in the first place and, if it were not destroyed, would continue to be an instigating factor! And, no doubt, Roman military genius dictated that they first appear to be about to attack Jerusalem so that those at Qumran would be deceived long enough for the Romans to get close and prevent their escape. This was the one eventuality that the Qumranites had not prepared for. And, once again, the Romans surely wanted the Copper Scroll too because they wanted the treasure listed upon it.

So, then, what do John the Baptizer and Jesus and their followers have to do with this? It is clear from a combination of biblical texts and from what we know from history that Jesus, contrary to common belief, did ***not*** actually prophesy that that he, or the Hebrew god, would destroy the temple in Jerusalem. But it is also obvious that he did make some sort of statement concerning the temple. *Matthew* 12: 6 states that he simply said "But I say to you that something greater than the temple is here." In fact, it seems that what he actually probably said was that the *Romans* would destroy the temple, just as they ultimately did in 70 CE. And, frankly, it would have taken little imagination for anyone to suggest that the Romans would eventually destroy the temple since the two previous to the one that existed at that time had been destroyed by conquering armies. But to openly say so in public invited retaliation from Roman authorities. And this is exactly what the Qumranites expected to happen in any case. And since the Roman General Vespasianus did order the temple to be destroyed as the messiah was supposed to do according to the Essenes, it is not so far-fetched to see him as messiah, is it?

Therefore the future destruction of the temple was already seen as the apocalyptic "end" by the Essenes at Qumran. They wanted the temple to be destroyed because they saw it as already desecrated. They did not believe that it could be purified, so it had to be destroyed and replaced by a new one. And it appears obvious that, as a follower of John the Baptizer, Jesus would have been seen by others as also an Essene. So, whether he made a statement about the temple's destruction himself or not, he was among those who clearly *wanted* it to happen. And, Jesus' statement concerning the "abomination of desolation" only makes sense if the ones who are to destroy the temple had first set up something *abominable* in or around the temple area. And this is in keeping with the relevant passage from the book of *Daniel*. So, when the "abominable thing" would be set up in or about the temple, then the expectation would be that the temple would be destroyed not too long afterward. And, again, the Qumranites actually wanted the temple to be destroyed so that a new age would be ushered in. And they had no expectation that the Romans would *ever* leave until after they had done exactly this.

The "abomination of desolation" is mentioned in *Matthew* 24:15 as well as *Mark* 13:14. And, in *Luke* 21:20 a related statement reads "But when you see Jerusalem surrounded by armies, then recognize that her desolation is near." Further, in verse 24 the writer continues; ". . . and they will fall by the edge of the sword and will be led captive into all the nations; and Jerusalem will be trampled under foot by the Gentiles until the times of the Gentiles are fulfilled". Still, as has been pointed out, these are not prophecies since the gospels were written after the fact.

Now, in the *Gospel According to Mark* it is stated that the witnesses at Jesus' trial gave *false testimony* when they said that Jesus had stated that *he* would destroy the temple (*Mark* 14: 56-59). So why was Jesus arrested in the first place if he had not threatened to destroy the temple? He was arrested because of his violent act which Christians call the "cleansing of the temple." When Jesus overturned the tables of the money changers he was probably initiating an insurrection (as well as masking the actions of his followers who stole scrolls from the temple)! He well knew that the Romans, once an insurrection had begun, would focus very much on the temple, where it all had started. His followers fully expected the Romans to do their part so that their new age could be initiated as they also fully expected to defeat the Romans *after* the Romans first destroyed Jerusalem and its temple (which they would rebuild to their liking once victorious over the Romans). But when it didn't happen that way, Jesus' followers were left to explain exactly *why* no parousia had taken place.

Their first tentative explanations for the fact that nothing had happened upon the death of Jesus can be found in the gospels in the story of the tearing of the temple veil, which Crossan calls a "symbolic destruction" (Crossan 357). Although this rending of the veil probably did not really happen, it was a plausible story and served to explain and substitute for an apparently failed prophecy. After all, they would have expected the temple to soon be destroyed after Jesus' death mainly because Jesus supposedly prophesied it. But that did not happen. So the tearing of the temple veil symbolized the *future* destruction of the temple and they expected that it would still soon take place. After all, had not the temple lost favor with the Hebrew god as exemplified by the tearing of the veil? And Jesus' followers *remained in or close to Jerusalem* so that, when the destruction did happen, they could be ready to help usher in the new age. It is well-known that the first century Christians expected Jesus to return within their lifetimes or very soon thereafter. Persecution of the Christians did nothing to dissuade them from their expectations, but instead fueled the anticipation. It made them believe it all the more.

The Roman Connection

There is also, as alluded to previously, a connection between the burning of Roma and the destruction of Jerusalem in that the destruction of Jerusalem was *a direct result of* the burning of Roma! Historians seem to collectively refuse to even allude to this in any way since I have found this in *no* historical work whatsoever. But, logically, it *has* to be the case. And it is actually key to everything. It is well-known that, in 64 CE, Roma was consumed by flames, the cause still to this day being unknown or uncertain. It began during the night of 18-19 July. It is *widely believed* today that the imperator, Nero Claudius Caesar (Nero), started the fire and that he played the lyre while watching Roma burn. This myth is repeated over and over as actual history today, but it is *absolutely untrue*. No ancient historian states that Nero started the fire. But Cassius Dio does state that Nero sang the *Sack of Ilium* as he watched the city burn (*Roman History* LXII, 16). This according to Gaius Suetonius Tranquillus (*Lives of the Twelve Caesars, Life of Nero*, 38), who used Dio's history, which is no longer extant. So, in a general hatred for Nero, everyone today latches onto this salacious bit of political/religious propaganda.

Publius Cornelius Tacitus, a much better historian, stated that Nero **was not even in Roma** when the fire broke out, but was at Anticum and makes it clear that it was nothing more than a rumor that Nero played the lyre while watching the city burn. He adds that, upon hearing what had happened, Nero actually rushed back to Roma to organize a relief effort and paid for it *out of his own funds*. But, more than this, he even opened up his own palace, which had actually been partially damaged in the blaze, to provide shelter for the homeless and destitute, arranging for the delivery of food to prevent starvation (Tacitus, *Annals* XV.39). Afterward he rebuilt Roma on a grander scale and, yes, built himself a new palace too. But the rebuilding was accomplished by the use of funds imposed on the provinces of the empire. No one in Roma or in Italy had to pay a thing (*Annals* XV.45). So much for the *evil* Nero! This was the real Nero here, according to the ancient historians, not the crazed maniac he has been made into over the centuries. That he did some bad things, as all did, is not in question. That he set the fire himself and relished in it - that is simply *false*.

However, when Nero, *having been falsely blamed by some* for starting the fire, in return blamed the "Christians" (*Annals* XV.44), this was no idle effort simply meant to cast blame on someone else, but was actually a direct declaration of war against Jerusalem because the Christians were still seen as Jewish! When the Christians were executed it was really because they refused to acknowledge the authority of the imperator and were, therefore, seen as subversives, perhaps even spies, from an enemy camp (after all, they also exhibited Zoroastrian tendencies). The Christians, still a Jewish sect who had come to the attention of Nero at least once before, and probably twice because of Paul, were believed by the populace to have set the fire, and Nero acted in accordance with this belief. It seemed obvious to the people at that time that the Jews (in the form of the Christians) had finally set fire to Roma as so many had for so long feared.

But why, again, would Nero or anyone else have singled out Christians, since they were pacifistic and weren't hurting anyone? That is the question people still ask, after all. Why, indeed, would the Christians, *if* they were recognizable from the other Jews, have been singled out? First, the actual word that Tacitus uses here is *Christianos*. He states (*Annals* XV.44):

> As a consequence, to get rid of the report, Nero fastened the guilt and inflicted the most exquisite tortures on a class hated for their abominations, called *Christianos* by the populace. *Christus*, from whom the name had its origin, suffered the extreme penalty during the reign of Tiberius at the hands of one of our procurators, Pontius Pilatus, and a most mischievous superstition, thus checked for the moment again broke out not only in Judea, the first source of the evil, but even in Roma, where all things hideous and shameful from every part of the world find their centre and become popular.

Tacitus was a genuinely good historian and he had no real axe to grind here. So, it is significant that, whereas he had come to the aid of Nero's reputation where the fire was concerned, he did nothing of the kind when it came to singling out the Christians, which is obviously what Nero was here doing. But did Nero really single them out simply because people hated them? After all, they hated practically all Jews, not just those who followed Christ. It is here that one has to see the actual key itself. The people who had been singled out were not just Jews who were still hoping for a *messiah*. These were people, Jews and others, who were eagerly anticipating their *Christ* - their new king - to appear. And *this* was subversion! And the subversive, Paul, executed only two years earlier, had also been a Christian. *This* is, in part, why they were singled out. They rejected the Roman imperator, Nero, in favor of Christ. And, as Tacitus continues:

> ... next, on their disclosures [confessions], vast numbers were convicted not so much on the count of arson as for hatred of the human race [a common accusation against the Jews]. . . . they were covered with wild beasts' skins and torn to death by dogs; or they were fastened on crosses, and when daylight failed were burned to serve as lamps by night. Nero had offered his gardens for the spectacle. . . . Hence, in spite of a guilt which had earned the most exemplary punishment, there arose a sentiment of pity, due to the impression that they were being sacrificed not for the welfare of the state but to the ferocity of a single man (*Annals* XV.44).

Many scholars dismiss the idea that Christians were recognized as a separate sect this early. But I will again posit that the idea of the Christian first developed exactly here, in Roma, not Antiokheia, and, with this event, they came to *truly* be recognized as different because it was with *this* event that the followers of Jesus came to be seen in one important way from the other Jews. They followed Christ and they expected him to return, to destroy the Romans, and to reign. This was substantially different from the Jewish belief that a messiah would appear - their messiah was not seen as someone who had previously been executed by Roman authorities and who would come back to take over. That is a subtle, yet inescapable difference. And, after all, there may still have been some Torah abiding Jews who were swept up in the frenzy that followed and executed along with the Christians. Nero had certainly heard nothing particularly good about Christians and once they "confessed" to having set the fire that burned Roma his fury knew no bounds! If he had not hated Christians and recognized them as distinct before this, he had certainly come to hate them here!

Following these mass executions for treason, for that is what they were according to Roman law, there can be no doubt that those who were able to escape did so. Well, where, then would they have gone? Back home - back home to places like Jerusalem and to *Antiokheia*, where the name was supposedly officially coined. In fact, it seems entirely plausible that, if Nero did not coin the name himself when referring to them, then those who returned to Antiokheia soon began to differentiate themselves by using this term (which had already been in use in Roma for some time) in order to show that *they* had suffered persecution and that *they* were somehow better than those who had not (like the ancient Hebrews/Israelites who had adopted circumcision) - never mind that they themselves had actually fled; that made no difference in the greater scheme of things. It would not have taken long after that for all other believers there to begin following suit and adopting the name for themselves. Thus, the first *true* Christians were created as obviously distinct from Jewish Christians.

And, of course, those who returned to Jerusalem were restless and had basically the same attitude of superiority. It seems to me that the Essenes and the Jerusalem church, along with those returning from Roma, were instrumental in instigating the rebellion of the Jews in Jerusalem, which began just two years later, in 66 CE, if for no other reason than the fact that they fought against and quarreled with one another. After all, there was also circulating an Essene tradition of a "messianic age" of forty years which some appear to have equated with the earthly Christian messianic age. And it had been almost that long since the beginning of the Christian age (Gaston 468). So it was time, in the view of some, to instigate the end and to *force* Christ to return! Once one realizes that there really was no gap between the Great Fire in Roma and the beginning of the first major Jewish revolt against the Romans, one has to ask if there is a connection and has to conclude that there *must* be. The connection has to be the Jews/Christians who fled from Roma during Nero's "persecution". Historians either conveniently or inadvertently gloss over this, writing in such a way as to lead the student of history to assume no causal connection. No one, to my knowledge, has ever linked these two events in any way whatsoever. It is truly one of the "forgotten" pieces of history.

The amazing conclusion here has to be that, if the persecuted people were not actually recognized as Christians at that time - if they were not actually seen as separate from Judaism, but simply as a sect within Judaism, then they *may* have been singled out, but the blame still actually fell upon the Jews in general! Thus a rather automatic declaration of war upon Judaism and Jerusalem by Nero. Certainly Tacitus later calls them Christians because, by his time, they were recognized as such a separate entity. In fact, it is unlikely that they were actually *seen* as a separate sect at all until after the Great Fire in Roma and into the time of the fall of Jerusalem, but the term "Christian" was still applied to these peculiar followers of Christ. The Great Fire in Roma and the fall of Jerusalem were the two historical events that truly made them distinct from Judaism overall. That is why, just a few years earlier, Paul could get away with still calling himself a Jew.

The Christian Connection

Now, Flavius Josephus states that this Jewish revolt was actually begun when a group of Greeks intentionally sacrificed birds in front of a local synagogue in Caesarea to provoke the Jews, but we know that there was more to it than that. In any event, the Jews were further inflamed because the Roman garrison stationed at Caesarea did nothing to intervene (Josephus, *War of the Jews* II. 14.5.). Nero appointed Vespasianus to crush the revolt, but this effort had to be completed by Vespasianus' son, Titus, as Vespasianus had to return to Roma following the death of Nero, becoming the next imperator.

So we had an actual war between Roma and Jerusalem; effectively facilitating war between Pauline Christianity and Jerusalem Christianity even though the churches in Roma and its allies were not very powerful as of yet and were not the driving force in this conflict. But their lack of strength was made up for by Roman might and there can be little doubt that, once Jerusalem had been destroyed at the hands of the Romans, the church in Roma and its allies would have seen it as the justice of god and would have been glad to see Jerusalem's downfall! Their competition had been effectively eliminated, but they could not "blame" Roma or the Romans for it. Nor could they blame the Romans for the death of Jesus anymore. No, the blame for everything had to fall *entirely* upon the Jews. And if Judaizing Christianity was also blamed along with Judaism proper, all the better.

Clearly, the hierarchy developing within the two separate groups was unique to each. Pauline Christianity's hierarchy is relatively well-described within the writings of Paul himself (and those attributed to him). That it eventually developed beyond his vision is simply natural. But no one ever seems to ask why the church in Jerusalem somehow became hereditary. After all, was not Peter supposed to have been the leader of the church? Then why would James, the brother of Jesus, have become the de facto leader and after him his cousin Symeon? And this even though Peter was obviously present at first and one of the leaders of the church there. It would appear that *a brand new priesthood* was being created by way of the family of Jesus. And this would have been the expectation of the Essenes - a new hereditary priesthood, but not directly through Jesus as Jesus had no male children, at least. Perhaps, however, they had forgotten that they would have to actually have sexual relations with women in order to keep this going. Or, more likely, they expected the parousia to occur very soon. But instead their own destruction occurred soon.

Again, once Jerusalem was destroyed, that effectively eliminated Pauline Christianity's competition since Jerusalem was the center of Gnostic, Judaizing Christianity. Some "Christians" were indeed killed in Roma after the fire, but the church there was not destroyed by this and many of them, again, left. Still, any church that existed in Jerusalem when it was destroyed would have basically ceased to exist. The only remnants of this Jerusalem church would have had to have fled before the siege of Jerusalem even commenced in order to have survived because the Romans systematically and ruthlessly executed *anyone* caught trying to escape after they surrounded the city. Now, again, to be truthful, a very few did manage to escape and, in one famous incident, the Romans actually allowed one Jewish Rabbi, Yoḥanan ben Zakkai, to go his way after he proclaimed Vespasianus to be the messiah and promised that all he wanted to do was to preserve his people's teachings and start a school elsewhere, with no revolution in mind. And he kept his promise! Also, a few Christian slaves *must* have been taken and transported to other parts of the empire.

The Roman Messiah Who Happened to be Pagan

Now, it is widely held that the *Gospel According to Mark* was actually written in Roma after the death of Peter and, perhaps, even before the destruction of Jerusalem. However, again, the actual writing of this gospel more likely took place after 70 CE and it was probably *not* written in Roma. Also, it is tradition that Mark went to Egypt following the crucifixion of Jesus and began the process of converting the Egyptians in about 42 CE. Whether there is any truth to this or not, it is certain that the spread of Christianity in Egypt began in Alexandria and began quite early. The *majority* of Egyptians were, in fact, already Christian by the beginning of the third century CE. And, although Egypt is said to have converted to Christianity in 384 CE, the truth here is that Egypt converted very early to Coptic Christianity for whatever reason and this region was overwhelmingly Christian well before almost any other region. The majority of Egyptians, especially in Alexandria, were Christian well before the year 384 CE, although this may have been considered some sort of "official" date. But few ever seem to ask why the Egyptians, of all people, were so receptive to a Jewish Gnostic/Essene mystery religion, i.e., Christianity. The Armenian nation and church will rightly point out that it was their nation that was the first to adopt Christianity as its official national religion in either 301 or 303 CE. But, again, by this time the majority of Egyptians had adopted the Christian faith, so Egypt, being much more populous than Armenia, was really first even if it was not done officially by that time.

In addition to all of this, there was a Jewish prophecy that was apparently then taken to mean that Vespasianus would be the messiah, according to the Jewish historian, Flavius Josephus. Also, this idea is found in rabbinic writings "such as Yoḥanan ben Zakkai's prediction (S & T, 34.) that Vespasianus would become emperor [according to] Isaiah 10:34 . . ." (Vermes 65). This prophecy, with the addition of some numerical wizardry, was taken to say that the *end of the world would* come exactly at the time of the temple's destruction, which was about to occur, they believed. As Josephus states:

> They had it recorded in their oracles that the city and the sanctuary would be taken when the temple should become four-square . . . An ambiguous oracle, likewise found in their sacred scriptures, to the effect that at that time one from their country would become ruler of the world. This they understood to mean someone of their own race, and many of their wise men went astray in their interpretation of it. The oracle, however, in reality signified the sovereignty of Vespasian, who was proclaimed Emperor on Jewish soil (Gaston 458).

General Vespasianus was, in fact, prosecuting this war and was in Judea when he was declared imperator, so he was effectively declared "king" on Jewish soil! This, coupled with the fact that a Jewish Rabbi had proclaimed him to be the messiah sealed the deal. Further, Josephus also states that Daniel had foretold the destruction of the temple as being by the hands of the Romans (Gaston 459-60). According to Gaston, the passage he had in mind was *Daniel* 9:24-27. This is the famous passage of the "Seventy Weeks" which also contains the statement that Jesus cited about the "abomination of desolation" (Gaston 461).

The king and messiah, therefore, for both Josephus and Yoḥanan ben Zakkai *was* the very Pagan Vespasianus who, along with his son, Titus, is known to have mainly worshipped the Egyptian goddess, Isis. Josephus clearly believed that these passages predicted a 490 year time period and that this 490 year period of time was just about to come to an end. The messiah would be the ruler of the world, and the ruler of the world was clearly Vespasianus. And to prove this, the siege of Jerusalem had lasted about three and one-half years, as Josephus also believed Daniel had predicted it would (Gaston 461-62).

Also, the exact moment when the temple was in flames and Roman standards were set up in the court of the temple as objects of sacrifice signified this "abomination of desolation". Deliverance, then, was expected to occur exactly on the day that the temple was destroyed because that very day was 9 Ab, which was the very day on which the first temple had been destroyed by the Babylonians, according to *Jeremiah* 52:12. So, 490 years had been completed by that date in fulfillment of prophecy (Gaston 462).

More clearly, the chronology proceeds as follows: The Babylonian exile - 70 years; Persian rule - 34 years; Seleucid rule - 180 years; Hasmonean rule - 103 years; and Herodian/Roman rule - 103 years. All of these time spans combined added up to 490 years. In further corroboration of this interpretation it must be added that Clement of Alexandria, Origen, Tertullian and other early church fathers understood this calculation to have been correct. So, for Josephus and some others, the messiah had indeed come. So, in effect, Vespasianus was seen by some Jews as "god's anointed" just as the Persian King, Cyrus, a Zoroastrian, had also been seen by them centuries earlier. After all, it seems that in some sects one did *not* have to be a Jew in order to be the messiah. But why would the expected messiah destroy the Jewish temple? These sects believed that the messiah was, in fact, *supposed* to cause the temple's destruction! And what sect was it that believed such a thing? The Essene sect at Qumran! The earliest Christians had shown Jesus as making such a prophecy so as to actually make him the divine instrument of the temple's destruction. If Jesus was not going to do it himself, at least it would have been done *because* of him! The hands of the Romans had been forced - the Christ would be forced to appear - and the result, contrary to expectations, was complete Roman victory.

Again, by that time the Christians in Roma and their allies were unwilling to antagonize the Romans, so they would not lay direct blame for the temple's destruction on the Romans. Furthermore, Josephus states that Titus wanted the temple to remain intact and actually did his utmost to prevent it from being destroyed, while the rest of Jerusalem was laid waste. After all, it is at least possible that Titus himself had heard the prophecy which stated that the Romans would destroy the temple and he, therefore, took great pains to prevent this from actually happening so as to prove the prophecy wrong. The destruction of the temple, Josephus states, was against the explicit orders of Titus, but in the frenzy of the situation an overly-zealous Roman soldier threw a torch into the temple, followed then by others (Mare 191). Then there was nothing left to do but to watch it burn. At least, that is the commonly accepted version of Josephus' history. But, as we will see, there is another version.

The True Gentile Church

After the destruction of the temple many Jews continued to make pilgrimages to the temple area, hoping to someday rebuild it (Mare 201). However, not until the ascent of the imperator Flavius Claudius Iulianus (Julian) did any authorization for such a project occur (although Constantine I apparently favored the idea), and even then it was barely started before it was halted because of Iulianus' death and, therefore, was never completed (Sinnigen & Boak 298). In any event, with the Jerusalem church gone and the apostles gone from Jerusalem, the Judaizing church was effectively eliminated. Elements of it apparently traveled northward into Galilee, but most of whatever was left moved into Egypt, mainly to Alexandria. It then, at that time, became all right for Christians to hate Jews. After all, the Judaizers had been effectively eliminated from power.

Why, indeed, had Jerusalem church leaders, such as James the brother of Jesus, been effectively written out of church history? Not because Pauline Christianity was embarrassed to admit that Mary had had other children, although this could have been a factor. No, it was part of the effort made after the destruction of Jerusalem to eliminate systematically any reference to any type of Christianity other than Pauline Christianity from history. These Gnostic Judaizers and Essenes simply *had* to be eliminated from the historical record because, otherwise, their influence would continue. Thus, even the disciples were effectively eliminated from history and later recreated into another, more acceptable, image as martyrs.

From at least the time of the Bar Kokhba revolt Gentiles were the majority within the Christian church. This could partially explain the gradual phasing-out of Jewish oriented material and the reinterpretation of that which could not be phased out, especially that which evidenced the previous conflict between Apostolic and Pauline Christianity (Evans &

Hagner 288). This could well also explain the gradual "Europeanizing" of Jesus and his earliest followers.

Since the Jews returning from Babylonian exile were influenced by the Zoroastrian religion, which kept a sacred fire burning, the returning exiles brought part of this sacred fire with them, which was said to have been kept burning for at least two-thousand years by that time, and, since there was no Ark for them to bring back with them among all of the other treasures that they were allowed to bring back, it seems that this sacred fire was effectively seen as a replacement for said Ark. And, as the Hebrew god would have actually resided in the Ark, the god was instead seen as residing within the flames of this fire. And this flame could also have represented the pillar of fire that had guided the Hebrews from Egypt to the so-called "promised land" centuries earlier, which was guiding them back at that time. No image, and yet a symbol of the very presence of their god, like in Zoroastrianism. However, it is known that this flame went out once they reached Jerusalem. Later, in the book of *Acts*, the disciples and others are said to have received "tongues of fire" upon their heads. Since the "wise men" of the *Gospel According to Matthew* were clearly Zoroastrian magicians or "Magi", another connection to Zoroastrianism seems clearly evident. Thus Jesus, through the holy spirit, is connected to the Ark of the Covenant since the Zoroastrian flame had effectively replaced the Ark.

Gnosticism, as we have already seen, was *not* just a Christian heresy that suddenly popped up during the second century CE as some of the ancient church Fathers would have us believe. It had origins not only within Jewish thought in Alexandria, Elephantiné and Leontopolis in Egypt, which created a form of Jewish Gnosticism, and also within Hellenization itself. This latter origin is best exemplified within ancient occult writings of Greco-Egyptian origin called the *Corpus Hermeticum*. And Jewish Gnosticism was often totally hostile toward the Jewish creator god, relegating him to a secondary position in creation, the actual act of creation having been performed by an angel, who eventually became equated with the "Son of Man"/messiah. They, again, referred to the Hebrew god as the *demiurge*. Of course, this was also their way of explaining the plural "gods" in the *Genesis* creation account.

> [I]n Alexandria, Gnosticism was the only recognizable type of Christianity until the end of the second century [CE]. The first orthodox Christian Bishop of Alexandria, so far as we know, was Demetrius (189-231). Before him, when the church fathers referred to Alexandrian Christians they meant Gnostic heretics, whom they thoroughly condemned. Two gospels, written in Alexandria, the so-called "Gospel of the Egyptians" and the "Gospel of the Hebrews," show every sign of being Gnostic creations [from the second century CE], and it is no doubt for this reason that they have not been included on the list of legitimate (canonical) books of the New Testament (Wilken 72).

Indeed, apocalyptic literature and the wisdom traditions were not exclusive to one another. They were sometimes combined within Jewish thought in the era prior to the advent of Christianity. And both of these traditions often referred to a remote god who was, more or less, completely separated from this fleshly world of chaos (Dart 57). Christian origins within Jewish sects in Egypt was further erased when Cyril, bishop of Alexandria expelled all Jews from the city, as previously noted.

Paul the Egyptian?

But it was impossible to erase every trace of it. As mentioned before, of all the strange statements in Christian writings, the question put to Paul by the Roman official who arrested him in Jerusalem is most puzzling; or is it? Plainly Paul is identified with some *Egyptian* who started a revolt. We do know of one, called "The Egyptian", who attempted a revolution and was killed by Roman soldiers along with his followers as they attempted to storm the walls of Jerusalem, believing that god would fight with them. But this passage from *Acts* indicates that the reference is to one who led his followers elsewhere and survived. The Roman, then, appears to have been thinking of someone else.

> "Do you know Greek? Then you are not the Egyptian who some time ago stirred up a revolt and led the four thousand men of the Assassins out into the wilderness?" (*Acts* 21:37-38).

Again, it is known that the Qumran community had direct ties to Egyptian Gnostic and apocalyptic communities and was by no means the pacifistic community that more modern scholars have sometimes painted it as being. Perhaps this Roman official believed that he had captured the ringleader of a revolutionary terrorist sect who had attempted to foment rebellion at the temple in Jerusalem, since that is basically the very accusation made against Paul - that he had desecrated the temple. And perhaps this Roman was not too far off the mark.

And it is, again, obvious, but not well known, from the actions of the Roman armies during the Jewish revolt of 66-74 CE that the Romans were aware of the fact that the Qumran community was *not* pacifistic. Other communities which did not openly rebel during this time, especially in Samaria, were spared such Roman destruction. Qumran, on the other hand, was annihilated! So it seems obvious that, either Qumran was taking part in the rebellion, or the Romans somehow knew that the origin of this revolt was from Qumran. Perhaps it was both. In fact, could it be that the two apparently separate, but not distinct, sects had planned to link up and begin this *holy war* - Egypt and Qumran, with Jerusalem in between?

Now, again, it is known from history that the Romans did, in fact, divert their attack on Jerusalem initially, having traveled all the way to the outskirts of the city, just long enough to go to Qumran and destroy that community *first*, after which they returned to siege Jerusalem. The question has to be asked again - just why would they divert their resources from what would justifiably be seen as their primary target to first destroy a bunch of fanatics out in the desert? I submit, again, that history has deliberately forgotten what the Romans knew out of hand - that the Essenes/Nazirites at Qumran had had a major part in instigating the revolt of 66 CE and that they also had the Copper Scroll. So the Romans wisely decided to strike them first before they were able to disperse. The Qumran community must have fully expected that the Romans would siege Jerusalem and that is exactly the appearance that the Romans gave, until they suddenly turned toward Qumran! This was exactly their plan from the start and it was done in brilliant, typically Roman, fashion. Once the Qumran community was destroyed, they were no longer any threat - they were unable to foment any more rebellions or attack from the rear because they no longer existed.

So, one can fully understand the astonishment in the tone of the Roman official when he is confronting Paul. He thought that he had come face-to-face with the very ringleader of that Qumran sect, or at least someone closely associated with it. "Then you are not the Egyptian . . . ?" He *knew* the connection between Egypt and Qumran.

Treading Upon Roman Victory, Before and After

And again, the reference to the "abomination of desolation" only makes sense if the ones who destroy the temple first set up something *abominable* in or around the temple area. So, when the abominable thing would be set up the expectation would naturally have been for the temple to soon be destroyed. The incident in the temple should be recounted here so as to exemplify the above statement. It reads as follows:

> As He was going, they were spreading their coats on the road. As soon as He was approaching, near the descent of the Mount of Olives, the whole crowd of the disciples began to praise God joyfully with a loud voice for all the miracles which they had seen, shouting: "BLESSED IS THE KING WHO COMES IN THE NAME OF THE LORD; Peace in heaven and glory in the highest!" (*Luke* 19:36-38). Then they came to Jerusalem. And He entered the temple and began to drive out those who were buying and selling in the temple, and overturned the tables of the moneychangers and the seats of those who were selling doves; and He would not permit

anyone to carry merchandise through the temple (*Mark* 11:15-16).

Now, the most obvious thing about this incident is that Jesus is portrayed as having instigated it on his own. For the crowds to have been following him, calling him "king" (as in, apocalyptic king and messiah) and for him to, therefore, proceed past the descent to the Mount of Olives to the temple and perform an extremely aggressive act must be seen for what it is - a clear act of insurrection! Jesus was intentionally attempting to instigate rebellion, and with the large crowds who were there, it is a wonder that it apparently did not take hold at that very moment! Here, Jesus clearly attempted to bring in the awaited apocalyptic kingdom *by force*, while probably also creating cover so that temple scrolls could be stolen and taken to Qumran. After all they, especially the Copper Scroll, had to be preserved if the temple were to be destroyed.

Also, in the *Gospel According to Mark*, it is stated that the witnesses at Jesus' trial gave *false* testimony when they said that Jesus had proclaimed that *he* would destroy the temple. It seems clear, then, that the testimony is false only because they said that he had stated that *he* would destroy the temple. And even though it seems clear that Jesus did attempt to initiate the necessary chain of events which were to lead to the temple's destruction, there is clearly no reason for us to believe, based upon the evidence, that he had stated that either *he* or god would destroy it. No, the *Romans* would do it! And the Romans apparently had Jesus executed exactly because he *did* stir up rebellion, *not* because the Jews wanted him executed. This was *entirely* a decision of the Romans. Because of this, he was executed by crucifixion since he was not a Roman citizen. That is what Roman law of the time called for. Jewish law had *nothing whatsoever* to do with it.

Still, the temple statements in the gospels had an unfortunate effect with reference to the later perception of Christians by others. Christians were seen as having advocated the destruction of the temple. In *Tos. San.* 13:5 the Christians are included among other mentioned *Minim* as "'those who stretched out their hands against the temple. . . .'" (Gaston 144). Perhaps this is the real origin, then, of the "blessing against he heretics". If the Christians were seen as anti-temple and since, in fact, the temple had been destroyed, then it would have been very understandable for Torah abiding, non-Gnostic Jews to have wanted to distance themselves from those *Nazoreans* or *Minim* who had helped to cause the temple's destruction.

Conversely, once Jerusalem and the temple had been destroyed, the Christians sect *had* to create its own identity, separate from any other aspect of Judaism which existed at that time. It had to create an identity that would allow it to be recognized as a distinct religion while not appearing to be "new". Already Romans were seeing Christianity as a "new" *superstition* and that was anathema to the Romans. So the Christians appropriated the Hebrew Scriptures, especially the Prophets, claiming them as their own and insisting that the Prophets had spoken of Jesus. The Christians questioned the Jewish claim concerning their inheritance from god as his chosen people, insisting that the Jews had rejected Jesus, whom the Prophets had foretold. And, after all, had not god rejected the Jews as evidenced by the destruction of the temple in Jerusalem? And, for these Christians, it was clear that the Jews did not even know how to interpret their own scriptures. Only Christians could properly understand the scriptures because only they had received the gift of the holy spirit (or the ability to interpret the scriptures allegorically), which directed their interpretation. In this way they began to create a distinct identity and to turn things around on the Jews while holding to the scriptures which, they believed, had pointed to Jesus, thus becoming the "new Israel". Later they would, in the same way, misappropriate even Greek philosophy in order to make it their own.

In the *Second Apocalypse of James* (59.12ff) we find the statement: "Therefore I say to you [in the name of the lord]: 'See, I have given you your house - this of which you say that God made it, (and) in which he who dwells in it has promised to give you an inheritance. This I will tear down, to the ruin and derision of those who are in ignorance (Evans & Hagner 280-81). Also [in the *First Apocalypse of James* (25.7-9)] "Jesus says, 'When you go away, then immediately war will be made with this land - therefore [weep?] for him who dwells in Jerusalem'" (Evans & Hagner 282).

Also, again, in the Mandaean *Letter of Truth*, reference begins to be made, several times, to "thou [or the] ruins, Jerusalem". To me, this clearly indicates that this book, at least in part, was written *after* 70 CE but still probably close enough to this date so that Jerusalem is still a concern of the writer, and that it is also *still* in ruins. Reference is also made to "a pure eagle-bird" who "destroyed the temple and laid fire to Jerusalem". This can be seen as nothing other than a reference to the Romans. Period. Also, it states that "He" (the eagle-bird) "brought downfall upon them and **in Jerusalem slew the disciples**" (Mead 70). To me, this latter passage clearly indicates that at least some of the apostles were actually *in Jerusalem* when she fell and were killed by the Romans, whatever tradition may state.

Now, Josephus has been cited and quoted in this work already a number of times. But, even though Josephus appears to be a reliable source in the main, he is not totally reliable as a historian. Or, at least the *versions* we have of his works may be called into question in certain places. Still, he is our only source for some historical details, so we have to take him at his word in most instances where there is no alternate history or version of his writings. But the second point is most important because it is true that there is *more than one extant version* of his histories and, in ancient times, it appears that there were still other versions that have not survived. So, the two main problems with Josephus is that, first, he was basically an apologist for the Roman rulers of his day since, after all, he did not want to say anything that might cause his execution and, second, it is obvious that his works have been edited, sometimes severely so, in some places by different people - thus, several versions of his works. In so many words, there were some powerful people, mainly the imperators (Vespasianus and Titus) and other politicians, who would not have liked what Josephus might have truly wanted to write, so sometimes he vaguely hinted at these things, and there were other equally powerful people, later Christian imperators and Christian religious leaders beginning with Constantine I, who did not like what he had written and had his works edited. These are simply *facts*.

Jesus, the Failed Warrior Messiah

Now, importantly, the Christian cleric Origen apparently had a version of Josephus' *Antiquities of the Jews* (the usual ancient title for said work actually being *Jewish Archaeology*) that indicated an opinion, he stated, that Josephus believed the troubles of the Jews and the overthrow of their nation was due to the murder of James, brother of Jesus. Josephus, according to Origen, praised James, recognizing his righteousness. However, he also states that Josephus did not recognize Jesus as messiah (*Contra Celsum*, i., 47). So, it appears obvious that here was at least one of those multiple versions, which Origen quoted or at least paraphrased from. If this is so, then it becomes obvious that sometime between the lifetimes of Origen and Eusebius of Caesarea "the uncomplimentary account of Jesus had been replaced in some way by that which now appears in the extant text (Brandon 112; Cf. Meyer, op, cit., I, p. 206).

First it should be noted that Josephus writes a short passage concerning John the Baptizer that is quite similar to the one written about James, brother of Jesus. George R. Mead quotes the extant version of that passage about John the Baptizer, in part, thus (*Antiquities* XVIII. V. 2, ed. Niese, iv, 161):

> Some of the Jews thought that Herod's army had been destroyed, and indeed by the very just vengeance of God, in return for [his putting to death of] John the Baptizer. For in fact Herod put the latter to death [though he was] a good man, nay even one who bade the Jews cultivate virtue and, by the practice or righteousness in their dealings with one another and of piety to God, gather together for baptism. For thus in sooth [John thought] the dipping (in water) would seem acceptable to him (God), not if they used it as a begging-off in respect to certain sins, but for purity of body, in as much as indeed the soul had already been purified by righteousness. . . . (Mead 3).

In effect, Josephus blames the defeat of Herod's army and, presumably, the defeat of the Jews on the execution of John the Baptizer.

In any case, I agree with S. G. F. Brandon in that there is really no reason that Josephus would have even entertained the idea that James was a righteous man while debasing Jesus. That is, unless Josephus thought like the Mandaeans and saw in Jesus a flaw in that he turned to violence when the others did not. It is also possible that Origen may have misread what Josephus actually stated, perhaps intentionally. Josephus himself would not have even known Jesus and most likely did not know James personally either (not to mention John). So whatever he might have written here would have been second-hand knowledge at best. Still, whatever version Origen had, it would have at least had more original material in it (or, perhaps, would have been *an* original version) than the later changed versions which exist today. This version must then have contained an account of Jesus that was offensive to Christian sensibilities. Indeed, Origen was adamant that Josephus did not recognize Jesus as the messiah and insisted that he should have stated that the downfall of the Jewish nation was a result of the death of Jesus, *not* James (Brandon 113-14).

Where I mainly differ with Brandon is with reference to his conclusion. Brandon posits that the Pharisees (who had marked Zoroastrian leanings) had seen James as righteous since he held closely to Torah, which is probable. But then he posits that they also probably believed that their own downfall was a result of the murder of James since he was such a close adherent of Torah. Here he is positing a close connection, as it were, between the earliest Christians in Jerusalem and the Pharisees, which I believe to be unproven (Brandon 114).

For me, what all of this shows is that Josephus did not attribute the downfall of the Jewish nation to the execution of Jesus because he did not believe in Jesus as messiah, so there would have been no causal connection. But the murder of James would have been more recent and a causal connection could easily have been established in that the various Jewish factions in conflict in Jerusalem, including the Christians, were the cause of the nation's downfall and the murder of James was the catalyst for all of it. That is probably what Josephus actually said with the addition that the murder of so righteous a man would naturally have brought down the wrath of god. But it was the quarreling and fighting among those in Jerusalem that more directly brought down the wrath of the *Romans*.

So, it would seem that this passage was edited/eliminated in later versions because (1) Josephus probably stated something offensive about Jesus that no one wanted to survive (or at least he did not attribute the downfall of Jerusalem to the execution of Jesus), which may have essentially proved that he was not the messiah and (2) the emphasis upon James and his adherence to Torah was not something that later Christians wanted to be remembered.

Here it actually becomes obvious exactly what it was that Josephus had written that was so offensive to early Christians, including Origen. The key is the fact that Origin, in referring to this passage, was writing against the work of Kelsos in his *Contra Celsum*. It takes us directly back to what it might have been that Kelsos knew about Jesus' early life and, I submit, Kelsos got his information for it from this work of Josephus! It was Josephus who, then, first wrote about Jesus being the illegitimate son of a Roman soldier and how Jesus had been brought up in Egypt and had returned to Judea after studying "magical arts". Kelsos had used Josephus to make his argument and Origen used the same passages from Josephus to counter Kelsos. It's really that simple. In later copies of his history, these offensive passages were edited or erased and, as is known from history, the works of Kelsos were systematically destroyed, so that no one could ever read what Josephus had written again.

But part of it has, in fact, survived after all. See, the references found in the Greek version of Josephus' *Jewish Wars* to Jesus and James, his brother, are considered by the majority of scholars to be Christian forgeries or additions. And it does seem to me that scholars are correct in this view. But, the references contained in the Slavonic version show some interesting variations which, some believe (as do I), may indicate another ancient source. Johannes Frey believed that said statements were indeed also forgeries, but that they were not done by a Christian, but by a Jew. He also believed that this forger had access to a source which might have been used by the gospel writers themselves.

If true, then this, he believed, would be the long sought for Q (from the German, *Quelle*) source.

One important difference between the Greek and Slavonic Josephus is that in the Slavonic version Jesus is *not* referred to as the *messiah* as he is in the Greek version. And the statements attributed to John the Baptizer are, as one would expect, revolutionary and apocalyptic in tone. For example, statement six of John's *Proclamation* reads, in part "... [H]e plunged them into the stream of the Jordan and dismissed them, instructing them that they should cease from evil works, and [promising] that there would [then] be given them a ruler who would set them free ..." (Mead 104). Of Jesus, in the section on Jesus' ministry, trial and crucifixion, sentences 11 and 12 state: "And *many* from the folk followed him and received his teachings. And many souls became wavering, supposing that thereby the Jewish tribes would set themselves free from the Roman hands" (Mead 106). Most importantly Josephus states, in sentences 15-17: *"And there [on the Mount of Olives they] gathered themselves to him of servants [slaves/disciples] ... a hundred and fifty*, but of the folk *a multitude*. But when they saw his power ... they urged him that he should enter the city and cut down the Roman soldiers and Pilate and rule over us. But that one scorned it" (Mead 107). Regardless of what Josephus says of Jesus at the very end (if he really wrote that part), Jesus was clearly about to lead a rebellion for there is no way that so many men would gather at one place ready to do battle and then *ask* Jesus to lead them. This had to have been pre-planned. Josephus subtly told us the partial truth here.

One can see reference here to the *multitudes*, as in the gospels, and to their messianic expectations. That Jesus is always shown as having entered Jerusalem by way of the Mount of Olives in both the gospels and in this passage is important in that it has been shown that in ancient times the only way to attack Jerusalem was from that direction - from the North. Jesus is *never* shown as entering Jerusalem from any other direction or place at all. Of course, this passage also states that Jesus refused to support the people's wish for rebellion, which is probably Josephus' way of being allowed to write about it without getting into trouble with the Romans. And here we finally have the passage (alluded to more than once previously in this work) that states that Jesus had 150 (and more) followers who had gathered on the Mount of Olives.

So, if nothing else has shown it, then this clearly indicates that Josephus' writing here was changed by someone at some later date as Josephus would likely not have believed in Jesus as the messiah. But Josephus somehow knew about the 150 "disciples", which no other source includes. Origen and other Christians would have found all of this to be completely objectionable, so they worked to eliminate it.

Also, concerning the trilingual inscription, the Slavonic translation states that it read: "Jesus has not reigned as king; he has been crucified by the Jews, because he proclaimed the destruction of the city and the laying waste of the temple" (Mead 109). It seems obvious here that the forger has to acknowledge that Jesus was indeed arrested for starting a rebellion after all. And his small, but concerning, army was dispersed.

Surviving Original Christianity

Now, documents of the Mandaeans, which are also ancient, repeatedly call the Jerusalem Christians *Nazoreans*. Could it be that the only surviving Gnostic Christian sect left in the world today might be an offshoot of the original Jerusalem church, which obviously held John the Baptizer in great esteem? They also were undoubtedly called Nazoreans themselves in past times. If these people were originally Gnostic, at first at least, as their ancient documents suggest, then a link has clearly been established showing that the Jerusalem church was indeed Gnostic in flavor. That they vehemently oppose mainstream Christianity today may well be a forgotten reaction not only to the destruction of Jerusalem as the end of what they considered the true church, but also to the fact that they were originally Gnostic Judaizers themselves who were opposed by and to Pauline Christianity.

In addition, "Gnostic heretics are not specifically mentioned anywhere in Jewish rabbinic literature, but some modern studies have shown that 'there were heretical Jewish Gnostics in Palestine, and they were referred to as *minim*. . . .'" In some cases, the *minim* may have been Jewish Christians, but Berger Pearson maintains that the polemic in rabbinic writings makes it clear that Jewish Gnostics, from the early second century on, if not earlier, 'posed a great threat in many Jewish circles'" (Dart 53).

As for the Pella tradition, which states that the apostles left Jerusalem before the siege and went to Pella (the one located in Trans-Jordan, not the one located in Makedonia), only to return later "[t]he oldest explicit reference . . . is preserved in Eusebius *HE* III.5.3:

> The people of the church at Jerusalem, in accordance with a certain *oracle* that was vouchsafed by way of revelation to approved men there, had been commanded *to depart from that city* before the war, and *to inhabit* (*oikein*) *a certain city of Peraea.* They called it *Pella.* And when *those who believed in Christ* had removed from Jerusalem . . . (Sanders, E. P., Jewish and Christian Self-Definition 163-64).

As Eusebius of Caesarea is considered to be untrustworthy at best by most scholars, I can only agree with Sanders in that "[t]he Pella-tradition has no historical value whatsoever for the question of what happened to the Christian community during the Jewish war" (Sanders 171). Indeed, if there is any value in this tradition at all it would be to show where they did *not* go. But, that leaves us to contemplate the fact that *some* disciples possibly went *somewhere.* Indeed, the Pella tradition is a paradox in that, it seems to me, it can be readily shown that, according to the gospels, Jesus did instruct his followers to leave Jerusalem when they saw armies coming to destroy the city. After all, they would not have needed an additional prophecy in order to obey their Lord, would they? It truly seems that, given this command to leave, there is still no reason to believe that, at least some of the apostles, ever actually *did* leave Jerusalem before its destruction in 70 CE. Tradition, including that of Pella, maintains that they *all* left and were later martyred (except for John) elsewhere while spreading the gospel. But it seems more likely that some of them remained in Jerusalem, along with their countrymen, and were either killed or sold into slavery. As Gaston states:

Although Jesus and the early church expected the promise of the kingdom to be fulfilled soon, and later the prophets nourished the hope for vindication of the persecuted church, only one actual date was set for the parousia: the fall of Jerusalem. We hear of a disappointment over the failure of the parousia to materialize only in two post 70 A.D. writings, Jn 21:23 and 2 Pet 3:3ff, where the problem seems to have been solved without too much difficulty. . . . It was expected at the end of the first generation, and then when it did not occur the church adapted with little difficulty to the longer perspective required by the Gentile mission (Gaston 457-58).

It seems obvious, then, that the destruction of Jerusalem and the temple there are both strongly connected to the early Christians. The gospels, as well as extra-biblical sources, all strongly indicate that the early Christians constantly reiterated their belief that the temple and the city would soon be destroyed by the Romans. And the Pella tradition cannot be trusted at all. Eusebius was a skillful liar, willing to state anything to make Christianity and his imperator, Constantine I, look good. And the people who had perpetuated the Pella tradition seem to have only craved recognition for their city. And it may also have been an effort to somehow compare the apostles, returning from Pella in Trans-Jordan and going out to other areas of the world to spread the gospel, with Alexander the Great, who was born at Pella in Makedonia and came from there to conquer the world. And perhaps it was also an effort to smear the great Alexander and his successes, showing the apostles as more important. But the question as to what happened to the apostles had to be answered, so this elaborate tradition along with that of martyrdom was developed to fill in the gaps. After all, Eusebius could not very well tell the truth - that some disciples were actually *killed* in Jerusalem and that those who were not fled to *Egypt*, of all places!

Conclusions

So now, at long last, we can have the real history of what happened during the first century CE rather than some vague ethereal belief or some dogmatic article of faith we must adhere to. We can now finally know that even the earliest gospel writers had no idea who Jesus really was and what happened to the original apostles, with the exceptions of James, brother of John, and Paul. We can know that there were divisions from the very first which practically ripped Christianity apart. We can know that there was much competition between the early apostles, even out in the field of the wider Roman Empire. But we still can't know everything, like what certain apostles did following the death of Jesus and who it really was who first went to Egypt to draw converts. And we can have no idea why none of them apparently went into Galilee, or at least had much of a ministry there.

The *truth*, for those who wish to understand it, is that Christianity, while it claimed to be the only way almost from the beginning, was also split and fragmented from the very beginning. There were often sharp disagreements between the various Christian sects even concerning the nature of Jesus - whether he was human, partly human, fully god or, frankly, even real. This question itself wasn't even "resolved" until the fourth century CE. And even today Christianity is at least as fragmented as ever while all sects still claim that they are the only way while also, to some degree, allowing that "other Christians" and even some people of other religions *might* also get to go to Heaven, *if* they live or somehow believe right.

The very fact that the *Gospel According to John* deals only with the last month or so of the life of Jesus, and almost exclusively with his death, shows two things, for those who wish to pay attention. First, it shows that the writer, or someone close to him, was indeed someone who actually knew Jesus and who had most likely witnessed these events personally, although it is also obvious that he inserted words into the mouth of Jesus which he probably never spoke. Second, this is exactly a distinct clue that it was *this* canonical gospel that was written *first* rather than last. What this indicates is that the others actually were *not* eyewitness accounts and that their accounts depended, in part, upon *this* gospel as well as the *Gospel of Thomas*. Therefore, *only this* canonical gospel was written relatively early, although the others soon followed. Attention to detail is helpful here as a thorough investigation of extant evidence simply mandates that this is the case. Scholars and historians have overlooked and/or ignored the obvious here for almost two-thousand years; those who re-wrote and rearranged history having done their job so well. Yes, the various New Testament books were deliberately mis-arranged in order to make it appear that the earliest were written last, etc. Once one takes the blinders of faith and tradition off, it becomes perfectly obvious that it was the *Gospel According to John* that was written first among the canonical gospels and that the *Gospel According to Luke* was written last among them. So, even though it only deals with, at most, the last few weeks of Jesus' life, if one really wants to know the real Jesus, then one has to look here, at least first.

And one really does have to ask here just why there is more than one canonical gospel in any case. And why do they all conflict with each other? After all, could not god have inspired someone, say Paul, to have written a gospel that was definitive for all? Indeed, why would there be more than one gospel unless they were all made-up? Logic would certainly suggest that this must be the case. Otherwise, there should only be one that is both definitive and authoritative, having been actually written *by* an apostle. Or, one simply has to posit that the devil inspired at least three of the gospel writers to make-up gospels and that only one, at most, can be real and definitive. After all, had not Satan anticipated all of this and already moved to counterfeit everything ahead of time? So which would be Satanic counterfeits and which true? One would have to presume, according to such a scenario, that the last written would have to be the real one since Satan would have counterfeited the previously written ones in his effort to delude people. So one would have to decide, then, which was last written in order to find the one that was valid for faith. But, of course, this is preposterous! In fact, considering all of the New Testament books, none of which are consistent with any other in entirety, even the Pauline epistles - why is it that we don't possess only one authoritative and definitive book written by, perhaps, Jesus, James or Paul, or even John the Baptizer? After all, did not Zarathushtra write his own books? Would not Akhenaten have done so had he lived long enough? Did not Moses, presumably, write his own books? Why, then, would Jesus have not written his own book or books?

Another real possibility here is that the disciples might not, generally, have known one another very well at all. When one reads the gospels one assumes that they were all together virtually all of the time, conversing and working together as they followed Jesus all over Galilee, etc. But that assumption may well be incorrect, at best, for even in the gospels we see conflicts between one group or another on occasion. And the brothers of Jesus had absolutely nothing to do with it, if one accepts the gospel accounts at face value, even up to the time at which Jesus was crucified. Yet, soon afterward, according to the book of *Acts* and according to Josephus, James, a brother of Jesus, becomes the de facto leader of the Jerusalem church. Just when he entered the picture is unclear at best, but this fact alone is really enough to show that the idea that the disciple, Thomas, was a twin brother of Jesus, as is traditional in some circles is also preposterous. After all, if Thomas were his twin, then why was he not the next church leader rather than James?

So, perhaps the disciples were not all together very much at all. In fact, perhaps they were only really all together during that very last weeks of Jesus' life, during which they may well have been preparing to do something big. But, it seems that only two of them, John and Thomas, may have written notes about it from first-hand experience. It seems possible, then, that those who remained in Jerusalem after Jesus' arrest and crucifixion only got to know one another well *after* Jesus was dead. This could be seen as precisely why different disciples seem to have had different accounts of who Jesus was. All of them only knew Jesus in part and some, like, perhaps, John, James (John's brother), Matthew, Peter and Thomas, knew him much better than others. So, if this is true, then most of the original disciples did not get to know Jesus very well at all, and much less so for later followers. And Paul did not know him at all. And that must therefore be exactly the reason why there are no canonical gospels attributed to these others. They didn't know enough about Jesus to have written about him, even if they were literate and able to write.

Conversely, some would not have written anything because they didn't want to write about what they *really* knew - about what had been planned and how it went terribly wrong (but Josephus apparently did, so it was known). And some of them, one has to admit, probably fell completely away. So they probably never all came together following the crucifixion of Jesus anyway. Most may have, but not likely all. After all, how dangerous would that have been for all of the followers of an executed criminal to come together anywhere when the Romans were undoubtedly looking for them? They would have had to have been brave indeed, as well as foolhardy, to have done it.

It is also obvious that there was a great difference between what the original disciples taught and what Paul taught. This brought them into conflict, culminating into two rather distinct camps and spheres of influence. As has been seen, the original disciples tended toward an Egyptian form of Jewish Gnosticism tinged with the old Atenism plus apocryphal and apocalyptic beliefs. But what has not yet been emphasized much is that Paul's teachings were much more like Zoroastrianism. Paul's teaching concerning the resurrection is a case in point. It's not that the others did not teach resurrection, but that Paul's teaching concerning this subject is distinctly like that which had been taught among the Zoroastrians. The final judgment is emphasized by Paul while stressing that the deceased seem to be in some sort of intermediate state, awaiting said resurrection, just as in Zoroastrianism, where there would no longer be old age, infirmity, decay, corruption or death (all things attributed to the corruptible body). And evil will have been vanquished forever. Saoshyant, the Zoroastrian savior, who was to be born of a virgin, would defeat evil and death and cause the general resurrection and the final judgment to happen.

> Whoever is righteous, and whoever is wicked, every human creature, they raise up from the spot where its life departs. Afterwards, when all material living beings assume again their bodies and forms, then they assign to them a single class (Oesterley 90; *Bundahish xxx* 7-9).

Roman officials, for their part, would still have seen the Christianity that existed in and around Jerusalem as Judaism, making no real distinction. But this Pauline Christianity would have been recognized rather quickly as something else altogether and the Romans would have detested it because it sounded so much to their ears like the Zoroastrianism of their arch enemies.

Yes, the history of Christianity was skillfully rewritten after the fall of Jerusalem because there was, for all practical purposes, no opposition to "orthodoxy" left. So they could re-write Christian history in any form that they pleased, especially once they had the backing of Constantine I. But that history, and the traditions created to support it, is a *lie*! The Pella tradition, for example, along with the stories of the martyrdoms of the apostles are pious falsifications. Sadly, what we have today is a whipped-up, homogenized, biblical pseudo-history that nicely fits the agenda of those who created it. It bears little resemblance to what really happened.

And, as we have seen, books such as the *Apocalypse of Adam* show clear signs of being of pre-Christian origin and they are also Gnostic texts. This book and several others focus on Seth, third child of Adam and Eve, establishing Seth as the community's hero, so to speak. These early pre-Christian Sethians may be related to or identical to the Nazoreans, the Ophites, or even the "heretics" mentioned by Philo. Later Sethian texts, such as *Zostrianos* and *Allogenes*, draw upon the previous Sethian texts and all extensively utilize Platonism and show no traces of what we call Christianity. Still, later Sethianism did incorporate Christianity as it grew, but Platonism was always clearly most important for them. Perhaps this is part of the reason why orthodox Christianity hated Platonism so much - because they really hated the Gnostic Sethians from Egypt and the Platonism found within Gnosticism overall. And the usurpation from Egypt did not stop there, but even extended to religious representations as Christians began to represent holy people and angels as possessing halos, essentially making them demigods, which anyone can see are taken from the symbols of the sun and the moon atop the heads of certain Egyptian deities. To ignore this is to be deliberately blind.

But why would the apostles, following the death of Jesus, continue to remain loyal to him, since the messiah was not supposed to die? Whether they were already acquainted with them or not prior to Jesus' death, the apostles or their later followers utilized scriptures from the Hebrew Bible that showed that the messiah was *supposed* to suffer and die to support their cause. Somehow, they really believed in Jesus and his mission enough to do this. But, one must not be too critical of them for this, after all, because the entire Greco-Roman world was well-acquainted with the belief that the hero must suffer and die, as best exemplified by the Greek hero, Herakles. But, instead of later Christians utilizing the example of Herakles to exemplify Jesus, they used the example of Sokrates.

Also, the Gnostics, it would seem, *did not persecute*. They were, instead, persecuted much like the Maccabean martyrs had been before them. Stephen and the earliest apostles and followers of Jesus who were persecuted and killed were, in fact, Gnostics. The later Christian church claimed them as their own. That effort began with the writer of *Acts*, but was greatly expanded by Eusebius of Caesarea.

And it is interesting to note that both cremation and circumcision were abhorrent to Christianity while, somehow, castration was not. Eunuchs were not uncommon at all within early orthodox Christianity. And this was essentially a replacement for circumcision with eunuchs being seen as superior because they gave up something for the Kingdom of Heaven. In any case, it becomes increasingly obvious here that books written by church leaders such as Paul, John, Peter and James were saved and preserved by the church for a specific reason. That reason is exactly *because* they were all martyrs. And this is really the only reason that Paul actually succeeded; (1) because he wrote the most books, (2) because he died as a martyr and (3) because Jerusalem was destroyed by the Romans.

Nero really wanted Paul badly after the riot in Ephesos and there can be little real doubt that, following his arrest, Paul did *not* appeal to Caesar. He would have been out of his mind to have done so! No, instead he attempted to more or less hide his identity and keep a low profile, hoping that some lower level magistrate might release him. But, once his identity came to light it was brought to Nero's attention and Nero, naturally, sent for him to be brought to Roma. Such a high-value target could not simply be executed out in the deserts of Judea! He had to be brought before Caesar himself and condemned. Still, Paul was not seen as soon as he arrived in Roma. Like Iulius Caesar before him, Nero was really in no particular hurry to execute his adversary. The concept of a speedy trial was not necessarily a part of the Roman psyche. He took his time, allowing Paul to languish in a Roman prison (probably *not* under house arrest) for some time. And, once Paul stood before Nero there was nothing he could have said that would have changed his fate. His execution was already a foregone conclusion.

Paul, the renegade and instigator of rebellion, hated by both Jew and Gentile - once caught and found out, his fate was indeed sealed. He had committed no act of violence, but he had still been an instigator. His trial would have been a farce. Nero had wanted this guy for a long time and even though he still waited a few years longer to try him, there can be no doubt that he had Paul brought directly before him when his time came. No doubt, Nero asked to hear Paul. But, when Paul was brought before him Nero, along with all of those present, undoubtedly would have mocked him and laughed at him. All of them would also have insulted him in various ways. Perhaps Nero even informed Paul that he had been caught because his own Christian brethren had caused him to be arrested in the first place, just to see Paul's reaction. And it probably would not have lasted long, even after all of those years of waiting. No great speeches on either side. Indeed, it would have been quite appalling to modern sensibilities. Then Paul would have been summarily executed somewhere just outside. That is, unless, by unlikely chance, Paul was still alive when the Great Fire broke out. If he was, then his fate was likely much more excruciating than a simple beheading following a short trial.

There is no surviving account of his trial. If one was ever written, later Christians made sure that it was destroyed and *never* referred to in any way again. For by no means could the hero of the faith have met his fate at the hands of the hated Nero! And it is as if the writer of the book of *Acts* didn't even know which Caesar was in power when Paul was arrested, so skillfully he avoided mentioning him by name. Why so, when he had mentioned Tiberius in the *Gospel According to Luke* and Claudius earlier in *Acts*? The reason had to have been that the writer really did not know who had been Caesar at that point in time; he wrote so late after the events in question. He was no first-hand reporter as has been believed for centuries. Knowledge of Tiberius and Claudius came from earlier Christian tradition which the writer utilized for his writings. But none of it was first-hand knowledge. The writer was not a witness to the events he wrote about and was not a companion of Paul. He probably didn't even know Paul. And he didn't know what actually happened to Paul either. And, contrary to what some other scholars have postulated in their efforts to explain all of the books purportedly written by Paul, Nero would have by no means whatsoever let him go, only to have to recapture him later. Paul did not get any more chances to incite further rebellion and subversion. And he didn't write any more books.

Claudius and Nero got rid of all four of the earliest, most important church leaders. They got Peter, John, Paul and finally, James. These were all the true leaders of the early church and there really never were any other effective early leaders. This is *really* why Christians vilify Nero, although they have forgotten this *as* the reason. If the writer of *Acts* knew this, perhaps his name was left out because he was *so* hated. More likely, however, is that his name was left out because the writer did not actually know which imperator had had these four executed; perhaps it was felt, his name did not deserve to be mentioned. But it is, if one pays attention, glaringly obvious that his name is not mentioned while others are. So there must at least be some reason for this.

Having been able to flesh out the truth concerning Nero and his role with reference to early Christianity, it must again be stated that the historian Josephus cannot always be trusted in his details. This may very well *not* be because Josephus himself lied, but because someone later in history chose to change parts of his history to reflect what they wanted to be the "true" history of Christianity - someone during the reign of Constantine I. Therefore, what Josephus states about Vespasianus and, especially, Titus, can be called into question. As already pointed out, it is generally accepted among modern-day historians that Titus did *not* want the temple in Jerusalem to be destroyed and even ordered that it *not* be destroyed, but that over-zealous Roman soldiers did it anyway. Frankly, this is just another means by which Josephus and/or later Christian editors of his history wished for Titus to be portrayed because, again, the Romans could not be blamed for *anything* at all. But the truth, as has been well pointed-out by Gedalyahu Alon in his book, Jews, Judaism and the Classical World, translated by Israel Abrahams, is that Titus *fully intended* for the temple to be destroyed and he opposed those who felt otherwise.

A Christian monk, Sulpicius Severus, of all people, in his work, *Christianity*, wrote that at the meeting of principal commanders, Titus himself insisted that the temple *had to be* destroyed because the root of Judaism and Jewish rebellion had to be eliminated and so that they would never again have a place from which to foment rebellion. This he apparently got from some now lost part of Tacitus' *Historae*. That most scholars and historians still favor Josephus in his multiple statements absolving Titus from wanting the temple to be destroyed speaks volumes. It is truly easier to simply believe Josephus, or whoever might have edited his works, but that does not mean that this position is correct. In fact, there is yet another tradition concerning this event, from the Jewish sages Tannaim and Amoraim (*Sifre Deuteronomy* x, §328; *Midrash Tannaim*, p. 202), who state that the temple was burned down on the orders of the "wicked Titus". They even went so far as to paint Titus as the very foe of Israel's god. Titus, therefore, was not so much at war with the Jewish people as with Judaism and their god (Abrahams 252-54). Now, one can expect the Jews to have felt this way about Titus and to have been, perhaps, just a bit less than objective. But Josephus had motives of his own and as a Roman slave certainly would not have stated anything that might have gotten him executed.

In any case, it is in fact known that some of the escapees from Jerusalem did go down to Egypt and attempted to foment rebellion against the Romans from there. And where did they go in their efforts to continue their revolution? To the very temple at Leontopolis. Alon states that Vespasianus' order that this temple also be destroyed was rescinded about three years later, but the sources do not seem to be clear on this and it is difficult to believe that the Romans would have simply ignored an edict by an imperator so that, three whole years later, he would have rescinded it. What? Did the rebellion simply fizzle out there? Doubtful. So, whereas I basically agree with Alon, I disagree strongly on this point. It simply does not fit the overall pattern of how the Romans tended to conduct themselves and their operations. After all, if Titus felt strongly enough about the temple in Jerusalem that it must be destroyed so that future rebellions could not be instigated from it, there is absolutely no doubt that the temple at Leontopolis would also have been destroyed for the very same reason. And one must not forget that Qumran had been wiped out before the temple in Jerusalem and Masada was taken and destroyed afterward.

So the Romans were by no means reluctant to destroy any center of rebellion and they were by no means finished once the temple in Jerusalem was destroyed. They didn't stop until rebellion was completely put down in *every* location! That was simply the Roman way. It is simply preposterous to think that the Romans intended to destroy the entire city of Jerusalem, but leave the shrine intact and it is equally preposterous to believe that the Romans would issue any order for the destruction of the Jewish temple in Leontopolis and then resend that order three or four years later, having somehow never gotten to it in the mean time while the opposition had time to gather there to continue their rebellion. It would not have happened. Period. So, either Josephus lied about the overall situation in order to keep his head or someone after him changed his history at this point, rewriting specific parts of it.

Either way, that which is left to us clearly favored Christianity because the Christians did not want anything to do with their origins to be reflective in a negative way on the Romans. The Christians wanted to stand in good graces with the Romans so they systematically erased any references to anything that would make it look like there was any conflict between the Romans and the earliest Christians. As Alon further states (Abrahams 267-68):

> Josephus' efforts to exculpate Titus and to speak in his praise are obvious in many passages, but special attention should be paid to his practice of finding 'excuses' for the destruction of the Temple in devious ways, as long as the emperor should appear innocent. . . . Despite his efforts, however, he did not succeed in whitewashing all their

deeds, and unwittingly (or possibly even wittingly?), he himself, through many slips of the pen, tells us the truth.

But, as Alon also astutely points out, the fact that the Romans allowed Rabbi Yoḥanan ben Zakkai to escape and to rebuild Judaism in another place simply ensured that the Judaism which they had worked so hard to crush would sprout again and become a force which would outlive the empire that they cherished. So they essentially destroyed their entire effort by doing so, not recognizing the impact that this one fugitive could have upon the future (Abrahams 269).

One may finally ask here whether we are finished with Jewish Gnosticism from Egypt. The reader may be tired of reading about it. Some may believe that the point has been made and that it is unnecessary to belabor it any further. Alas, more is in store because I disagree. The main reason is that there is one final twist to the whole thing. It is the reason that the point has not been completely made yet. That twist is that I have come to understand that there were not just two opposing Jewish Christian groups during the first century which conducted rather separate missions, but also that there were essentially two sets of gospel writings, two New Testaments, as it were, which were not totally exclusive but not totally or easily compatible either. Try as we might, even today we find it difficult to make these books with separate viewpoints mesh. We have tried to reconcile the two competing camps rather ineffectively over the centuries. Frankly, we may as well acknowledge that they were two opposing camps at last and deal effectively with that knowledge as it stands. So that is further drawn out in the remainder of this book.

5

THE NEW TESTAMENT, THE DEAD SEA SCROLLS AND THE NAG HAMMADI MANUSCRIPTS

The Problem of the Canonical Gospels

The books that make up the New Testament canon were mainly written by Paul, or a scribe at the direction of Paul. It is not my purpose here to provide much detail about each book. It is more important to focus upon certain books within this collection, as well as some outside of it, because they are important to this work. The canonical books that should mainly be focused upon are the gospels, *Matthew, Mark, Luke* and *John* along with the books of *Acts, Hebrews* and the *Apocalypse of John* (otherwise known as *Revelation*), but not necessarily in that order. Others will be mentioned as appropriate.

The first thing that should be noted is that, contrary to popular belief, the gospels were not necessarily written by the apostle named in its title. Church councils over time deemed that they either were or probably were, but the titles themselves, in Greek, actually do not state this. They are the gospel *according to* the apostle named (except for *Mark*, who was not an apostle). This means that these gospels could very well have been written, instead, by a follower/disciple of the person the teaching found within is attributed to. So, again, it would have been the gospel as taught by, i.e., *according to*, the apostle named. This knowledge in and of itself changes the probable date of the first writing of each gospel as Christians have tended from the beginning to date each book according to the belief that each had actually written it. That some also purport to have been written by said apostle is also irrelevant since it was not considered to be a falsehood if a disciple wrote a book in the name of his teacher and actually stated that it had been written *by* that teacher. We today would consider such to be a falsehood, but they did not because it was supposed to be a true representation of that which the teacher believed and taught in any case.

Also, it is well-understood among scholars that each gospel was written predominantly for the use of a particular faith community, although the outlines of these communities are no longer certainly known. So, this line of thought posits that there was a community that followed the apostle John, one that followed Matthew, one that followed Paul and one that followed Peter (and this is very much in line with the division already detailed between, at least, James, John, Peter and Paul). Obviously, since more gospels than the four canonical gospels have been found, there were even more such communities. These communities, perhaps, followed Thomas, James, etc. and were of more Gnostic persuasion. But this is not necessarily the case. After all, there can be little doubt that some apostles went about spreading the word and that others later wrote down what they had taught. And they undoubtedly *believed* in Jesus as the messiah, regardless of his death, because they believed he would return.

So, it is fairly obvious that these gospels and other books were written by persons who had received teaching that could be attributed to the apostle or other authority in question. Otherwise we could expect to have multiple versions of the *Gospel According to Mark*, for example, all written by separate persons and all purporting to be his teaching or Peter's teaching through him. No one could know what to believe in such a scenario! If we had multiple gospels attributed to the *same* apostle then we would have even more conflict than we do and even greater questions of authority. And, in any event, if the writer wanted real authority, then why isn't there a Gospel According to Jesus or a Gospel According to James the brother of Jesus or a Gospel According to John the Baptizer or even a Gospel According to Paul? No, each writer in question had to have had at least some connection with the person the work was attributed to, however indirect that connection might have been. So they wrote each separate gospel as they had been taught to the best of their memories. And this easily accounts for the discrepancies between each. But that does not really explain Gnostic books like the *Apocalypse of Adam*, for example, which clearly could not have any genuine relation to Adam, if he even existed to begin with. The connection here must be to ancient Jewish communities from which these books were taken and modified by later Gnostic Christian groups.

In any case, the intricacies of these various communities are not necessary to attempt to draw here. What is important here, however, is the fact that others have also come to the conclusion that, *if* Mark's gospel was indeed the first to be written (and, I submit that it wasn't), that it may well have been written in response to "heresies" which sprang up within Mark's community. The main proponent of such a possibility has been Theodore Weeden in his work Mark: Traditions in Conflict (Fortress Press, 1971). He proposed that Mark's gospel was written in response to a *Gnostic* "divine man" heresy (Johnson 98). Sound familiar?

However, that which seems to be absent from these other analyses, including Johnson's, is that (1) Mark's gospel may well *not* have been the first written and (2); that if such heresies had cropped up, prompting a response from these communities, then "heresies" made themselves known quite early within the Christian community - within the first sixty or so years; and (3) this "divine man" controversy clearly appears to possess earlier *Gnostic* elements, i.e., with reference to the phrase "Son of Man". But, one has to ask, then, from whence could these Gnostic groups have come if Gnosticism within Christianity did not appear until the second century CE? The fact of the matter, as already shown, is that Gnostic Christianity was around *at least as early* as Pauline Christianity was. This is something that scholars tend to ignore because they are often still too wedded to the idea that Christianity began as a solid orthodox movement with a standard teaching from which some later strayed. This is a viewpoint which was propagated by early church fathers and by Constantine I and his followers, such as Eusebius, in order to create the type of history for Christianity that they wanted. But this history is false.

John Was FIRST!

In any case, the traditional date for the writing of each of these books is as follows: *Mark* (60-70 CE), *Matthew* (60-85 CE), *Luke* and *Acts* (60-90 CE), *Hebrews* (63-90 CE), the *Apocalypse of John* (68-100 CE) and *John* (80-95 CE). The first thing to be noted about this order here is that the *Gospel According to John* is believed to have been written either last or next to last, depending upon when the *Apocalypse of John* was written. I, again, submit that this arrangement is incorrect and that the *Gospel According to John* likely came *first* among the gospels.

Now, the earliest extant known fragment of each book is dated as follows: *John* (125-160 CE), *Matthew* (150-200 CE), the *Apocalypse of John* (150-200 CE), *Hebrews* (late 2nd to early 3rd century CE), *Luke* (175-250 CE), *Acts* (250 CE) and *Mark* (350 CE). It is stunning to see that the order here is dramatically different, especially when one notes that the *Gospel According to John* is first and the *Gospel According to Mark* is last. Does this really make a difference, though? Well, first, the fragment of the *Gospel According to John* in question is the *Ryland's Library Papyrus P52*, which came from an original papyrus codex (a book, not a scroll). It is a fact that there are many people who still do not know, somehow, that the first actual bound books began to be made around the time of the writing of the first Christian texts. It is a mode that Christianity quickly adopted while Judaism proper continued to prefer scrolls. And, now, it should be added that this fragment, according to some scholars and linguists, could actually have been penned as early as 100 CE, rather than 125 CE. As we will see, this *really does* make a significant difference, if true.

Again, it is the earliest fragment of any New Testament book in existence today, as far as is known. It was written in Greek and found in Egypt, having been purchased on the Egyptian market. Now, scholars almost insist that it was originally first penned at Ephesos, which is located in the province of Asia in Anatolia. This belief is held because it is presumed to have been written by the apostle John, who is traditionally said to have resided at or near Ephesos during his latter years They posit, therefore, that if this book was originally penned about between 80 and 95 CE, it would have taken time for it to have been copied once or twice and by this process make its way to Egypt. But, this scenario is improbable.

Many scholars, biblical and otherwise, are also determined that the *Gospel According to John* and the *Apocalypse of John* **must** have been written by one and the same person. Those of faith are certainly unable to see it otherwise. But, it simply may not be the case that both were written by the same person. In fact, it is actually more likely that these two books were *not* penned by the same person. But, if they were, then it becomes obvious that both of these books were written by a man known as John the elder, no doubt a disciple of John the apostle. But the gospel was *not* written by John the apostle by any means, as will be shown. In so many words, it is my belief that John the apostle did write the *Apocalypse of John* and that the gospel and pastoral works are written by his disciple, John the elder, utilizing notes from John the apostle.

The means by which we arrive at this conclusion reveals the hideous deception in all its ugliness! The *Apocalypse of John* was written early and has absolutely *nothing to do with* the supposed end of the world, but, instead, had to do with the expected return of the messiah within the lifetimes of the first Christians. But later Christians twisted it to suit their own ends since the parousia did not occur when Jerusalem and the temple were destroyed. So, an entirely new scenario than that which is traditional is called for here. Let us begin, correctly, with the *Apocalypse of John*. The *Apocalypse of John*, if one actually considers the internal evidence, **must** be seen as having been written (1) during the reign of Nero, (2) before the Jewish Revolt of 66-74 and the fall of Jerusalem and, (3) after Paul wrote *1 Corinthians*. That would initially place the writing of the *Apocalypse* as being between the years of about 54 CE to 65 CE. Add to this the probability that John was arrested before Paul wrote *1 Corinthians* as shown by internal evidence, as we have seen, and that would mean that the *Apocalypse* would have been written a little later, probably about 55 CE. From all of this, it seems reasonable to infer that the *Apocalypse* was written relatively soon after John's arrest.

But how do we arrive at this determination? First, put very simply, the following internal facts have to be recognized. Almost all scholars, and even the faithful, accept that the designation "666" refers to the Roman imperator, Nero. Some try mightily to explain this away or to somehow prove that it references a fear that Nero would return after his death and they often point to some prophecy concerning this. These scholars and researchers are determined that Nero was, in fact, deceased by the time of the writing of this book. After all, this is the only way to really make this a prophecy of the *future* - of the end times. But, in fact, it was instead a prophecy of the destruction of the temple in Jerusalem. After all, there is absolutely NO direct reference whatsoever to the actual historical fall of Jerusalem or the destruction of the temple within this book. In fact, the *Apocalypse* reads exactly as if Jerusalem and the temple are still extant at the time of its writing. But, at the same time, the hatred toward the Romans is more than evident. Also, the *Apocalypse* is clearly *looking forward to* the destruction of the temple, which was to be replaced with one descending from Heaven. And this is, more or less, what the Essenes expected to happen.

But the real key here is the reference made to the two prophets who are killed in Jerusalem and then rose again. If Jerusalem was already destroyed, how could this happen? **It couldn't.** Finally, the multiple admonishments to churches in certain cities of those who eat meat sacrificed to idols indicates the known rift between Jerusalem Christianity and Pauline Christianity referenced in the book of *Acts*. And the seething hatred exhibited within the pages of this book for those who disbelieved is very much like that found within the pages of apocalyptic literature found among the Essenes in their Dead Sea Scrolls. Finally, in both cases, the conflict was between two opposing sects *within* Judaism. This is made clear by multiple references to the "true Jews", etc. Christianity had not yet fully separated from Judaism when the *Apocalypse* was written.

The latter point is pivotal. It seems obvious both from the *Apocalypse* and from the book of *Acts* that during his first two missionary journeys Paul actually avoided the area of Anatolia (the Roman province of Asia) where these churches existed for the most part, moving on into Hellenic areas instead. After all, there is really no reason to suppose that Paul had no competition outside of Palestine for converts, and that is exactly what has played out here. John was his main competitor in Anatolia and the churches listed in the *Apocalypse* were John's territory and he wanted to keep Paul's influence out of that area because he did not like Paul's teachings! So John's sphere of influence encompassed the cities of Ephesos, Smyrna, Thyatira, Pergamon, Sardis, Philadelphia and Laodikea, to whom he likely wrote epistles and/or letters about 50 CE. Ephesos must have served as a base for John's ministry. So one can reasonably postulate that John had written letters to his churches, except for the one at Ephesos, just the same as Paul wrote letters to his churches, as mutely indicated by the *Apocalypse* itself. Those letters, which are, unfortunately, no longer extant, would likely have been written from Ephesos shortly after Paul wrote *1 Corinthians* and in response to it. That would place their writing sometime in mid-to-late 50 CE or soon thereafter. And please recall that one did not have to be literate in order to write letters. One only needed to have a scribe to write letters for you. These letters never made it to Egypt and, thus, are not preserved by the sands of time as other documents were. This is one good reason why the *Gospel According to John* was more likely written in Egypt even though the *Apocalypse* was not.

Now, in the *Apocalypse* reference is made twice to the "Synagogue of Satan". This is done with reference to the churches of Sardis and Philadelphia (*Rev.* 2:9; 3:9). In both cases the writer identifies them as those ". . . who say that they are Jews and are not". But why on earth would the writer, whether he were the apostle or a disciple of the apostle, be concerned about people who called themselves Jews, but weren't? That those the writer is referring to are other Christians can hardly be doubted. So why would he refer to them as Jews? Peter Bergen answers this question in the following way: "The book reflects a situation in which Christians understood themselves to be a distinct group within a Jewish context, and even thought themselves to be true Jews" (Evans & Hagner 200; *Polemic in the Book of Revelation*). This, I submit, is almost exactly correct and one of the main reasons that we must accept the fact that this book was written quite early - **before** the full separation of Christianity from Judaism. So what he misses here, I submit, is that the Jewish faction called "Christianity" was also divided and the writer of the *Apocalypse* is really talking about "true Christians" and "false Christians". Jerusalem Christianity and Pauline Christianity are seen here. The writer of the *Apocalypse* did not like Pauline Christianity.

Scholars will often point out that when the writer of the *Apocalypse* refers to Babylon, he actually means Roma. I submit that the writer means exactly that. The writer of the *Apocalypse* also stood against that which was happening within the Roman area of Christian influence. So he used the name of a city that was universally hated by almost all Jews of his day in order to emphasize his stand against that which was being taught in this locality - those in Roma being influenced by Pauline Christianity even though it had been founded by Peter, those in Sardis and Philadelphia having strayed from John's strict teachings in a similar way. Why would this be the case, though? Because after Paul and Barnabas freed Peter from the prison in Jerusalem Peter began to be more open to accepting Paul's viewpoint and eventually did accept it, if not in total, almost in total. And one cannot escape the fact that Roman Catholic Christianity *is* Pauline Christianity almost in total, with additions; much more so than Eastern Orthodox Christianity is.

But what of the *Gospel According to John*? Well, first, many modern scholars make a big deal out of the supposed fact that it is seemingly very anti-Semitic in tone. But they are often at a loss to explain this since it was supposedly written by the apostle John, who was a Jew. But, if one reads this gospel as it is written without the "advantage" of faith and the belief that it must have been written by the apostle, then it is easily seen that this book really is *not* anti-Semitic at all *and* that it was *not* written by the apostle after all. It was simply written by someone who was *not* a Jew himself, but who had been a follower of the apostle John. So the writer's continual reference to "the Jews" is explained by this. He *may* have personally disliked Jews in general, since he was not one and since he personally blamed the Jews for the destruction of Jerusalem, but his tone really is *not* very anti-Semitic.

Still, in the end, does the writer blame the Jews for the crucifixion of Jesus? Yes, he does. This gospel writer started the trend of blaming the Jews as a people, rather than the Romans, for the destruction of Jerusalem and the temple there. But why would the writer do this? Because the writer was of the sect of the Christians who followed the apostle John, who did write the *Apocalypse*, while, in his mind, those Jews to blame were not. Whether his belief was historically accurate in any way is unlikely, but this is what the writer really wished to portray.

For him, it was the other sects of Judaism that were responsible, not the Christian sect. So he stops at almost nothing to paint them as the villains from the very beginning, but this was not really hatred due to race or ethnicity.

The early Christians, as Martin McDonald astutely points out (Evans & Hagner 237-38; *Anti-Judaism in the Early Church Fathers*) had three major expectations that did not materialize as they had hoped: "(1) that Jesus would soon return to the earth and establish his kingdom, (2) that the city of Jerusalem would become the religious capital for the Christian faith, and (3) that the nation of Israel would soon come to accept Jesus as the promised messiah." The earliest Christians were sure that the Jews would soon see that Jesus was indeed the promised messiah and convert to Christianity. The fact that this did not occur was something that greatly concerned the church well into the European Dark Ages. The response to this was that the church first made many attempts to convert the Jews, sometimes by force. But these efforts proved largely unsuccessful. Because of this, many began to hold to the opinion that the Jews had been rejected permanently by god. But since the "old Israel" continued to exist and even to prosper, this constituted a major theological problem within the church (Evans & Hagner 238).

The success of Jewish proselytization continued into the fourth and fifth centuries CE and had become so pervasive and noticeable that many Christians were greatly concerned that the Jews were gaining so many converts from Pagan ranks. Many Pagans simply found Judaism more appealing than Christianity, attending Jewish festivals, seeking healing from Jews through prayers, incantations and even by wearing Jewish amulets. And let us not forget the Jewish emphasis upon marriage and the family, which was very much like that of the Pagans already, and which Christianity predominantly lacked. These are things that Christians found it difficult to compete with; so much so that Ioannes the Khrysostomos (Ἰωάννης ὁ Χρυσόστομος, c349-407 CE), Khrysostomos meaning "golden-mouthed", known today as John Chrysostom, even felt that he had to warn Christians against converting to Judaism (Evans & Hagner 239). For, in 387 CE, he wrote:

If [the Jews] are ignorant of the Father, if they crucified the Son, and spurned the aid of the Spirit, cannot one declare with confidence that the synagogue is a dwelling place for demons? (241; *Discourse* 1.3.3).

Khrysostomos had gone so far as to state that Jewish synagogues were houses of idolatry and of devils. And he even went further than this by stating that the Jews did not even worship the same god, but worshipped devils instead (Evans & Hagner 199; Peter Borgen, *Polemic in the Book of Revelation*). And, unknown to most Christians today, he wrote one very sickening diatribe against the Jewish people entitled *Why I Hate the Jews* as well as several homilies against them. The Christians later also made exactly the same accusations against the Pagans. But Christian hatred of the Jews really had its genesis here and lasted well into the European Dark Ages, when Christians would blame the Jews for anything that happened to them that was ill or unpleasant.

Finally, as Robert Kysar points out (Evans & Hagner 118-21; *Anti-Semitism and the Gospel of John*), there must have been a singular situation that prompted the writer of this gospel to stereotype Jewish leaders as he did - influenced by evil. He points out that, although these two were not the first to make such a proposal, J. Louis Martyn (History and Theology in the Fourth Gospel (rev. ed.; Nashville, Abingdon, 1979)) and Raymond E. Brown (The Gospel According to John (AB 29 and 29a; Garden City, N.Y.: Doubleday, 1966)) both posited that the occasion for the writing of this gospel was the result of an experience of expulsion of the Christian sect from their local synagogue.

But, of course, there is no direct evidence of this even though it is a plausible theory because situations like that described must have indeed occurred. More likely, because it is more likely to be true to what we really know of history, however, is a scenario in which disciples of the apostle John, who were alive when the destruction of Jerusalem and the temple occurred, saw that pivotal event in world history for exactly what it was - the destruction of everything they had known and held dear, stripping them of their cultic center. Because of this, their polemic against those whom they saw as the cause of this great loss became severe. And who were to blame other than Jews who had not accepted

Christ? Thus, those of the Christian sect saw themselves, for the first time, as a separate body that needed to find a way to reshape its identity in an effort to survive. So the response toward mainstream Judaism had to be a polemic of an either/or schema (like that found among the Essenes toward other Jews) - one of "us verses them". So, if one accepts the internal evidence, this gospel was really written by, probably, a follower of the apostle John who was actually a Gentile, but not by the apostle John himself. And, even though he harbored a dislike for Jewish people, he was not anti-Semitic and, after all, loved his Jewish mentor and sought to emulate him.

One other main reason that we can conclude that this gospel was written by an actual follower of the apostle John is that both the gospel and the *Apocalypse* constantly emphasize the number seven. In fact, the gospel has been called "The Book of the Seven Signs" while the *Apocalypse* begins with the seven churches in Asia and proceeds from there. Seven must have been an important number for the apostle John, for surely he could have written to more churches if he had so wished. But, perhaps, these were the most important ones in his sphere of influence.

The Esoteric Christ

It is also interesting to note that, in the *Apocalypse*, reference is constantly made (1:4ff; 1:8ff; 4:8ff; 11:17ff; 16:5ff) to "Him who is and who was and who is to come" or to those "who are and who were". In the *Apocalypse* this refers to the Christian god and/or to Jesus. But the reference actually comes from a source that one would not expect. It was actually part of the invocation used at Dodona when referring to *Zeus*. But why on earth would the writer of the *Apocalypse* use this formula? Whatever the reason, this is an example of very early appropriation of Paganism, wrapping it in Christian guise, something that continues even to this very day.

It is interesting to note that the *Gospel According to John* does not go into very much detail about who Jesus was as a person. The Jesus of this gospel is a full-fledged spiritual being in human garb. This is the first, but not the only, indication that it was a work of Gnostic origins. But we will not dwell very much on that fact here. Suffice it to say that scholars agree that this is *the most* Gnostic gospel of all of those which have been accepted into the New Testament canon. And its focus is on the final weeks of the life of Jesus. There is really no interest shown in his early life at all. And, for all practical purposes, it actually begins with the "cleansing of the temple", which is supposed to be one of the last acts of Jesus prior to his arrest and execution. So, essentially, this gospel is all about the final days of Jesus and his life upon this earth, ignoring his prior life and ministry for the most part. *This*, more than anything else, is the thing which clearly indicates that it was the *first* gospel written, not the last. And it is a clear indication of Gnostic origins since Jesus as a man is not really important.

Directly after the "cleansing of the temple" by Jesus, in this gospel alone, follows the arrest of John the Baptizer. In all of the other gospels, John is arrested *prior to* the ministry of Jesus. But, in *John*, it seems that Jesus himself *actually causes* the arrest of John the Baptizer by his actions and then embarks on a short ministry. Why, if this is so, would John be arrested for the actions of Jesus? For exactly the reason previously expounded - that the mission of Jesus and his disciples here was to distract the Romans and the temple authorities long enough to steal precious documents from the temple. Who would they have given them to? John! Who would John have given them to? Those Essenes from Qumran! The whole and only reason we still have any of these documents, which were found among the Dead Sea Scrolls, is exactly because of **this** incident!

Now, the *Gospel According to John* never actually states that John the Baptizer was ever killed or executed. But it does state multiple times that, immediately after the "cleansing of the temple" the Jews sought to kill Jesus. And, according to this gospel, they were instrumental in so doing. But, once again, those who are referred to here are the Jews who do not follow Jesus, not all Jews. In addition, it is clear by the final verses of this gospel that it was written *after* both Peter and John had died, whenever that was. And it indicates that Peter had been executed. Also indicated here is what appears to be a fact that is generally overlooked - that the apostle John actually did write some things down, which this writer utilized in order to pen his gospel. And that which is presented in this gospel writing is only a select part of what the apostle John had written down.

John and Peter

Now, it also appears obvious that the writer of the book of *Acts* knows that the apostle John had left Jerusalem at a certain point because he never refers to him again after a certain point. It is the same for the apostle Peter. At a certain point in this book neither are referred to again. And, whenever the book of *Acts* was written, both Peter and John were already deceased.

It seems obvious, then, that John was deceased shortly after he wrote the *Apocalypse*, which, like certain writings of the Essenes at Qumran, teaches that a *New Jerusalem* would descend to earth after a ferocious conflict between good and evil forces, and virtually no one disputes this. The question is *just when* this book was written. It is only during Paul's third missionary journey that he actually travels through Phrygia to Ephesos and spends any significant time in this area, although he had visited the Ephesians briefly and hurriedly during his second missionary journey. It seems obvious that the apostle John had been arrested by this time or Paul would not have been able to spend so much time there. And this missionary journey would have begun in about 52-53 CE, Paul remaining near Ephesos for two years. In the mean time, John is on Patmos and writes the *Apocalypse* about 55 CE. Soon after this, contrary to tradition, John, having never returned to Ephesos, but remaining on Patmos, dies or is executed there, about 56 CE.

But what of Peter? Well, again, contrary to the viewpoint of most modern scholars, it seems that the term *Christian* was used quite early. That the book of *Acts* was written quite late is obvious by use of internal evidence. The term Christian was certainly being used by the time this book was written, although it is unknown how widespread its use actually was. If one observes Peter's absence in *Acts* one sees that he is absent just after the point at which the Jerusalem Council delivered its decision. The writer of *Acts* either does not know or does not want to write about where Peter may be or what he is doing because he is essentially another competitor of Paul. What this shows is that Peter is probably on a missionary journey of his own. And where might Peter have gone? First to Asia to work with John and then to Roma. That is why he wrote to the churches in Asia from Roma.

Again, the Jerusalem Council appears to have taken place about 46 CE. Now, it has always been tradition that Peter somehow founded the church at Roma, but no one seems to know just when this might have taken place. Most believe that it must have taken place during Peter's later life and yet, a church had already been established there quite early. This is simply irreconcilable and so tradition here is widely ignored by scholars. But it seems to me that the key here is to accept the fact (for I believe this to be a fact) that the pastoral epistle of *2 Peter* was *not* written by the apostle Peter, but that *1 Peter* was. If *2 Peter* is eliminated as an apostolic writing, as it must be, and one accepts that *1 Peter* was indeed written from Roma, as most scholars do, one can easily see *1 Peter* as having been written quite early. It's writing has absolutely nothing to do with the time of the writing of *2 Peter*. And, if Peter was in Roma just after the time of the Jerusalem Council, then this writing could easily and very reasonably have been penned while he was there, in about 47-48 CE, much earlier than most scholars will even consider possible. And, if this is true, then Peter does become the de facto founder of the church in Roma. And one must also remember that Paul did not write *Romans* until toward the end of his second missionary journey, which would have been about 51 CE. So I submit that Peter *did* establish the church in Roma, but much earlier than people tend to believe. As to just when Peter died; that remains uncertain. It appears obvious, according to the *Gospel According to John*, that Peter did die before John did. Whether he was really executed or not can probably never be known, but this seems probable (but not by crucifixion upside-down as tradition holds). And, if the supposed bones of Peter were to be examined we might find out whether the person whose bones they were was crucified or not. But permission for this is very unlikely indeed. And, even if this were to be done, there is no proof that the bones are really those of Peter. But, it does seem reasonable to assume that Peter did die at Roma about 49 CE and probably never returned to Jerusalem. Perhaps it was he who had been stirring things up there over Christus!

Finally, the writer of *Acts* surely knew that Paul was deceased by the time he penned his work. But he did not know what had happened to Paul, so he ended his work with Paul still living at Roma. The writer of *Acts* did not know what had happened to any of the disciples/apostles except for James, the brother of John, and James is the only one whose death is, therefore, written about. If the writer had known about the others, he surely would have written about it. So, he knew that they were deceased, but did not know the circumstances of their deaths.

When Were the Books Actually Written?

Now, *all* of the gospels were written after the fall of Jerusalem. An objective look at the internal evidence can lead only to this conclusion. The main reason, as many scholars have correctly pointed out, are the temple statements found in each and every gospel, including those which were not accepted into the canon. The statements about the destruction of the temple are the key. They are couched as prophecies, but they were not prophecies. The gospel writers, including that according to John, refuse to admit that the temple has already been destroyed but, instead, portray its destruction as a prophecy of Jesus. This is best shown as the writer of the *Gospel According to John* even makes the glaring error of placing into the mouths of "the Jews" that it had taken forty-six years to build the temple (*John* 2:20). No one could have known that unless they had written *after* the temple had been completed. *No one* during the lifetime of Jesus would have said this! Period.

Not only were all of the gospels written after the destruction of Jerusalem and the temple, i.e., after 70 CE, the first canonical gospel to have been written was, again, the *Gospel According to John*. The last one was the *Gospel According to Luke*, with those of *Mark* and *Matthew* in-between. The writers of both *Mark* and *Matthew* tried to add details about the earlier life of Jesus to both of their gospels because people felt the need to know more of these details. *Luke*, with the most details about everything, including the earlier life of Jesus, was written last among them, soon followed by *Acts*. So, once again, the term *Christian* was used earlier than most scholars will allow for. It most likely came into vogue in Roma itself (even if it might have first been a derogatory term used essentially against the sect) even though the writer of *Acts* states that it was first used in Antiokheia. As far as he knew, this was true, so this was no deliberate falsification on his part.

The *Epistle to the Galatians*, it is generally accepted, was the first New Testament book written - that by the apostle Paul, probably from Antiokheia just after the conclusion of the Jerusalem Council. I concur with this. This book, which would have been written about 46 or 47 CE, strongly alludes to the disagreement between Pauline and Peterine (Jerusalem) Christianity, Paul claiming to have generally bested Peter and others in this dispute. This book started a series of responses between the two factions - the Pauline Jewish Christians and the Gnostic Judaizing Christians. For no one was really going to the Gentiles yet, but to Jews in the Diaspora and Jewish converts from Paganism. So, they may have sometimes called themselves "Christians" already, but at the same time still thought of themselves as loyal Jews and, frankly, as better Jews than the ones they blamed for the death of Jesus.

However, contrary to the observation of most scholars, it seems more than reasonable to presume that the *Epistle of James* was written also just after the Jerusalem Council, partly in response to the *Epistle to the Galatians*. So the *Epistle of James* would have been the second canonical book, having been written about 47-48 CE. And this book is rightly seen as "the most Jewish writing found within the New Testament". Therefore, "clear allusions to James by the fathers are infrequent" (Evans & Hagner 185-86; Robert W. Wall & William L. Lane: *Polemic in Hebrews and the Catholic Epistles*), because they did not like it. Why? Because it was clearly of Judaizing flavor and because Jewish Gnostic apocalyptic thought are a source for his theological perspective (Evans & Hagner 188).

> The mark of membership in "the faith" is mercy (2:12-13), especially toward the eschatological community's "last and least" - a class whose borders are symbolized by the socioeconomic distress of "widows and orphans" for

whom merciful deeds are most necessary. . . . Christ is *the model of mercy for the eschatological community*: He observed "the royal law" [an allusion to Melchizedek?] (2:8) perfectly and was approved by God as Messiah on that basis (Evans & Hagner 189). . . .

Jesus is seen here not only as interpreting Torah correctly, but also as obeying it perfectly. So, whereas James and other Gnostic Judaizing Christians emphasized the life and works of Jesus as evidence that salvation came through him (while still not emphasizing the personhood of Jesus so much), Paul and his followers emphasized the cross and the death of Jesus as the salvific point of importance.

At about the same time *1 Peter* was probably written from Roma. So the first three canonical books were written, most likely, from three of the original four Christian power-base camps - Jerusalem, Antiokheia and Roma (excluding Ephesos). Then, toward the end of his second missionary journey, about 51 CE, Paul wrote the *Epistle to the Romans* (after all, if he and Peter had made up and if Peter, therefore, had been espousing Pauline Christianity in Roma, then Paul would be the natural person to take the leadership role in Roma after Peter's death) as well as *1 Thessalonians* (which teaches the concept of what is today called the "rapture") from Kórinthos, where he was staying for about eighteen months.

Nero became imperator in 54 CE. By that time Paul was already well under way on his third missionary journey. And it was about this time, about 54 CE, that Paul wrote *2 Corinthians*. *1 Corinthians* had touched off a firestorm within the church with the advice Paul provided concerning the eating of meat sacrificed to Pagan deities. This was just too much for the Judaizing Christians, especially for the apostle John. So he wrote the letters mentioned in the *Apocalypse* in about 50 CE (probably while still at Ephesos shortly prior to his arrest), which are no longer extant today, plus, following his arrest, his *Apocalypse* in about 55 CE from Patmos, just before Paul was arrested and sent to Caesarea, in about 56 CE. Probably not long afterward, John died in about 56 CE.

So Peter was dead. John was also dead, or soon would be. There was no one who had any real authority who could still have come to the aid of Paul had they wished to do so (Peter might have but John likely would not have). Barnabas had long abandoned Paul. James, the brother of Jesus, stood completely unopposed when examining Paul. And Paul knew this. That is the reason he submitted to the test that James suggested to him. Then men from John's territory of Asia (*Acts* 21: 27), no doubt tipped-off by others, witnessed his duplicity in the temple, there could be no other real outcome than that Roman authorities would intervene, lest a riot ensue, and would arrest Paul. And there is also the possibility that James might have done this not just to get rid of Paul, but also to get in good-standing with Roman authorities, who certainly wanted that subversive, Paul. And perhaps Paul agreed in an effort to disguise himself and escape.

Paul was eventually taken to Roma from where he wrote the epistles "*Ephesians*", *Philippians* and *Colossians* as well as the pastoral letter of *2 Timothy* during the years 60-62 CE. It seems more than obvious that Paul never wrote *1 Timothy* at all and that it was written much later by someone else trying to create the monolithic church that never existed in Paul's time. *If* Paul was executed, it was soon thereafter, in about 62 CE, and he never wrote any more books at all. He did not write *Titus*, for example. Still, neither Peter nor Paul have been proven to have been martyred or even executed. But, whatever happened to them, they died prior to the beginning of the Jewish revolt in 66 CE and the destruction of Jerusalem in 70 CE. That can safely be said.

The Torch Passes Back to Egypt

Again, the most likely place for the survivors to have fled before the Romans destroyed Jerusalem was the closest and easiest place within the Roman Empire to go, where they could still easily hide among a large Jewish population. That place was *Egypt*, either Leontopolis or Alexandria. Support for this theory comes from the surviving documentation itself. Not only is it a fact that the oldest fragment of the *Gospel According to John* was written in Greek and found in Egypt, but that is also the case for all of the other canonical gospels as well as the book of *Acts*. The *Apocalypse of John* was also found in its earliest extant form on a papyrus (P 98) which was also written in Greek and, scholars believe, was probably actually written, but not first penned, in Egypt. And, interestingly, the book of *James* (P 20) was also found in Egypt, although this papyrus fragment is somewhat later than the others, having been copied sometime during the early third century. One must remember that James was the leader of the Jerusalem church before he was killed there and before the destruction of Jerusalem and the temple there. And the Epistles of John were also found, written in Greek, in Egypt. The exception to all of this - the book of *Hebrews* and the Pauline epistles of *Romans, 1* and *2 Corinthians, Galatians, "To the Saints"* (*Ephesians*), *Philippians, Colossians* and *1 Thessalonians*, all of which were found on a papyrus book fragment in that order (P 46). However, the provenance of this papyrus is unknown. It is surmised that it may have been made in a monastery, probably also in Egypt, and the papyrus fragment containing all of this material is dated to between 175 and 225 CE - rather late.

All of these fragments, the earliest known today, were written in *Greek*. But the fact that the oldest known fragments were found in Egypt cannot be significant, after all, since the desert routinely preserves ancient documents there, can it? In other words, can this mean that some of these books might have been first penned in Egypt rather than elsewhere? The answer to these questions can be responded to with a question - why not? Are we so wedded to tradition and the traditional places of original penmanship that we must close our eyes to such a possibility? Frankly, Alexandria, Egypt would have been the natural, most logical place for most of these books, except for the Pauline writings, the *Apocalypse of John* and the *Epistle of James* as well as *1 Peter*, and *Hebrews*, to have been first penned. From there alone they could have best spread to other areas of the empire and beyond. There would have been no place else better for it, within or without the empire.

Again, traditionalists posit that the *Gospel According to John* was written at Ephesos in Anatolia. But they can't adequately explain how a text, which is quite Gnostic, would have been written there rather than in the hotbed of Gnosticism, Alexandria, Egypt. They also never adequately explain how a text that is so Gnostic in flavor would have been written "by" a disciple of Jesus so early - well before Christian

Gnosticism supposedly emerged. Also, as already indicated, it is obvious that several extant early Gnostic texts, such as the *Apocalypse of Adam*, were actually pre-Christian and focused on Seth, the third son of Adam and Eve. And it is also believed that these early Sethians, as some call them, may be related to or identical to the *Nazarines*. From these groups, scholars believe, emerged, at least in part, the Gnostic movements of Mandaeism and Manichaeism.

But the disciples were mainly rude, uneducated, perhaps illiterate, fishermen, according to the gospels themselves. Still, perhaps some were not fishermen and may have been literate (although they did not need to be if they employed scribes). Indeed, the three who are said to have written the canonical gospels are surely the most likely to have been literate in Aramaic and/or Greek. But whether they actually wrote said gospels is problematic because one traditionally has to posit that they did so toward the end of their lives after Paul wrote most or all of his letters. But instead all of the gospels were actually written after the Romans destroyed Qumran and Jerusalem. So it is more likely that all of these gospels were written by disciples of said apostles.

For those who did not remain in Jerusalem and were, perhaps, killed - knowing that there was a connection to Qumran, which was also destroyed - where was the most logical place for any of them to go? Egypt. Which ones? Mark? Thomas? Why would they risk going deeper into the Roman Empire anywhere else during or right after Jerusalem's destruction? Going outside of the empire was not necessarily a good idea for them either because anywhere they would go - Arabia, Persia, Armenia - they would have been recognized as Jews, who were hated and who were refugees and possibly even criminals (making them easy prey for those who would like a reward from the Romans - not a safe bet to make). But going to Leontopolis or Alexandria would have worked.

So, the safest place for them to have gone would have been, probably, Alexandria, Egypt. Thus, Alexandria effectively replaced Jerusalem as the primary Christian power-base, Antiokheia remaining basically intact and Roma a bit weakened, but still extant. And Ephesos had long since ceased to play any important role. This is exactly why Christianity took hold so early in Egypt - because most, if not all, of the surviving/ escaping apostles/disciples went *there*. And the very reason that we find so many Gnostics and Gnostic texts in Egypt is exactly because of those who fled from Jerusalem to Alexandria, Egypt. Jerusalem Christianity effectively transferred itself to Alexandria. But, again, only a few of the apostles/disciples did actually survive. It seems clear that the survivors were probably Thomas, Mark and Matthew along with John the elder and possibly Luke. Probably no others survived to make the trip.

Again, they did *not* go to Pella, as tradition has posited. The reason is that Pella was too close to Jerusalem and, if they had gone there, they could easily have been hunted down by the Roman authorities. In Egypt they could easily hide among a large Jewish population in Alexandria. They could even proselytize a bit after the war was over and they were no longer in so much danger. They had escaped, gradually regrouped after the war was over, and then eventually separated, gathering disciples of their own. These disciples are likely the ones who actually wrote the gospels "according to" each apostle/disciple named therein. Also, the *Gospel According to Thomas* may actually be the only one actually written *by* an apostle that is still extant. And this is probably the ever elusive "Q" source. Yes, Thomas served well as the "Didymos" Oracle! Also, again, it seems reasonable to acknowledge that the apostle John did, in fact, go to Ephesos and that he also did die on Patmos. *This* tradition seems to have some historical basis for belief. The other surviving apostles, except for Paul (and Peter, in part), are lost to history now because the traditions concerning them are simply not trustworthy.

The Dead Sea Scrolls

Now, that which is known as the Dead Sea Scrolls were originally various collections of manuscripts found west of the Dead Sea, the first seven, representing over five-hundred books, having been found in 1947 by an Arab goatherd, Muhammad adh-Dhib, with more being found in the years following. The region where the most important manuscripts were found were near Qumran, Murabba 'at and En Gedi. Although most scholars focus on the documents found in eleven different caves at Qumran itself, it should be noted that the documents found at the other two sites relate to the time of the second major Jewish Revolt

(Bar Kokhba) against the Romans (132-135 CE). What this shows is that, although the caves at Qumran remained unoccupied following the First Jewish Revolt, this site having been so thoroughly destroyed by the Romans, nearby caves became occupied during the time between the two revolts by more apocalyptically-minded people. Remember, they were no longer allowed to reside in Jerusalem, which had in the mean time been transformed into Aelia Kapitolina, a Pagan Roman colony.

Once the fragments were put together it was found that all of the books of the Hebrew Bible or Old Testament were represented, sometimes multiple times, with the sole exception of the book of *Esther*. The scrolls also included commentaries on these books as well as books of community rules and regulations and order of worship. The liturgical texts show that the Qumran community utilized a different calendar from that utilized within the temple in Jerusalem. The calendar utilized by the Qumranites was of an entirely solar nature similar to the calendar mentioned in the *Book of Jubilees*, this book having been written about 100 BCE. So the Qumranites, in effect, worshipped the sun or at least saw their god as a solar deity, like Akhenaten and the Atenists had done hundreds of years before them.

According to a study of the ancient handwriting and also carbon dating of the linen that some of the manuscripts were wrapped in, all of these documents were penned during the last two centuries BCE and the first century CE - no later. And the nearby community called Khirbet Qumran was found, due to coins found in various places in that area, to have actually been occupied from about 130 BCE to 70 CE. So at least most of these books (most being copies) were likely penned *at* Qumran and/or within these nearby caves by those whom the Romans destroyed. The main exception to this would be the Copper Scroll.

In any case, two main phases of habitation occurred at this site and these phases were separated by a period of about thirty years when no habitation was extant there. Following the thirty year interval occupation resumed in about 4 BCE, the year Herod the Great died (and the presumed year of the birth of Jesus). Indeed, the area of Khirbet Qumran was probably first occupied by a group called the Hasidim, which temporarily allied with the Maccabeans in their effort to defeat

Antiokhos IV Epiphanes. However, this alliance broke up after the Maccabean victory in 142 BCE mainly over the issue of the priesthood. Those Hasidim from which the Essene community at Qumran developed insisted that the sons of Zadok (sounds similar to Melchizedek, doesn't it?), who had held the priestly office during the time of Solomon, were the only ones who could legitimately hold the high priesthood. Therefore, the Hasmonean priesthood was seen as illegitimate and was even seen as "wicked". And, in their writings, they refer to one member of the Hasmonean priesthood as especially wicked because he had persecuted the sect and its organizer, the "Teacher of Righteousness", at some unknown time in the past, likely sometime about 100 BCE. It seems that this community at first expected that their new age would dawn during the lifetime of this organizer, but he died. Still, they continued their hope in their perceived new age even after this. When the Romans proved to be even more oppressive than those who had come before this community began to focus upon the Romans as those who would be the recipients of divine judgment at the hands of the community. All they had to do was to wait for the appropriate time. Everlasting righteousness would be established following the "War of the Sons of Light against the Sons of Darkness". And, again, the traces of Zoroastrian influence are here greater that that found within wider Judaism. Also, according to the *Zadokite Work* (as already mentioned), Damascus is shown to have been an "outpost" of this Qumran or Essene community and it is significant that the apostle Paul spent some early time there following his conversion to Christianity (Cavendish 609-11, F. F. Bruce, *Dead Sea Scrolls*).

Again, the Qumranites were hardly a pacifistic sect as demonstrated by their own writings. And they were also in constant conflict with mainstream Judaism. This is demonstrated by the fact that they called their opponents by epithets such as "prophets of falsehood," "seers of deceit," and *"hypocrites."* Calling their opponents hypocrites is significant in that this was a favorite term for Jesus to use against his opponents, according to the gospels. Beyond this, they would label their opponents as having "devised plans of Belial [i.e., Satan] against" the true teacher of god (Evans & Hagner 7). This becomes important when compared to certain references made in the *Apocalypse of John* and other canonical New Testament writings. When the writer of the *Apocalypse* references the church at Pergamon he states:

> But I have a few things against you: because you have there some who hold the teaching of Balaam, who kept teaching Balak to put a stumbling block before the sons of Israel, to eat things sacrificed to idols and to commit *acts of* immorality (*Rev.* 2:14).

The writer of the *Apocalypse* is here referring to the reference in the book of *Numbers* (25:14) in which some Israelites had married foreign women and began to worship foreign (Canaanite) deities. And this is clearly against Torah. Further, Peter Borgen shows that the "Synagogue of Satan" in the *Apocalypse* is synonymous with the "congregation of Belial" (1QH 2:22) mentioned in the writings found at Qumran. He states that the Hebrew word that is utilized here which we translate as "congregation" is ēcdāh, which can be translated as "synagogue" and often is because it is the word most often used in the Septuagint to refer to synagogue (Evans & Hagner 205; Peter Borgen, *Polemic in the Book of Revelation*). The Qumran community, then, saw itself in a dualistic confrontational relationship with other Jewish sects, especially to mainstream Judaism as it existed in Jerusalem. All other sects were seen as demonic. More than this, the Qumran community looked forward to a coming parousia at which time they would, as the elect of god, take an active part in the punishment of faithless Israel (ibid 8; 1QpHab 5:3-5).

Now, again, the Dead Sea Scrolls include all of the books of the Hebrew Bible, as it stands today, with one exception, the book of *Esther*. One cannot read too much into this omission since a copy of this book probably did exist at Qumran, but no copy was still extant there in 1947 due to the ravages of time. In addition, there were a good number of other manuscripts also found in various caves. They included scrolls with names sometimes provided to them by the archaeologists who found them, or by scholars once their contents became understood. These scrolls included the *Apocryphal Prophecy*, *Apocryphon*s of *David* and of *Moses*, the *Community Rule*, the *Copper Scroll*, the books of *Enoch* (including the section called the *Book of Giants*), *Festival Prayers*, the *Genesis Apocryphon, Hymnic Composition, Instruction, Jubilees, Judicial Text, Liturgical Texts 1 & 2, Liturgy of the Three Tongues of Fire, New Jerusalem, Peshers* on *Habakkuk, Isaiah, Micah, Psalms* and *Zephaniah*, the *Mysteries*, the *Rule of the Blessing*, the *Rule of the Congregation*, the *Temple Scroll*, the *Testaments* of *Judah* and of *Levi, Thanksgiving Hymns*, the *War Scroll*, and *Words of Moses*. The *Book of Giants* (by the way which Mani, who started Manichaeism, held in great esteem), details how angels who rebelled against god mated with human females and produced giants, called the Nephilim, whom god sent the flood to destroy.

Some things jump out at the reader just by reading the titles of these works. First, and most important, there are several apocryphal works, which are "secret" writings. Also included is a *War Scroll* and one entitled *New Jerusalem*, both apocalyptic in nature. Interestingly, there is a scroll entitled *Liturgy of the Three Tongues of Fire*. And, finally, there is a scroll on the *Mysteries*, also known as the *Book of Secrets*. All of these scrolls were written either in Aramaic or in one or another form of Hebrew. So *none* were written in Greek.

The Nag Hammadi Library

Conversely, the Nag Hammadi Manuscripts, found in Egypt in 1945, are all believed to have originally been written in Greek and later copied into the Coptic language. These books were probably buried in 367 CE as they would have been seen as heretical. There are three categories among these books; (1) the *Corpus Hereticum*, which are Egyptian-Greek wisdom texts mainly dialogues between a teacher, usually "Thrice-Greatest Hermes", and a disciple, written during the second and third centuries CE, (2) a partial translation/alteration of Platon's *Republic*, which has been changed to include Gnostic concepts (as Neoplatonists would have preferred it), and (3) other assorted Gnostic texts.

So, the books which still exist within this latter collection are the *Acts of Peter and the Twelve Apostles, Allogenes*, the *Apocalypse of Adam*, the *First* and *Second Apocalypse of James*, the *Apocalypse of*

Paul, the *Apocryphon of James* (most likely written no earlier than the first half of the second century CE), the *Apocryphon of John*, *Asclepius 21-29*, *Authoritative Teaching*, the *Book of Thomas the Contender*, *Concept of our Great Power*, *Dialogue of the Saviour* (clearly first penned in the latter half of the first century CE and, like the *Gospel of Thomas*, used by the writers of *Mark*, *Matthew* and *Luke* and to a lesser extent, *John*), *Discourse on the Eighth and Ninth*, *Eugnostos the Blessed*, *Exegesis on the Soul*, the *Gnostic Apocalypse of Peter*, the *Gospel of Philip*, the *Gospel of the Egyptians* (as separate from the one quoted by Clement of Alexandria), the *Gospel of Thomas*, the *Gospel of Truth*, *Hypsiphrone* [She of High Mind], *Interpretation of Knowledge*, the *Hypostasis of the Archons*, *Letter of Peter to Philip*, *Marsanes*, *Melchizedek*, *On the Anointing*, *On Baptism* (A&B), *On the Eucharist* (A&B), *On the Origin of the World*, the *Prayer of the Apostle Paul*, Plato's [Gnostic version] *Republic*, the *Sentences of Sextus*, the *Sophia of Jesus Christ*, *Testimony of Truth*, *Thought of Norea*, *The Thunder, Perfect Intellect*, the *Trimorphic Protennoia*, *Paraphrase of Shem*, *Prayer of Thanksgiving*, *Second Treatise of Great Seth*, *Teachings of Silvanus*, *Three Steles of Seth*, a *Treatise on the Resurrection*, the *Tripartite Tractate*, a *Valentinian Exposition*, and *Zostrianos*.

Among these, the *Testimony of Truth* seems significant in that it presents the story of Adam and Eve differently than the book of *Genesis* does. In it, the serpent in the garden is shown as good and as only providing Knowledge to humankind, through Eve, because god actually wanted them to have this Knowledge. So Eve, through the agency of the serpent, essentially becomes the savior of humankind by giving them Knowledge. Thus, as in the Sacred Mysteries, it was the feminine principle who gave Knowledge and enlightenment.

One should note here that Nag Hammadi is really not that far from the island of Elephantiné. It is entirely possible that those monks who later lived near Nag Hammadi and buried their treasured scrolls there might have been in some way influenced by the ancient Jewish/Samaritan colony at Elephantiné. *It is entirely possible.* In fact, some of these books could have originally come directly from Elephantiné.

Now, knowing that the Nag Hammadi collection of manuscripts is incomplete (because a few were inadvertently destroyed) and many

Apocalypse and Armageddon, The Secret Origins of Christianity:

scrolls most likely did not survive the millennia, that which is still extant is telling. *No* canonical biblical books are present, of course, because they were not heretical and would not have had to be hidden. Included are several apocalyptic books and several apocryphons. Like the Essenes at Qumran, there are authoritative teaching books and books of community order. Also included are several gospels, some of which are otherwise unknown. And, obviously, along with these Gnostic texts are several Pagan texts - *Asclepius* and the *Republic* being the most notable among them. Seth appears to have been held in great esteem among this particular group (perhaps they were Sethians), whoever collected the manuscripts. And, finally, included is a book about *Melchizedek*.

The Nag Hammadi Manuscripts and the Dead Sea Scrolls have several similarities, other than those already mentioned. But they also have differences. The most obvious difference is that the former are overwhelmingly Gnostic while the latter are not so much so. BUT, Gnostic influence *is* seen within some texts of the Dead Sea Scrolls. Still, the most important thing that both communities had in common was and emphasis upon apocalyptic and apocryphal literature.

The Apocalypses

Unbeknownst to most people today, there was also a vast array of apocalyptic literature (not found at Nag Hammadi or at Qumran) that was written during the first and second centuries BCE and CE. The pre-Christian works included the *Apocalypse of Abraham*, the *Apocalypse of Baruch*, the *Apocalypse of Daniel*, the *Apocalypse of Elijah*, the *Apocalypse of Ezra*, the *Apocalypse of Gabriel*, the *Apocalypse of Lamech*, the *Apocalypse of Metatron*, the *Apocalypse of Moses*, the *Apocalypse of Sedrach*, the *Apocalypse of Zephaniah*, and the *Apocalypse of Zerubbabel*. In addition, there existed an *Aramaic Apocalypse*.

The "Christian" apocalyptic books that were not included in the New Testament were the *Apocalypse of Golias*, the *Apocalypse of Methodius*, the *Apocalypse of Samuel of Kalamoun*, the *Apocalypse of Stephen*, and the *Apocalypse of the Seven Heavens*. It should, by now, be obvious to anyone that apocalyptic literature was decidedly more important to these ancient peoples than any other type of literature and that is exactly why there are so many early apocalyptic writings still extant (for who knows how many may have perished forever?). There are significantly more apocalypses than gospels, for example and, I submit, apocalypses came before gospels. That is why there are apocalypses of apostles such as James, but no purported gospel written by James. After all, if this scenario holds, what need would there have been for him to write a gospel if he wrote an apocalypse?

So, to make the point, there were several gospels that were also ultimately not accepted within the canon, including the *Gospel of Eve*, the *Gospel of Judas* (condemned as heretical by a church council in 180 CE and found in Egypt in 1978; another so-called *Gospel of Judas*, either written between 280 and 330 CE or, more likely, being a modern forgery, having purportedly been found on the Egyptian market in 2006), the *Gospel of the Hebrews* (most likely penned during the late first century or early second century CE), and the *Gospel of Mary* [of Magdala] (and even a few more gospels which I will not get into), all of which are likely ancient forgeries. In addition, the disciples of the Gnostic teacher Prodicus are known to have boasted that they possessed the *Secret Books of Zoroaster* (Zarathushtra), of all books for them to purport to possess!. This shows as well as anything can that gospels were simply *not* important to the earliest church while apocalypses were. And the earliest gospel written was most likely that of Thomas.

The so-called *Gospel of Mary* was found at Akhmim, Egypt in 1896. It is, unfortunately, missing the first several chapters. But, in it Mary is clearly the repository of secret knowledge given to her by Jesus, which the other disciples did not receive. Peter becomes upset that she would say the he had told her anything that he had not told anyone else, but she is vindicated. The book, overall, appears to be an effort to say that Peter was not really the "rock" of the church, but that Mary was. So one has to posit here a Gnostic community, most likely located in Egypt, in which the feminine was elevated above the masculine and in which the leader might well have been female. In fact, since this book was *found in* Egypt, the Gnostic community in question could easily have been one that had formerly worshipped Isis and, in their own way, transferred the attributes of Isis to Mary of Magdala. The later church obviously suppressed this movement, but still transferred the attributes of Isis, not to this Mary, but to Mary, mother of Jesus. In any case, it was clearly first penned during the second century CE, so it must be considered as a part of the Gnostic resurgence of that century.

Again, the *Apocalypse of Moses*, which was written in Greek, was actually a more detailed account of the lives of Adam and Eve and of their children. The Latin version is entitled *The Life of Adam and Eve*. In this work, the third son of Adam and Eve, Seth, was one given to them by god to replace Abel and Seth was, then, the good son. And the couple go on to have thirty more children, explaining the proliferation of humanity from them. The real point, though, is that this was a Gnostic text suppressed by the orthodox church and that Seth, as the good son, was thus staged as the precursor hero for the already mentioned Sethian Gnostics (one should recall that the Egyptian god who killed Osiris was his brother, Seth), thus, another reversal.

Finally, there were several other "Christian" works that ultimately were not accepted into the New Testament canon, some of which were generally quite good and almost did make it. These included the *Apocalypse of Peter*, *First* and *Second Clement*, the *Didache* [the Teaching of the Twelve Apostles], the *Epistle of Barnabas*, the *Protevangelium* [infancy gospel] *of James* (first penned no earlier than the mid-second century CE), the *Infancy Gospel of Thomas* (based in part on Luke and first penned no earlier than the mid to late second century CE), the *Shepherd of Hermas* and the *Third Epistle* [purportedly of Paul] *to the Corinthians*. And, having mentioned the ancient text known as the *Apocalypse of Peter*, it also must be mentioned that there was a *Gospel of Peter* (most likely first penned during the latter half of the second century CE) which was found buried with a Christian Monk in Egypt in 1886, he having been buried in about 700 CE during Medieval times. Again, this Gnostic text could not have been written earlier than the second century CE and was probably written later than that, making it yet another pious fraud. And, at last, there was a so-called *Gospel of Māni*, which really was not a gospel so much as it was a book of his revelations and call to ministry.

Frankly, apocalyptic and apocryphal literature was the "fiction" of the day. Most readers probably knew that there was no way that these works had been written by those they were attributed to. These works were greatly entertaining for the people of that time period who could read them. Most readers would have taken them allegorically. But some did take them literally, and *that* is when they became dangerous. The person who took such writings literally could not conceive of how utterly ridiculous it was for him to do so - believing that someone like Moses or Adam, for example, had been subjected to an apocalyptic vision of the end times which someone, perhaps himself, had actually written about! But, because they believed it, they took the contents to an absurdity, effectively living their lives by it.

Conclusions

In his letter *"To Theodore"*, which was discovered by professor Morton Smith in 1958 at the Greek Orthodox monastery of Mar Saba in Palestine, the early church father, Clement of Alexandria, denounced the Gnostic Carpocratians. In this letter Clement mentions a previously unknown version of the *Gospel According to Mark*, known as the *Secret Gospel According to Mark*. But instead of denouncing this "secret gospel", he states that it is "a more spiritual gospel" and even, essentially, calls Jesus himself a hierophant [one who guided initiates into the Greek Sacred Mysteries] and refers to "those who are being initiated into the great [Christian] mysteries". And, according to Marvin W. Meyer in his work The Ancient Mysteries: A Sourcebook, this version of the *Gospel According to Mark*, which is known only from the above mentioned letter of Clement *"To Theodore"* may well be older than the version found within the New Testament (Meyer 232). In fact, that is the common consensus among scholars today. But how could it be that any other gospel might have been written *prior to* what is generally accepted to be the first gospel written? Practically everyone agrees (except for myself) that the *Gospel According to Mark* (whichever version one may be referring to) was the first written, although, as I have shown, it likely was not. In this letter, Clement states, in part:

For, even if they [the Carpocratians] should say something true, one who loves the truth should not, even so, agree with them. For not all true things are the truth, nor should that truth which merely seems true according to human opinions be preferred to the true truth, that according to the faith.... But when Peter died a martyr, Mark came over to Alexandria, bringing both his own notes and those of Peter, from which he transferred to his former book [the Secret *Gospel According to Mark*] the things suitable to whatever makes for progress toward knowledge. Thus he composed a more spiritual Gospel for the use of those who were being perfected. Nevertheless, he yet did not divulge the things not to be uttered, nor did he write down the hierophantic teaching of the Lord.... he left his composition to the church in Alexandria, where it even yet is most carefully guarded, being read only to those who are being initiated into the great mysteries (Meyer 233).

Clement goes on to tell how a presbyter of the church in Alexandria had been beguiled by the Carpocratians and had, therefore, given them a copy of this *Secret Gospel According to Mark* and that they went on to use it in a misguided way, seducing other people with it. In addition, the *Gospel of Philip* (67, 27-30), which is obviously heavily Gnostic, declares:

The Lord [did] everything in a mystery, a baptism and a chrism and a Eucharist and a redemption and a bridal chamber (Meyer 235).

It must here be said, however, that, for all we know today, books like the *Gospel of Philip* might instead have been "secret gospels" themselves. In other words, there may have been even more secret gospels than *Mark*. After all, they do purport to contain secret sayings of Jesus and the like. And indeed this was the case in, for example, the *Gospel of Thomas*.

Is there a direct connection between the two communities? Not unless at least some of the Essenes of Qumran did, in fact, originally come from Egypt and not unless such literature as that found at Nag Hammadi was somehow representative of Christian communities in Egypt as descendants of the community at Qumran and the community that they originally emanated from, which was in Egypt. This was simply a round-about way of stating that the Qumran community originated in Egypt and, upon its destruction, elements of this community spread back into Egypt, resulting in communities, whether monastic or not, that closely resembled it, such as the one near Nag Hammadi. So the answer is "yes", as has been shown.

Egypt *is* the source for both. The Qumranites mainly came out of Egypt and, later, most of the Christian gospels and some other books were almost undoubtedly first written *in* Egypt. And one must not forget that the Israelites supposedly came out of Egypt. And whether some sort of Exodus ever really happened or not, it is almost unquestionable that, if Moses really did live, he was an *Egyptian* as Sigmund Freud astutely pointed out in Moses and Monotheism (a book that most take as pseudo-history, but which I take as extraordinarily insightful).

The Apostolic Gnostic church in Jerusalem, which was clearly the Judaizing church, was destroyed, for all practical purposes, by the Romans when they destroyed Qumran and Jerusalem. Whatever was left of it went to Alexandria and sprang back up there. That is the fact which has been hidden from the folk ever since at least the fourth century CE. This fact cannot be ignored anymore unless one wishes to ignore that the preponderance of the evidence shows that every real connection that the early church had was to *Egypt*, whether directly or indirectly. Both in its origins and its renewal, the place was *Egypt*, the hotbed of various combinations of Hellenization, Neoplatonism, Gnosticism and apocryphal as well as apocalyptic literature. And the *Sibylline Oracles*, a book of completely fictitious oracular statements attributed to a fictitious Hebrew Sibyl (copying the Greek Sibyls), were also written in Alexandria, Egypt by a Jew who resided there and were, in a way, a precursor to all of this. This being a perfect example of the fact that people would make things like this up all of the time and others would accept these writings as authentic.

The apostles/disciples could not reasonably have fled to any place outside of the Roman Empire, especially into areas of Arabia, because if they had they would have been seen as two things, (1) Jews, who were hated and, (2) refugees who might also have been criminals. This would simply have not been a safe bet to make. And Pella, in Trans-Jordan, was all too close to such territories too and also too close to Jerusalem. The safest place for them to have gone would have been to Egypt - to Alexandria. This is exactly why Christianity took hold so early in Egypt - because most, if not all, of the surviving/escaping apostles/disciples went there. In Alexandria they could easily hide among the large Jewish community there. They could have even proselytized a bit while there, especially after the war was over because places like Alexandria were such a hotbed for a variety of thought.

They had escaped, gradually regrouped, and eventually separated again, gathering disciples of their own wherever they went. These second disciples are likely the ones who wrote the gospels. Frankly, one has to come to the realization that if Gnosticism did not suddenly begin in the second century CE, as church tradition would have us believe it did, then we *have* to admit that original, apostolic Christianity was stamped out by the destruction of Qumran and Jerusalem, only to revive in force, although changed, during the second century. So the scenario that has been passed down to us for almost two-thousand years was invented during the time of Constantine I, when the various traditions of the saints, martyrs, etc. were also invented.

To illustrate the impact of this more fully one only has to recall that, if my scenario holds, Peter had "converted" over to Pauline Christianity after Paul and Barnabas helped him to escape from prison in Jerusalem and only afterwards founded the church at Roma. And after Peter died, Paul briefly cultivated his brand of Christianity there (by writing *Romans*) prior to his own arrest and perhaps further cultivated it afterward as Peter's de-facto successor when taken there as prisoner. Otherwise, the history of Christianity would certainly have unfolded very differently. Jerusalem Christianity would have been transported to Roma instead and Pauline Christianity would likely have come out the loser overall rather than the winner.

Still, as it turned out, the two places that became the major Christian power-bases following the destruction of Jerusalem and prior to the ascendancy of Konstantinopolis (Constantinople) were, in fact, Roma (still rather weak) and Alexandria (for Antiokheia and Ephesos simply declined as such power-bases). And this remained the case until power was basically usurped from Alexandria by Konstantinopolis. Constantine I and his successors enacted a diabolical plan to destroy all books of Pagans as well as Christian "heretics" so that they could have greater control of that which remained. Then they used the oldest texts that remained and, after re-writing everything in their own image, they destroyed the oldest canonical texts too, wherever they could. They did all of this so that the rest of history would unfold as *they* wanted it to. They changed the past so that the future would also be changed thereby. It is exactly the same as resurrection of the human body disrupting the natural cycle of life, death and rebirth, which cycle the ancient Pagans had understood as essential from time immemorial. Another reversal.

It seems that the books that the established church hated the most were actually the ones mentioned by the early church fathers and, I submit, that they are the very ones that are *most* likely to have been authentic and "authoritative" - actually written by the very persons they are attributed to. The *Gospel of Thomas* would be among these. But the established church made sure that *these* books would be destroyed and, if not for modern archaeology and science, they would have forever succeeded in this effort. But this is not the story that has been passed down through tradition. No, if Paul was executed for being a Christian, then all of the other apostles had to be too, it was thought. So that was the picture that they painted for us of the apostles as Christian martyrs.

It should finally be added that, as has surely become obvious to the reader, not only do I find that the gospels and the *Apocalypse* were written in a different order than is commonly believed, but some of the other books of the New Testament were also. I find that *1 Cor*inthians was written before *Romans* because it seems obvious that when Paul wrote *1 Corinthians* he did not know that "Cephas" had already died. And Prisca and Aquila had clearly returned to Roma by the time he wrote *Romans*. In addition, Paul's reference to the field opening up wide for him at Ephesos in *1 Corinthians* 16:9 is, to me, a clear indication that

John had by the time of its writing been arrested and was, effectively, out of Paul's way. So all of this territory was suddenly opened up for Paul to make his own inroads into, but he was never to be able to effectively take advantage of it to any appreciable degree after all. Still, he did as much as he could to turn the converts in those areas more to his way of thinking before he was finally tried and executed.

1 Peter is shown as having been written much earlier than is commonly believed by the simple fact that he wrote to the churches in Anatolia, some of which were in the province of Asia and were, thus, those of John's purview. This because he had previously assisted John before moving on to Roma. Otherwise, why would Peter have been writing to these particular churches if he had never had anything to do with them previously? And he was clearly away, so where else might he have been other than Roma? For the book of *Acts* never mentions him again after a certain point so he is unlikely to have ever returned to Jerusalem.

I have also proposed that John had, in fact, written letters to the seven churches in Asia, probably just before he was arrested, from Ephesos (thus, no letter to Ephesos) and that he is referring to these letters in his *Apocalypse*, written a few years later. These letters, sadly, are no longer extant. But he basically tells us the content of these letters in any case. The impetus for these letters must have been the revolt of Jerusalem that took place in 49 to 50 CE. The expectation of the return of Jesus prompted him to write them but, when this revolt was short-lived and Jesus did not return, perhaps these letters were of little importance to the churches and they were discarded.

And I also now propose that *Hebrews* was NOT written by Paul since it is much too Gnostic and Essene in flavor, but was instead a book written by the opposing faction in Jerusalem toward the time of Paul's death and circulated *AS* a book written by Paul in an effort to modify the beliefs of his churches, the key being Melchizedek. And, since it was quickly accepted as a writing of Paul, the ploy generally worked. After all, it is included, along with other authentic Pauline writings, in the earliest extant corpus of Pauline writings, the *Papyrus 46* document, which is likely to be dated just after the end of the first century CE.

After all, the whole concept of Melchizedek is Atenist from the start and we know this thanks to Sigmund Freud and his book Moses and Monotheism. He was "priest of the Most High God" in Jerusalem according to *Genesis* (to whom even Abraham was subservient), which was effectively Aten. He is further found in *Psalm 110* (therefore, he appears in the "Prophets" rather than in the "Law"), and in the Dead Sea Scrolls found at Qumran, therein referred to as "Elohim" who would proclaim the "Day of Atonement". He is also found in *1 Qap Gen* (*The Genesis Apocryphon*). Philo Judaeus of Alexandria mentions him along with the "Logos". He is found in the second book of *Enoch* and, obviously, in *Hebrews*. And, of course, he is finally found in the Christian/Gnostic work *Melchizedek* (found within the Nag Hammadi library), which actually refers to him as Jesus Christ, much as in *Hebrews*. Frankly, Melchizedek is nothing more than an incarnation of the Aten, given the name of an ancient Canaanite deity (Moloch/Tzedek) to hide this fact and his real name.

So *Hebrews* was an effort to modify Paul's obvious Zoroastrian influences with the more Atenist viewpoints of the apostles and the Essenes. And it was deliberately circulated among the Jewish/Christian Diaspora in a final effort to erase Paul's influence as much as possible. It is anonymous exactly so that those who had known Paul or had been directly influenced by his teachings would not immediately recognize it as a forgery and dispute its authenticity and so that it would quickly be adopted as Pauline by those who wished to do so without it having to be defended as such directly. Very shrewd indeed! All that was required was that it be planted among other Pauline books so that people would assume it to be a work of Paul. And, if one takes internal evidence, then it is also clearly written *before* the destruction of the temple in Jerusalem, probably about 61 or 62 CE. It was the very last work that the Jerusalem church would put out, although they may well have intended to put out even more books. But circumstances would not allow this to take place.

Frankly, the generally accepted timeline for New Testament writings is shown by the preponderance of the evidence to be completely fictitious and inherently illogical. To begin with, it is assumed that the book of *Acts* had to have been written somewhere close to the time of

Paul's death. This, as has been shown, occurred about 62 CE, although most place it instead a little earlier in about 61 CE. So they assume that *Acts* was penned in 61 CE with *Luke* being penned just prior to that in 60 CE. But they never answer the question as to just why the church would have needed a history, let alone a gospel, so early in its existence when the parousia was still expected to take place any day. And, as has been shown, since *Luke* is the most complicated of the gospels, containing the most traditional material, it must have been written *last* among the canonical gospels. However, scholars posit that both *Mark* and *Matthew* might have been written as much as a decade prior to *Luke* and that *John* must have been written toward the end of the first century, the *Apocalypse* also being written about that time. As one of my favorite former history professors used to say; "Poppycock!" Their scenario doesn't even hold, logically or otherwise. There was no need whatsoever for a history or a gospel prior to the destruction of Jerusalem and her temple in 70 CE. Period.

So the Apostolic/Atenist faction, mainly based in Jerusalem, was very Gnostic/Essene, pro-Torah, Jewish-centered and apocalyptic in outlook. Conversely, the Pauline/Zoroastrian faction, mainly based in Antiokheia, was very orthodox/pentecostal, anti-Torah, more Hellenized and more present-tense in outlook. In no way could these two opposing factional viewpoints stand together without the insertion of the gospels. And in no way could they connect to the Hebrew Bible without the gospels. The gospels were the bridge that allowed literary union of these two factions. The gospels, then, were effectively a bridge that was added later along with *Acts* in order to make the story "complete". It's time we dispensed with blind faith and acknowledged the facts as elucidated by extant evidence. All of these things are detailed in the following charts.

SELECT HISTORICAL TIMELINE:

18 BCE - Herod begins the rebuilding of the Jewish temple in Jerusalem.

9 BCE - The Ara Pacis Augustae (temple to Augustan peace) is consecrated.

5/4 BCE - The Jewish temple in Jerusalem is dedicated, although still incomplete.

c4 BCE - The Passover Massacre takes place. Jesus is born (no "Massacre of the Innocents" takes place). John was born a bit earlier at some unknown date.

c6 CE - The families of John and Jesus flee Judea for Egypt after a Jewish revolt against the Romans (the first failed apocalypse), led by Judas and Zadok, fails. Judea is made into a Roman province following the revolt.

c17 CE - Jesus returns to Judea from Egypt and is soon baptized by John.

19 CE - The Roman imperator, Tiberius, expels Jews from Roma.

c29 CE - Jesus stages the "Cleansing of the Temple", initiates a rebellion (the second failed apocalypse), and is executed by the Romans.

c31 CE - Jews were expelled from Roma and compelled to return to their ancestral homes, many returning to Jerusalem. The stoning of Stephen takes place in Jerusalem. Saul of Tarsus is a witness to this.

c32 CE - Saul of Tarsus goes to Damascus and is converted to "The Way".

c34 CE - Peter's encounter with the Roman Centurion, Cornelius.

37 CE - The Roman imperator, Tiberius, dies.

c41 CE - The Roman imperator, Caligula, orders that his image be set up in the temple in Jerusalem. Caligula is soon assassinated and the order is never carried out.

TIMELINE OF APOSTOLIC (SEPARATE, SECRET, HIDDEN) VS. PAULINE (REVEALED) EFFORTS:

Apostolic/Atenist:	Pauline/Zoroastrian:
c43 CE - John begins his mission in Asia.	Paul and Barnabas free Peter from a Jerusalem prison.
c44 CE - Peter joins John in Asia.	Paul's first missionary journey begins.
c45 CE - "Men from Judea" trouble church at Antiokheia.	
c46 CE - The Jerusalem Council.	First missionary journey ends. Paul, Barnabas and Timothy go to Jerusalem.
c46-47 CE -	Paul writes *Galatians*.
c47 CE - Peter moves on to Roma.	Paul's second missionary journey begins.
c47-48 CE - James writes his epistle. *1 Peter* is written from Roma to the churches in Asia and Anatolia.	
c49 CE - Peter dies at Roma. Claudius expels Jews from Roma. (The third failed apocalypse takes place as Jerusalem revolts for about a year).	

c50 CE - John writes letters to the seven churches in Asia. John is arrested and sent to Patmos.

c51 CE -

c52-53 CE -

c53-54 CE -

54 CE -

c54-55 CE -

c55 CE - The *Apocalypse of John* is written.

c56 CE - The apostle John dies.

c58-59 CE -

c60 CE -

c60-c62 CE -

c61 CE - *Hebrews* is written.

c62 CE - James "The Just" is killed in Jerusalem. Symeon takes over.

Paul first meets Prisca and Aquila at Kórinthos. Paul writes *1 Corinthians*. Prisca and Aquila return to Roma

Paul writes *Romans* and *1 Thessalonians*. Then, Paul's first, short, visit with the Ephesians on his way back to Antiokhea.

Paul's third missionary journey begins.

Book-burning at Ephesos.

Nero becomes Imperator.

Paul writes *2 Corinthians*.

The temple of Artemis incident at Ephesos.

Paul is summoned before James "The Just". He is found in the temple, a riot almost ensues, and he is arrested.

Paul's hearing before Felix

Paul arrives in Roma.

Paul writes "*To The Saints*" (*Ephesians*), *Philippians*, *Colossians* and *2 Timothy*.

Paul is tried and executed in Roma.

64 CE - The Great Fire in Roma takes place. The Jewish temple in Jerusalem is finally complete in all of its detail.

66 CE - First great revolt of the Jews (the fourth failed apocalypse) against the Romans begins.

68 CE - Nero dies.

70 CE - Jerusalem and the temple are destroyed by the Romans.

73 CE - The Jewish temple at Leontopolis is destroyed by the Romans.

74 CE - Masada is taken by the Romans. The revolt ends.

c75 CE - The *Gospel of Thomas* is written in Alexandria, Egypt. Afterward, all of the other gospels and *Acts* were written.

131-35 CE - The Bar Kokhba Revolt against the Romans (the fifth and final failed apocalypse) takes place. The Roman response is severe and genocidal.

EPILOGUE:
A CALL FOR A BRAVE NEW
(NON-APOCALYPTIC) WORLD

It seems to me that one of the most important things that should be gleaned from the previous analysis is the strong probability that the *Apocalypse of John* was written quite a bit earlier than has been generally believed. If this book truly was written prior to the destruction of Jerusalem and the temple there, then it *cannot* be seen as a prophecy of humanity's future in any way, shape, or form. That would also mean that its use in this way over the centuries has resulted in an unmitigated catastrophe - a catastrophe of mental illness among those who allow themselves to accept such a notion. Said another way - if this is not a book about, even in part, the future for us; if the writer did truly expect its fulfillment within his own lifetime in the form of the destruction of Jerusalem - then we have been greatly misguided for many centuries. We have been tricked into believing in some end of the world for us when the end of the writer's world, which is what he was writing about, took place in 70 CE!

So humanity has succumbed to this and is fearfully waiting for some end of the world that is not coming. That is, unless we cause it to arrive ourselves, which I submit is exactly what is happening today. We are creating an apocalypse that would never happen if not for *this* book and belief in it. Every time we "recognize" some event as having to do with the end of the world - as being a sign of the end, we feed into this and work toward making it a reality, unwittingly. Every time we say things like the Mayan calendar is predicting that the end of the world will take place in December of 2012 (which, obviously, did not happen) or that Nostradamus called Adolf Hitler an antichrist, we feed into this potential calamity of our own creation. And now we even have Islamic forces attempting to create their own apocalypse by drawing western nations and their allies into a direct conflict with them. This is a perverse and irrational thing to do, but it is the very thing that apocalyptically-minded people will do to further their ends. And there can be no doubt that some Christian somewhere is drawing all of this out and making it all fit with his or her concept of the book of *"Revelation"*. *This* is the tragedy of the *Apocalypse of John* as it is misused today. This is not the way it was meant to be used, but this is the way it has been and still is used, just like the fact that the *Gospel According to John* is not really anti-Semitic, but it has been used to elucidate anti-Semitism (although that does indeed occur) for centuries. These are tragic misuses of these books. If the *Apocalypse of John* had not been placed last in the canon so that it was made to appear as something that Christians are to look forward to, then we would be able to laugh off anyone with apocalyptic expectations. Instead, we are watching history unfold as it is today with horror.

And the gospels, as if this really needs reiteration, were *not* written before the fall of Jerusalem in 70 CE. This because they were clearly *not* needed by the earliest church, which expected the parousia to take place within the lifetimes of the earliest church members. Jesus was to return *any day*. What need could there be to write about him? The fact that so-called "infancy gospels" were not written until the second century CE, long after anyone would have remembered a thing about the birth and early life of Jesus, is a perfect example of the fact that no one was interested in such until after the parousia did not occur. But when he didn't return, the writing of the gospels and other books became necessary. The lie is that the disciples and any of the earliest followers of Jesus thought beyond their own lifetimes until it became clear that Jesus was not going to return. So the *Apocalypse* could only have been written early, before the fall, if it was written by the apostle at all or even his student. It had, therefore, to have been written *before* any of the gospels. But this book has been twisted around to appear to have been written last, or at least late. Armageddon was supposed to have been about the defeat of the Romans. But, once the Romans blazed past

Megiddo, the Jews regrouped at Jerusalem itself and that was a mistake. For the followers of Jesus; Jesus did not return to save them. For the other Jews; no messiah appeared to save them. No parousia occurred for either.

Once again, the first canonical gospel to have been written, if my scenario holds true, is that according to John. He was an eyewitness and whoever wrote this gospel, whether it was him or, more likely, a student, had talked with him and, therefore, had direct eyewitness testimony. And the clear emphasis within this gospel is on the "Word" or "Logos", which meant Knowledge or Wisdom. This is one reason why the Gnostics loved this gospel. Those according to Mark or Matthew were written next, probably in that order. Let it be said, then, that whether *Mark* was the next one written or not, it can be seen easily as the one that seeks to present the divine Mystery. One quote will suffice to illustrate this (*Mark* 4:22):

> For nothing is hidden, except to be revealed. Nor has *anything* been secret, but that it would come to light.

Two similar statements from Luke (*Luke* 8:17; 12:2 respectively) read:

> For nothing is hidden that will not become evident, nor *anything* secret that will not be known and come to light. . . .
> But there is nothing covered up that will not be revealed, and hidden that will not be known.

And similar statements are found within the *Gospel of Thomas* as in 5.2 "For there is nothing hidden which will not become manifest" and 62 "Jesus said, 'It is to those [who are worthy of My] mysteries that I tell My mysteries. Do not let your left hand know what your right hand is doing'". So, regardless of what Clement of Alexandria may have stated, the *Gospel According to Mark* was already emphasizing Mystery and if there was really another (complete) one that emphasized this even more it is sad that we don't have it today, for it would have provided us with much that the present one does not. But, perhaps that is exactly why it no longer exists.

That according to *Matthew*, for its part, is definitely the most apocalyptic of all of the earliest gospels. And, by apocalyptic, in this instance, I do mean looking past the destruction of Jerusalem. In other words, the church still needed for apocalypse to be a part of its identity and, therefore, this gospel served that purpose. It was a different kind of apocalypse than the *Apocalypse of John*. That is most likely why early church councils chose to place this gospel as the very first one. It was an effort to ensure that Christians would look forward to a still future apocalypse rather than remembering the previous one, which had failed.

Finally, that according to Luke, who is believed to have been a Greek, came last. It is the most complicated gospel of all and actually has several inherent themes. But it seems that the most important one of all was the emphasis on the "holy spirit", which is equated with Wisdom. Miracle and the mystical are also important themes for the writer of this gospel. And this gospel alone truly emphasizes the *feminine*. In fact, unlike that according to John, the holy spirit is never referred to as masculine in the Greek. This would be in keeping with the general trend of the time, or at least of a century earlier.

So, Qumran and Jerusalem, along with her temple, were destroyed and made desolate. Most of the Jews who resided there were captured and sold into slavery and exported to every part of the empire and beyond. Then the pockets where Pauline Christianity had taken hold survived and made a concerted effort to change history so that it would appear to have been the only form of Christianity from the beginning. After this, the Christian Gnostics revived during the second century, but eventually waned. Pauline Christianity, with the help of the unwitting Romans, had won the day.

But it was still early in the game. Christianity had by no means spread and been accepted by very many within the Roman Empire as of that time, regardless of what the book of *Acts* leads the reader to believe (for centuries later, only about ten percent of the population of the empire in the West could be called Christian although a slightly larger portion were Christians in the East). No, people did not convert in droves until, rather quickly, the empire became Christian under the régimes of Constantine I, Constantius II and their successors. No, we have a long way to go from here before that happens. In the mean time the Roman Empire went along much as it always had, with only this irritating new belief system pestering it from time to time. The Romans generally tried to ignore its existence. And that was to the empire's detriment.

When Nero had Christians executed by way of animals and burning at the stake, he was resorting mainly to the old Roman laws called the *Twelve Tables* although he also went a step too far for the populace when he seemed to be doing this simply out of malice. The Romans generally turned on him for this as it seemed unusually cruel even for those accused of arson. Centuries later the first Christian régimes revived the *Twelve Tables* again in a very sinister way as a means toward religious cleansing. And, as we have seen repeatedly from history, this is what monotheistic dictatorships do. They revive archaic laws and use them for their own purposes. A prime example today is seen as the Islamic terrorist organizations as they revive strict Medieval Sharia, misusing it for their own twisted and perverse purposes.

During the time of Jesus Judaism had for some time been working toward a sort of evolution from the strict observance of Torah, this evolution generally taking the form of the sect of the Sadducees. But the Pharisees generally wished to keep the strict observance of Torah intact. Saul (who later changed his name to Paul) had been a Pharisee and was so when he witnessed the stoning of Stephen, something that was done because of a strict interpretation of Torah following an influx of Jews returning from Roma. The gospels, which were written later, then essentially painted Jesus as a Sadducee (though not directly calling him one, making him more into a Sokratic philosopher) who argued with the Pharisees. One should recall that the Sadducees did not believe in the afterlife (like the Atenists) while the Pharisees did believe in the afterlife (like the Zoroastrians). But the gospels deliberately leave out Jesus' (and John's) Essene roots, completely eliminating this background altogether in order that these Essene roots might be forgotten to history.

It seems that Jesus started out as anti-Torah as John probably also did, but John remained so while, following John's arrest, Jesus decided to espouse Torah along with a violent overthrow of the Romans. He expected his Essene associates from Qumran to rally to his side since he was about to initiate the war against the forces of darkness. But the expected Qumranic assistance never materialized and Jesus was captured and executed. Because of this some factions rejected Jesus as a failure and false messiah, the Mandaeans being their modern successors. Judaism in the main also rejected Jesus and eventually, along with him, they also rejected the apocalyptic.

Paul turned from his former Pharisaic outlook when he went to Damascus and converted to a more or less combined Essene-Zoroastrian point of view, like those at Qumran and Damascus. So, in effect, he tried to bring nascent Christianity back more in line with the original benevolent teachings of Jesus (and he himself, while instigating certain events, never performed any overtly violent act) while others, those mainly in Jerusalem, remained determined to strictly follow Torah and follow the Jesus who incited rebellion. Frankly, John and James were akin to terrorists in that they were determined to finally have that war against the forces of evil. So they promulgated this in the form of apocalyptic writings just as the Jewish Gnostics and Qumran Essenes had and worked to stir things up in Jerusalem until a revolt ensued. That was the one major element that Paul did not take from the Qumran Essenes while the other major players did, although Peter later modified his position. So, ultimately, Paul and Peter were much more pacifistic, although Paul had instigated a book-burning and a riot at Ephesos. The Mandaeans later followed suit in this general pacifism.

The Jerusalem Christians tried to combine Torah, apocalyptic expectations and Gnosticism, but were ultimately unsuccessful. In addition, according to the book of *Acts*, this segment of the church was rather communal or communistic, but it is anyone's guess as to just how long that lasted. And it was dynastic in nature with church leadership passing from one relative of Jesus to the next until it was destroyed by the Romans along with Jerusalem and her temple. Frankly, the idea that Jesus actually had been married sometime during his earlier lifetime seems implied in the canonical gospels when he tells others that they must be willing to leave family, including wife and children, in order to follow him. After all, would he tell others to do something that he was unwilling to do himself (and that he probably had actually done)? It is essentially implied that he left, but did not divorce, a wife and it is directly shown that he left his own extended family. And he may well have had at least one child, but not by Mary of Magdala, as some speculate. Still, tradition has implied that he did have at least one child, a girl. Whether this was a clever lie or not, at least it explained why his son would not have become the leader of the Jerusalem church following his death because he didn't have a son, even according to tradition. Either way, the various theories about the daughter of Jesus are nonsense and unworthy of scholarly research, in my view. Their sole objective is to cause Europeans to believe that their royalty are descended from Jesus. In any case, Pauline Christianity basically rejected the Gnosticism only to have Barnabas and Marcion revive it and try to combine it with Pauline orthodoxy during the second century CE. The renewed Gnostic effort was short-lived as it was also doomed to failure. And by that time the church order described in the pseud-Pauline letters of *1 Timothy* and *Titus* was clearly beginning to take shape.

This is the strange soup that was earliest Christianity. It was anything but monolithic and fully-formed from the beginning. But it eventually coalesced, combining Pauline freedom with a touch of Torah, leaving the Gnosticism out completely and writing the Essenes completely out of the script. So the two most important foundations for earliest Christianity, Jewish Gnosticism and the Atenist Essene movement, were basically erased as much as possible. And, in the end, it added the "Old Testament", which had finally been codified about 100 CE and which Marcion had rejected, along with its demiurge god, and kept the gospels as the bridge between Judaism and what Christianity had become. That Christianity would then become more a political than a religious force is pretty much a given, just as Judaism had before it and Islam would after it.

In the end, however, to perhaps coin a phrase, a religion is more than the sum pf its parts. One cannot judge Zoroastrianism simply by reading the Avesta. One cannot judge Judaism simply by reading Torah and the rest of the Hebrew Bible. One cannot judge Christianity simply by reading the New Testament. And one cannot judge Islam simply by reading the Quran and the Hadith. All religions, as well as the adherents to them, grow and evolve over time and this should be recognized most of all. All of these religions have had their "Renaissance" sometime during their own histories. So, while it is important to study their origins, it is dangerous and detrimental to attempt to take them back to their roots. This is especially true of embracing the apocalyptic, which really only leads to perversion of a given religion. The absurdity of this mode of thinking is demonstrated by the desire among some today that the Jewish people should return to Israel. Judaism, during the last approximately three-thousand years, has grown beyond a small, clearly-defined state. It is really a part of "Jewishness", if you will, to possess and embrace that legacy of the Diaspora. They have truly become citizens of the world and any attempt to circumvent this evolution is preposterous. Judaism has also grown past the apocalyptic while still retaining its essential mystery. That is important for people to understand. But apocalyptically-minded fundamentalists don't see it that way, so they propose that all (or at least most) Jews should return to Israel because it is somehow the will of god. This is what apocalyptic thought leads to.

Finally, for those able to bear it, the shroud is the same as the swaddling clothes. Death is the same as life. This is the one real truth found within the pages of the canonical gospels. Obviously, the Shroud of Turin has been proven to be fake, but that does not mean that no shroud ever wrapped the body of Jesus (although he was instead likely to have been wrapped in strips of cloth) any more than it can be assumed that he did not wear swaddling clothes as a baby. Of course he did because all babies were wrapped in swaddling clothes and all deceased bodies, when possible, were wrapped in strips of cloth. If, by chance, the followers of Jesus had kept his shroud or strips of cloth, which is unlikely since they were looking forward to his return and were not focused anymore upon his death as Gnostics who believed in a soon-to-take-place apocalypse, and the gospels do not mention that they took it, it would undoubtedly have been kept in Jerusalem. Thus, it would likely have still been there when the Romans destroyed Jerusalem and the temple in 70 CE. But, if some of the fleeing apostles took it before this event occurred, then they would have taken it to Egypt! In a way, this would have amounted to a return of Jesus to Egypt where he was brought up. Thus, another in a series of reversals explicitly tied to Christianity.

But everyone focuses on Jerusalem as if he had never left - as if he were still there or at least would return there from above. In this respect, people don't care who Jesus really was because the person they are awaiting is not the one who lived. These people only care who Jesus is to them in an apocalyptic sense. It is thought by both Christians and Muslims that Jesus will return to Jerusalem to fight his enemies, including the Antichrist, when the remnant of believers is very few in number. The mindset is that Jerusalem was lost in the last apocalyptic battle and it must be won back in the future battle. It's that simple. But such a scenario sets us up for a war that otherwise would never be fought. It is my opinion that this should be avoided or we risk plunging the world into a worldwide Dark Age which may take hundreds, if not thousands, of years for us to be extracted from. It's time we learn from real history and act accordingly.

ACKNOWLEDGMENTS

Grateful acknowledgment is made to the following publishing houses for permission to reprint previously published material:

Augsburg Fortress Press: Anti-Semitism and Early Christianity: Issues of Polemic and Faith, © 1993, Jewish and Christian Self-Definition: The Shaping of Christianity in the Second and Third Centuries, Vol. 1. © 1980 and The Religion of Jesus the Jew. © 1993. Reprinted by permission of Augsburg Fortress Press.

HarperCollins Publishers: Brief quotes from: The Historical Jesus: The Life of a Mediterranean Jewish Peasant. ©1991 by John Dominic Crossan (pp. 32-3, 232, 287 and 355) and The Ancient Mysteries: A Sourcebook of Sacred Texts, Edited by Marvin W. Meyer. ©1987 by Marvin W. Meyer (pp. 2 and 233). Both Reprinted by Permission of HarperCollins Publishers.

Moody Press: Ryrie Study Bible, Expanded Edition; New American Standard Bible. ©1995. Reprinted by permission of Moody Press.

University of Nebraska Press for the **Jewish Publication Society of America**: Movements in Judaism: Hellenism, © 1920 (now in the public domain). and The Jews of Egypt, From Rameses II to Emperor Hadrian, © 1995. Reprinted by permission of University of Nebraska Press.

Watkins Publishing: The Gnostic John the Baptizer: Selections From the Mandaean John-Book, © 1924. Reprinted by permission of Watkins Press.

SELECT BIBLIOGRAPHY

Abrahams, Israel, trans. of Alon, Gedalyahu. Jews, Judaism and the Classical World: Studies in Jewish History in the Times of the Second Temple and Talmud. Jerusalem: The Magnes Press, the Hebrew University, 1977.

Aland, Kurt. Synopsis of the Four Gospels. USA:, 1985.

Allegro, John M. The Sacred Mushroom and the Cross: A Study of the Nature and Origins of Christianity Within the Fertility Cults of the Ancient Near East. London: Hodder and Stoughton, 1970.

Barnstone, Willis. The Other Bible: Gnostic Scriptures, Jewish Pseudepigrapha, Christian Apocrypha, Kabbalah, Dead Sea Scrolls. San Francisco: Harper & Row, 1984.

Barnstone, Willis and Marvin Meyer. Essential Gnostic Scriptures. Boston, MA: Shambala Books, 2010.

Benko, Stephen. Pagan Rome and the Early Christians. Bloomington: Indiana U. P., 1984.

Bentwich, Norman. Movements in Judaism; Hellenism. Philadelphia: Jewish Pub. Soc. of America, 1920.

Beyer, Catherine. *About.com* Guide. *Who was Zoroaster (Zarathushtra)?; The Origins of Zoroastrianism.*

Bible Secrets Revealed: *"The Forbidden Scriptures"*. The History Channel, 2013.

Bindley, T. Herbert. Religious Thought in Palestine in the Time of Christ. London: Methuen & Co., LTD., 1931.

Black, Matthew. The Scrolls and Christian Origins: Studies in the Jewish Background of the New Testament. New York: Scribner, 1961.

Boccaccini, Gabriele. Beyond the Essene Hypothesis: The Parting of Ways Between Qumran and Enochic Judaism. Grand Rapids: William B. Eerdmans, 1998.

Boles, Kenneth L. The College Press NIV Commentary; Galatians & Ephesians. Joplin, Missouri: College Press Pub., 1993.

Brandon, S. G. F. The Fall of Jerusalem and the Christian Church. London: S. P. C. K., 1974.

Breasted, James Henry. The Dawn of Conscience. New York: Charles Scribner's Sons, 1934.

Breasted, James Henry. The History of Egypt. New York: Scribner, 1906.

Burrows, Millar. The Dead Sea Scrolls. New York: Viking, 1955.

Cantor, Norman F. Medieval History, The Life and Death of a Civilization, Second Ed. New York: Macmillan Pub. Co., 1969.

Chuvin, Pierre. A Chronicle of the Last Pagans. Cambridge: Harvard U. P., 1990.

Collins, John J. and Craig A. Evans. Christian Beginnings and the Dead Sea Scrolls. Grand Rapids: Baker, 2006.

Conzelmann, Hans. A Commentary on the Acts of the Apostles. Fortress P., 1972.

Cross, Frank Moore. Canaanite Myth and Hebrew Epic. Cambridge, MA: Harvard U. P., 1973.

Crossan, John Dominic; Robert J. Miller, ed. The Complete Gospels, Everything You Need to Empower Your Own Search for the Historical Jesus: Anotated Scholar's Version. Salem, Oregon: Polebridge P., 1994.

Crossan, John Dominic. The Historical Jesus, The Life of a Mediterranean Jewish Peasant. San Francisco: Harper Collins Pub., 1992.

Dart, John. The Jesus of Heresy and History: The Discovery and Meaning of the Nag Hammadi Gnostic Library. Cambridge: Harper & Row Pub., 1988.

Elsman, Robert H. The Dead Sea Scrolls and the First Christians. Shaftesbury: Element, 1996.

Evans, Craig A. and Donald A. Hagner. Anti-Semitism and Early Christianity: Issues of Polemic and Faith. Minneapolis: Fortress P., 1993.

Fox, Robin Lane. Pagans and Christians. HarperSanFrancisco: Harper Collins Pub., 1986.

Fredriksen, Paula. From Jesus to Christ, The Origins of the New Testament Images of Jesus. New Haven: Yale U. P., 1988.

Freedman, David Noel. The Anchor Bible Dictionary. New York: Doubleday. 1992.

Freud, Sigmund. Moses and Monotheism. New York: Vintage Books, 1939.

Garland, Robert. The Greek Way of Death. Ithaca, New York: Cornell U. P., 1985.

Gaston, Lloyd. No Stone On Another: Studies in the Significance of the Fall of Jerusalem in the Synoptic Gospels. Lieden: E. J. Brill Pub., 1970.

Gebhart, Jacob. www.ancient-hebrew.org/39 exodus.html. "Ancient Hebrew Research Center Plowing Through History, from Aleph to Tav" "How many came out of the exodus of Egypt?"

Golb, Norman. Who Wrote the Dead Sea Scrolls? The Search for the Secret of Qumran. New York: Scribner, 1995.

Grant, Robert M. and David Noel Freedman. The Secret Sayings of Jesus. Garden City, NY: Doubleday & Co., Inc., 1960.

Hans, Jonas. The Gnostic Religion (3rd ed.). Boston: Beacon P., 1958.

Hedrick, Charles W. and Robert Hodgson, Jr. Nag Hammadi, Gnosticism, & Early Christianity. Peabody, Mass: Hendrickson Pub., 1986.

Hodgson, Peter C. and Robert H. King. Readings in Christian Theology. Minneapolis: Fortress P., 1985.

Hogg, C. F. and W. E. Vine. The Epistle of Paul the Apostle to the Galatians; With Notes Exegetical and Expository. London/Glasgow: Pickering & Inglis, 1922.

Johnson, Luke Timothy. The Real Jesus: The Misguided Quest for the Historical Jesus and the Truth of the Traditional Gospels. New York, N.Y.: HarperSanFrancisco, 1996.

Kaufmann, Walter. The Portable Nietzsche. New York: Penguin Books, 1982.

Kraabel, Thomas. "The Roman Diaspora: Six Questionable Assumptions". The Journal of Jewish Studies, Vol. 33, 1982, pp. 445-464.

Legge, Francis. Forerunners and Rivals of Christianity, From 330 B.C. to 330 A.D. New York: University Books, 1964.

Lightfoot, J. B. The Epistle of St. Paul to the Galatians; With Introductions, Notes and Dissertations. Grand Rapids: Zondervan Pub. House, 1865.

Longenecker, Richard N. Word Biblical Commentary, Vol. 41; *Galatians*. Dallas: Word Books, 1990.

Mead, George R. The Gnostic John the Baptizer: Selections From the Mandaean John-Book. London: John M. Watkins Pub., 1924.

Meyer, Marvin W. The Ancient Mysteries: A Sourcebook; Sacred Texts of the Mystery Religions of the Ancient Mediterranean World. HarperSanFrancisco: Harper Collins Pub., 1987.

Meyer, Marvin and James M. Robinson. Nag Hammadi Scriptures: The International Edition. Harper One, 2007.

Miller, Robert J. The Complete Gospels. Sonoma, CA: Polebridge P., 2010.

Modrzejewski, Joseph Mèléze. The Jews of Egypt, From Rameses II to Emperor Hadrian. Philadelphia: The Jewish Publication Soc., 1995.

Oesterley, W. O. E. The Jews and Judaism During the Greek Period: The Background of Christianity. Port Washington, New York/London: Kennikat Press, 1941.

Pagels, Elaine. The Gnostic Paul: Gnostic Exegesis of the Pauline Letters. Philadelphia: Fortress P., 1975.

Pagels, Elaine. The Other Gospels: Non-Canonical Gospel Texts. Ron Cameron, ed. Philadelphia: The Westminster P., 1982.

Parke, Herbert W. and D. E. W. Wormell. The Delphic Oracle, Vol. I, The History. Oxford: Basil Blackwell, 1956.

Parrot, André. Samaria: The Capital of the Kingdom of Israel. New York, Philosophical Library, Inc., 1955.

Perowne, Stewart. Hadrian. London: Hodder and Stoughton, 1960.

Porten, Bezalel, ed. and Jonas C. Greenfield. Jews of Elephantine and Arameans of Syene (Fifth Century B.C.E.) Fifty Aramaic Texts with Hebrew and English Translations. Jerusalem, Israel: Copyright Bezalel Porten, 1974.

Ramsay, William M. A Historical Commentary on St. Paul's Epistle to the Galatians. Grand Rapids: Baker Book House, 1965.

Ryrie, Charles Caldwell. Ryrie Study Bible, Expanded Edition; New American Standard Bible, 1995 Update. Chicago: Moody P., 1995.

Sanders, E. P. Jewish and Christian Self-Definition: The Shaping of Christianity in the Second and Third Centuries, Vol. 1. Philadelphia: Fortress P., 1980.

Sanders, E. P. Judaism Practice and Belief, 63 BCE - 66CE. London: SCM Press, 1992.

Sanders, Jack T. Schismatics, Sectarians, Dissidents, Deviants: The First One Hundred Years of Jewish Christian Relations. Valley Forge, Penn.: Trinity Press Int., 1993.

Schweitzer, Albert. The Quest of the Historical Jesus: A Critical Study of Its Progress from Reimarus to Wrede. New York: Macmillan, 1968.

Sheres, Ita and Anne Kohn Blau. The Truth About the Virgin: Sex and Ritual in the Dead Sea Scrolls. New York: Continuum Pub., 1995.

Silva, Moisés. Explorations in Exegetical Method: Galatians as a Test Case. Grand Rapids: Baker Books, 1996.

Sinnigen, William G. and Arthur E. R. Boak. A History of Rome to A.D. 565. New York: Macmillan Pub. Co., Inc., 1977.

Slingerland, Dixon H. Claudian Policymaking and the Early Imperial Repression of Judaism at Rome. Atlanta: Scholars P., 1997.

Terry, Milton S. The Sibylline Oracles: Translated from the Greek into English Blank Verse. New York: Eaton & Mains; Cincinnati: Curts & Jennings, Reprint of 1899 ed., 1973.

Thackeray, H. St. J., and Ralph Marcus, ed. Josephus; Jewish Antiquities, Books V-VIII. London: William Heinemann LTD, 1950.

van der Toorn, Karel; Bob Becking and Pieter van der Horst. Dictionary of Dieties and Demons in the Bible, 2nd ed.. Leided, Netherlands: Brill, 1999.

Vermes, Geza. The Religion of Jesus the Jew. Minneapolis: Fortress Press., 1993.

Walters, James C. Ethnic Issues in Paul's Letter to the Romans: Changing Self-Definitions in Earliest Roman Christianity. Valley Forge, Penn.: Trinity Press International, 1993.

Wilken, Robert L. The Christians as the Romans Saw Them. New Haven and London: Yale U. P., 1984.

Williamson, G. A., trans. Eusebius: The History of the Church From Christ to Constantine. London, New York: Penguin Books, 1989.

Yamauchi, Edwin. Gnostic Ethics and Mandaean Origins. Piscataway, N. J.: Gorgias Press, 2004.

ABOUT THE AUTHOR

The author grew up on a farm in rural America, studied to become a minister, holds three advanced degrees in religious studies, and has served in the US Army, having been deployed to the Middle-East twice. And, over the course of his lifetime, the author has either studied or taken part in nearly every religious movement extant today, especially with reference to the various Christian denominations.